GOODIES	BADDIES
DOWDING	SHOLTO DOUGLAS
KEITH PARK	DOUGLAS BADER
	TRAFFORD LEIGH MALLORY
	"SIR" JOHN SALMOND
	"SIR" HUGH TRENCHARD
	← NEWALL *
	LORD CHERWELL

DOWDING
AND HEADQUARTERS
FIGHTER COMMAND

DOWDING
AND HEADQUARTERS
FIGHTER COMMAND

Peter Flint

Airlife
England

First published in the UK in 1996
by Airlife Publishing Ltd

British Library Cataloguing in Publication Data
A catalogue record for this book
is available from the British Library

ISBN 1 85310 534 1

Typeset by Hewer Text Composition Services, Edinburgh
Printed in England by Livesey Ltd, Shrewsbury.

Airlife Publishing Ltd
101 Longden Road, Shrewsbury SY3 9EB

Dedicated to the memory of Czech airman Frankie Truhlář.

The royalties from this book I am pleased
to donate to the Blond McIndoe Centre at the
Queen Victoria Hospital, East Grinstead.

Contents

Acknowledgments

Many people have given me support in creating this book. Sadly, a number of them have passed away during the years the work has been in progress. Naturally most help came from those with a Service background; civilian scientists working in the field of radar development were also generous with their time. I am particularly indebted to:

The late Group Captain R.M.B. Duke-Woolley, DSO, DFC.

Group Captain 'Gerry' Edge, DFC, with whom I had many discussions about fighter tactics and learned much from his expertise.

Wing Commander Joe Kayle, DSO, DFC, OBE.

The late Air Vice-Marshal H.A.V. Hogan, DFC.

Air Vice-Marshal 'Peter' Chamberlain, CB, OBE.

The late Air Chief Marshal Sir Theodore McEvoy, KCB, CBE.

Group Captain John Cunningham, DSO, DFC, CBE.

Air Vice-Marshal 'Sandy' Johnstone, CB, DFC, AE.

Squadron Leader M.A. Liskutin, DFC, AFC.

'Ada' Vrana, No. 312 (Czech) Squadron

Cliff Kenyon, Deputy Controller, Operations Room

Professor R. Hanbury Brown, A.C., D.Sc., F.R.S.

Professor R.V. Jones

Archibald Potts (Operational Research) Fighter Command

Lady Betty Pretty

Dr Vincent Orange, Dept. History, University of Canterbury, New Zealand

Christopher Elliot

Peter Elliott, Keeper of Aviation Records, RAF Museum

A host of ex-WAAF members, too many to mention here, gave freely of their time when corresponding with me and all their contributions proved to be of value.

There were many other people who gave assistance; to them I give my thanks.

Successive Memorabilia Officers at Bentley Priory – Squadron Leaders Al Turner, Brian Canfer, Phil Atlay and Flight Lieutenant Bill Fawcett generously gave their time and hospitality during our visits.

My thanks are due to the publishers Adam Hilger for permission to quote an extract from *Radar Days* and similarly Collins for *Years of Command*.

Group Captain Tom Gleave, C.B.E., the official historian of the Battle of Britain Fighter Association, died when the book was in the latter stages of preparation. He was a constant source of encouragement and carefully read the final draft of the manuscript. His contribution to the recording of air defence history will be sorely missed.

The support given me by my wife, Iris, has been more than can be reasonably expected of anyone; without it there would be no book.

Introduction

When considering writing a book on the Headquarters of Fighter Command at Bentley Priory, I had little idea of the magnitude of the subject, the extent of my knowledge being that it had been at the heart of fighter operations during the Second World War. A small amount of research soon proved this to be an extremely narrow view. Bentley Priory was also Headquarters of Anti-Aircraft Command and of the Royal Observer Corps; down the hill at Stanmore Park, and directly related, was the Headquarters of Balloon Command. In short, it was the central point of the United Kingdom air defence system. To do justice to these other important organisations, each would require a volume of its own: similarly the house and estate, with a long and fascinating history, was also worthy of detailed recording. As the project progressed, it also became evident that even the period during which the Royal Air Force has been in residence would need to be restricted and it would be necessary to confine the history to the original concept of being almost solely Fighter Command, and terminate it at the end of the war. Even then, many well known personalities would not be mentioned, and some important items left out.

Improvements in procedure and equipment produced a state of continuous change within the raid reporting and fighter control organisation. To give an idea of how it functioned, it becomes necessary to select a particular time in its evolution. Unless stated otherwise, descriptions given in reminiscences by those working within the system roughly relate to the 1940 period. It was a time when it was far from being a smooth-running machine. That it achieved so much is due to the dedication and discipline of those involved. This period also embraces the time when it was being subjected to the heaviest pressure, and incidentally when its leadership and use of its weapons were being brought into question. The administration and responsibility for the air defence covered a very wide spectrum of activities which on occasions extended into debate at Cabinet level and the higher direction of the war.

It is now generally accepted that the Commander-in-Chief, Sir Hugh Dowding, was badly treated and, in the light of recent evidence, this now appears to be something of an understatement. The view that he was due for retirement when relieved of his Command is incorrect; the time limit on his tenure as Commander-in-Chief at Fighter Command had been lifted two months earlier. Neither is the notion correct that at the time the achievement of Fighter Command in winning the Battle of Britain was not fully realised. The facts were there to be seen; The *Luftwaffe* had withdrawn its heavy daylight attacks after not having attained its objective. Those who were seeking to discredit him and bring about his dismissal eventually succeeded. Knowing little of the intriguing which brought about his removal, he could only speculate in later life as to what had happened; by then his memory was becoming blurred and some events had become telescoped.

Bentley Priory had greatly influenced the outcome of the war by helping to preserve a base from which Germany could be threatened. That threat, in the form of Allied air power, later became overwhelming. During the weeks prior to D-Day, the launching day of operation OVERLORD, and until the ground forces were firmly established on the continent, the leaders controlling this great force met daily in the underground operations block to decide strategy and select targets. Prior to this, United States and British staffs had been working for many months in and around the Priory organising and creating the necessary support for the landings and subsequent move across Europe.

The mansion and estate, now but a shadow of its former splendour, had nevertheless taken on an importance far greater than its earlier occupiers could ever have envisaged.

Chapter 1

Private House to
Fighter Command Headquarters

B y the time Fighter Command Headquarters moved into Bentley Priory on 14 May 1936, the estate had had a very chequered history. From a rather insignificant small house owned by Mr James Duberley, it had risen in size and status to become a highly prestigious country estate in the possession of The Honourable James John Hamilton, later 9th Earl and First Marquess of Abercorn. In 1789 he had engaged the eminent architect Sir John Soane to carry out a massive extension of the house and buildings at considerable cost. Bentley Priory was subsequently owned by Sir John Kelp, a building contractor; it was turned into a private hotel by a Mr Frederick Gordon and later became a private boarding school for young ladies. With much of the estate having been sold off and the house and gardens now in a dilapidated condition, the Royal Air Force acquired it in March 1926 and two months later, on 26 May, it became Headquarters of Inland Area, administering a number of air force home establishments under the command of Air Vice-Marshal Tom Webb-Bowen CB, CMG.

As part of a major reorganisation of the Royal Air Force, Fighter Command was created in July 1936 under Air Marshal Sir Hugh Caswell Tremenheere Dowding KCB, whose career had originated in 1900 as an Army Subaltern with the Royal Garrison Artillery and continued with the Royal Flying Corps during the First World War, Dowding was well qualified to become its first Air Officer Commanding-in-Chief (AOC-in-C). He had commanded Fighting Area in the earlier Air Defence of Great Britain (ADGB) organisation in 1929–30 and thereafter for six years was employed as Air Member for Research and Development on the Air Council. In this capacity he was well placed to gain knowledge and exert influence on selection and future development of equipment, one example being support of the Radio Direction Finding (RDF) principle (later termed Radar). During this period technological progress

1

brought about a great transformation in air fighting, particularly with the development of the fast monoplane fighters; the effectiveness of their speed and firepower in combat was, however, still to be proved.

Dowding was a man of strong character with a mind capable of deep thought and foresight, and had very positive views on how his new Command and the air defence system should develop. He was of a naturally reserved nature with a disinclination towards most forms of socialising; his seemingly humourless, often grumpy image portrayed to those not of close acquaintance, plus a facility for quick acid comment, gained him enemies and a reputation for being difficult. He sought the favour of no-one. From his early service days the nickname 'Stuffy' endured.

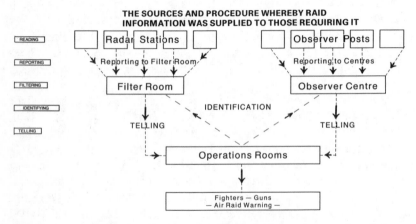

Prior to the official installation of Fighter Command at Bentley Priory, discussions were taking place on the function a Command Headquarters Operations Room would be expected to fulfil. On 10 June Dowding attended a high level meeting held to lay down the basic requirement for the room and its associated communications. It was concluded that all intelligence on aircraft in flight supplied by the various observation sources, including Radar, should be transmitted through the most direct channels to Group Headquarters and Sector airfields. It was thought that it might be necessary for the long-range readings from the proposed Radar stations on the coast to be initially transmitted direct to Bentley Priory and plotted on the large map there; maps at Groups and Sectors would basically show only the Group's area of responsibility. Reports from Secret Services sources and enemy radio interceptions would normally be of a strategic nature and, as such, would be passed to Fighter Command and not directly

2

to Groups. The Admiralty should have a direct link with the air defence system through Fighter Command.

When discussions turned to the initiation of air raid warnings, it was realised that there were advantages in having this de-centralised and operated from the Group Headquarters who would have shorter telephone links with the areas affected; alternatively, if responsibility was at Fighter Command Headquarters, the map's more general view, covering enemy raids throughout the whole defence system, would make it possible to deduce their future course and threatened districts in their path could be warned earlier. Either way, the initiation of warnings was considered to be the responsibility of the Home Office and it was agreed that a representative should be either present in the Operations Rooms or in contact through direct telephone links. It was considered necessary to have liaison with Bomber Command, enabling relevant information on bomber routes and movements to be pre-recorded; if the need arose, the record could be amended at a later juncture. With this knowledge on hand, an Intelligence Officer should be able to distinguish friendly from hostile tracks being plotted on the Operations Table.

One aspect of the deliberations, which later was to create great controversy, was the reinforcement of one Group by its neighbour. It was thought that

'it might be desirable, owing to the importance of speed, for a Fighter Group to call upon an adjacent Group for assistance of a fleeting nature involving small forces. As, however, the Fighter Command would have full intelligence respecting every enemy raid, reinforcements, even of this nature, might possibly originate there . . . The Fighter Command should normally issue instructions for inter-Group reinforcements but the power to order fleeting minor reinforcements might be delegated to Fighter Groups at the discretion of the Fighter Command.'

With regard to the Operations Table at Bentley Priory, it was not thought necessary to display all the detailed information carried on those at Group level; just sufficient to allow the Commander-in-Chief to see the geographical position of each raid without any indication of numbers or height. An indication of the far-seeing approach of the members at the meeting came in the suggestion that for the present information would have to be displayed by hand but ultimately it might be possible to record it by some optical means using a television reproduction of the proposed three Group operations tables. Possibly this idea was dropped because of the need for television to be viewed in subdued light, creating difficulties for those performing other activities in the same room.

Dowding was asked to formulate proposals for the information he desired to produce on the table, what type of operations table was required and the number of personnel this would involve. He was asked to restrict the amount of displayed information to the essential minimum; enough for him to decide, if necessary, when a raid passed near the boundary dividing two Groups, which one should intercept, and also he should be able to see if a raid was passing round to the rear of the defended areas and, by so doing, surprising the defences. The question of the security of Operations Rooms was also dealt with.[1] These, then, were Dowding's terms of reference for the Fighter Command Headquarters Operations Room at the Priory, a basis to work on.

He was, at this time, dealing with some Command correspondence from his home at Wimbledon Hill, in South West London, but by the beginning of July had begun working from Bentley Priory. On 2 July he wrote from there to the Air Ministry outlining his plans to set up an Operations Room and specifically asking for permission to install an experimental board (Operations Room Table).

He wrote,

'The Ball Room appears to be most suitable for the purpose although this of course may not be desirable as a permanent location owing to the fact that the Priory is extremely conspicuous from the air and the rooms would be very difficult to render gas proof. I do, however, wish to make a start immediately so that the delay in the production of my permanent Operations Room may be reduced to a minimum and only by immediate experiment can be determined the requirements necessary for the purpose.'

He then went on to say that the board would fill most of the unoccupied space in the Ballroom and the area on the board (Operations Room table) covered by the map would be from Edinburgh to the French coast, to Cherbourg, and from the Welsh border to the East of Belgium. The circular room (The Rotunda) would serve as a subsidiary for housing teleprinters, switchboards, etc. A gallery would be necessary along the North and West sides of the Ballroom. Following closely the recommendations of the earlier meeting, information displayed on the table map would be obtained by 'telling' from Group Boards (maps); that is to say aircraft movements showing on their maps would be rapidly 'told' over the telephone to Bentley Priory, thus making it possible for the countrywide picture to

4

be established. No movements of friendly fighters would be shown. Reports from the long-distance Radar would perhaps be received direct, and relayed to the Groups Headquarters. Intelligence information would certainly be received first at Bentley Priory and circulated in a reversed procedure. Every movement of bombers, both friendly and hostile would be tracked. The total cost of the experimental layout would not exceed £500.[2] This sum was approved by the Air Ministry three weeks later.

In the rooms designed nearly a century and a half earlier the first practical step was taken in the building of an entirely new concept in air defence, when radar would provide early raid warning and the locations of friend and foe could be established on a map. Techniques were being developed whereby Group/Sector control rooms could direct fighters into the vicinity of raiding aircraft. The system and its aircraft were developing together.

Squadron Leader Jim Griffiths was then a Leading Aircraftman (LAC) and moved to Bentley Priory from Hillingdon House, Uxbridge when ADGBHQ Fighting Area became Fighter Command. He stayed until posted to Egypt in April 1938. He stated

'On the formation of Fighter Command the support branches were transferred from Headquarters Fighting Area to Bentley Priory; from memory they were Engineering, Armament, Signals and Equipment.

'My duties were those of shorthand-typist to four officers of the Engineering Branch. This was a most exciting period; it was the time of the re-equipment of the fighter squadrons with the Hurricane and, as you can imagine, this involved a number of teething troubles some of which led to redesign and modification.

'At Command level the Officers (Engineering Branch) would act as advisers to the Air Ministry; I think during the early re-equipment days Hawkers had an engineer or two based at the Stations concerned. I cannot recall any major difficulty with the Hurricane, but every defect was reported to us on a Form 1022 which contained information as to what the problem was and a recommendation as to action required when considered beyond the capabilities of the Station concerned. When the same component, over a period of time, had been the subject of six Forms 1022, which were very comprehensive reports, any further failures were reported on a monthly Form 1023 until remedial action was completed; this prevented any defect being overlooked. Group Captain F.G.D. Hards, DSC, DFC, followed by Air Commodore F.F. Howard-Williams, was the Senior Engineer Staff Officer.

'To me, an LAC, Air Chief Marshal Dowding lived in a different world. His personal clerk was one Corporal Custance and when he went on leave I had the privilege of being his 'stand-in'. Apart from being called upon to take down pages of shorthand upon highly secret fighter defence matters, I have little recollection of the Air Chief Marshal, except that he was stern but kind. Of the other Officers, in those days 95% were of the General Duties Branch and all were pilots, each having to perform a number of flying hours per year. The pre-1939 RAF Officer was most emphatically an Officer and a gentleman and, as such, had Service and social obligations. The more senior ones were ex RFC or RNAS. The only time we saw any of our Officers in uniform was when they were going on a Staff visit, Armistice Day, King's Birthday or other such occasion; normally they came to work in lounge suits. Headquarters Units were not commanded by a Commanding Officer but by a Camp Commandant, and ours was one Flight Lieutenant Gearing.

'Looking back, I can only say that at Bentley Priory we were an extremely happy set of people; I cannot recall any unpleasant words or deeds. *Esprit-de-Corps* and morale were of the highest order. In the very stable and civilised conduct of affairs in the United Kingdom at that time security was almost unnecessary, but there was always a Duty Staff Officer, a Duty Clerk, Duty Signals Personnel and an Air Ministry civilian policeman or two on duty.

'The only disciplinary matter that I can recall was the Court Martial of a LAC Fitter MT who, with a Corporal, took a vehicle out on a run without a Form 658 (Authorisation of Journey). Every effort was made to help the LAC and he was found Not Guilty having convinced the court that he had had trouble with the brakes, had worked to get the vehicle serviceable for use the next day and had taken it out on a road test!

'At Hendon was No. 24 Squadron which was a Communications Squadron. The only aircraft I can remember being there were the Tiger Moths. Officers from Bentley Priory used these aircraft on occasions to do staff visits, and I recall on one occasion being told by one Squadron Leader Hardy that I was to go with him on a visit to Church Fenton. Shortly after take-off we ran into a headwind of some 40 mph and since our speed was about 80 mph the Squadron Leader decided to abort the visit since it would have taken some time to reach Yorkshire.

'Another visit I remember was to Highbury Stadium to see Arsenal play Blackpool. This was reward for our services (another LAC and myself) given by Squadron Leader Hardy and we were treated to seats in the stand at 7/6d. each.

'The same Squadron Leader Hardy had been given a Rolls/Bentley by his wife as a birthday present, and one day when he had this car at Bentley Priory, he asked if I would like a trip in it. We travelled along Western Avenue at some 100 mph.

'Our off-duty time was controlled by our financial reward. As a LAC my weekly income was 31/6d., part of which (10/6d.) was placed in a Post Office Savings Account. My most memorable times were spent playing sports, the occasional dance in the NAAFI, visits to theatres, cinemas and pubs, week-ends occasionally at home with my parents, normal healthy relations with a girl friend. We airmen were most fortunate in that we had our own room (no barrack room life), food was first class, only an occasional parade and lots of hard work over long hours.'

On taking up his new appointment, Dowding was invited to become Chairman of the Home Defence Committee's Sub Committee on the Reorientation of the Air Defence Great Britain, a position held until then by Air Marshal P.B. Joubert de la Ferté, who had remained at Uxbridge when it became Headquarters of No. 11 Group (Fighter). At the first meeting under Dowding's Chairmanship on 29 October 1936, they had preliminary discussions on a Memorandum put forward by the Minister for Co-ordination of Defence, Sir Thomas Inskip, who requested them to make a study and submit their findings on a hypothetical, money-and-supply-no-object, 'ideal' air defence system which would reach fruition in 1939. This task was given to a small sub-committee consisting of Lieutenant-Colonel K.M. Loch, representing the War Office, Captain J.M. Fuller, from the Admiralty and Wing Commander J. Andrews, of the Air Ministry, who were asked to work out the detailed requirements; any points on which guidance was needed could be listed for later attention.[3] An existing plan for expansion, agreed in 1935, was for an establishment of 21 Fighter Squadrons, which was due to reach maturity at the end of 1938 or early in 1939; there were to be 68 Bomber Squadrons. At this time, in reality, the home defence fighter strength had reached nineteen squadrons formed from fourteen No. 11 Group 'regulars', three Auxiliary Air Force Squadrons, who had converted from bombers in July 1934 and were part of No. 6 Auxiliary Group, plus two University Air Squadrons who were attached to Fighter Command.

The Committee went about their work with alacrity and a twelve page Draft Report on an 'Ideal' Air Defence System was produced which covered all facets of the defences, including guns, searchlights, the London Balloon Barrage and provision of fighter aircraft; the representatives had sought and received guidance from the respective departments. The question of fighter strength caused a large measure of disagreement among the representatives; one thought uppermost in their minds was the possibility that a future enemy, namely Germany, might attempt a massive 'knock-out' blow using all their available strength to destroy the country's ability to resist in one fell swoop. It was this prospect and how to cope with it that received much attention. The debate centred on how much reliance could be placed on the threat of a retaliatory blow by British bombers deterring such a move and, if this failed, what fighter strength there should be available to parry the 'knock-out' blow. One principle was agreed; the most important function of the air force was offensive action by bombers, but that a defensive system was also necessary.

With hindsight, it is perhaps a little odd to find the representatives of the War Office (Army) and Admiralty (Royal Navy) strongly opposing the Air Ministry's opinions on fighter strength. The Air Ministry had advised;

'Having regard to this fundamentally important aspect of the air defence problem, the Air Staff have concluded that it would be unsound to propose a large increase to the fighter forces allocated to the Home Defence Organisation. They consider that such a policy would unduly retard, so far as the practical possibilities of the next three years are concerned, the development of the necessary offensive strength. They, therefore, propose that during this period addition to the Home Defence fighter strength should be limited to four fighter squadrons, which they at present contemplate might be auxiliary squadrons. These four squadrons would enable two new aircraft sectors to be established, the Auxiliary Squadrons being distributed through the defence system.'

This statement brought forth strong reaction and it was recorded:

'The Admiralty and War Office representatives are not satisfied that the proposed increase in fighter strength by four squadrons is in any way adequate.'

They related how the existing scheme was based on 21 squadrons being able to combat an estimated German bomber strength of 900 aircraft; with the German force expected to reach 1,700 aircraft, if fighter aircraft were to be the primary weapon of air defence, the suggested increase to 350 fighters was not enough, especially having regard to the fact that only a portion of this strength could be concentrated over a given area. The report continued:

> 'The argument that the real answer is the counter-offensive is a weighty one, but the Admiralty and War Office representatives are not convinced that the counter-offensive against Germany is likely to produce immediate results. Unless, therefore, the counter-offensive can guarantee an immediate and appreciable lessening of the weight of attack on this country, it cannot be regarded as a sufficiently effective counter in conjunction with a meagre fighter strength to a "knock-out" blow by Germany.'[4]

It was noted that Dowding was 'reluctant to put forward any suggestion which could not be implemented in practice' and he also regarded the 'ideal' as bound to be, in his opinion, somewhat of an academic question. He submitted to the committee that he would be prepared to undertake the defence of Great Britain with thirty-four squadrons provided that certain ground establishments were improved. The Committee recommended forty-five squadrons as being the 'ideal', four of which would be relinquished to an Expeditionary Force at the outbreak of hostilities on the assumption that they would be sent to support ground troops engaged in a Continental conflict.[5] This figure was, of course, calculated on current estimates of German air strength and on the basis of German long-range bombers raiding directly from Germany not, as was later the case, from airfields located a few miles on the other side of the English Channel. No thought was given to Germany being able to operate single-seater fighters over the British Isles.

To explain the Air Staff's viewpoint requires looking at British air strategy on a much wider basis. Broadly speaking, since 1933, no doubt because of the great strength of the Navy, it was generally thought that an invasion of British shores was only a remote possibility. Therefore, the biggest threat to security came from the air, and the idea that an overwhelming early 'knock-out' blow aimed initially at London became prevalent.* If Germany invaded the Low Countries and succeeded in securing bases there, it would have a double-edged advantage for them; firstly their bombers would be able to carry a heavier bomb load, which

---

* The expected catastrophic effect of aerial bombardment of civilians had a great influence on both military and political policy. A strong body of opinion pressed for disarmament, then an attempt at the international (*continued on p.10*)

would be made possible through the shorter range requiring less weight of fuel; secondly, for the RAF to strike at important targets in Germany it would be necessary to fly over that occupied country which would now be hostile. Thus it became convenient that a small army should be supporting the French, keeping the front line as far away from Britain as possible and also minimising the range for British bombers striking at Germany. The emphasis, therefore, was placed on having a strong, powerful bomber force. This would act as a deterrent to Germany's territorial ambitions and be of great value both politically and diplomatically. Later in the 1930s the view that having bases in France was of vital importance changed and the accent was directed towards raiding Germany directly from Britain; the Air Force then would be acting independently of the Army. To sustain the deterrent principle, it was imperative that the bomber force should be seen to, at the very least, equal that of Germany; parity and the retaliation deterrent became the cornerstone on which home security was based.

The Air Ministry, when giving advice to the 'Ideal' Committee, showed it was less concerned about the principle of what could be 'implemented in practice', proposing that the bomber force should be trebled, bringing it up to 2,500 aircraft, an increase of 1,500, which they estimated would by then be fifty percent greater than that of Germany. The Army's 'ideal' Anti-Aircraft gun strength was to be 1,256 heavy and up to 300 pom-poms, and at night 4,700 searchlights should be in support.[6] The realisation that these figures could not be achieved until after 1939, making an interim scheme necessary, gave Dowding the opportunity to insist that a properly organised system of control from the ground and all Operations Rooms should be completed in peacetime.

By 11 December 1936, work on the Experimental Operations Room was sufficiently advanced for Dowding to write to the Air Ministry requesting installation of GPO telephone lines for which, incidentally, an estimate for expenses likely to be incurred was necessary.

At the same time he informed them of the intention to limit the field of experiment to a single link-up with No. 11 (Fighter) Group, and in so doing, concentrating effort in developing and proving a prototype component of the future organisation.

In May 1937, which incidentally saw the creation of No. 12 Fighter

cont'd
abolition of the bombers was made. Either way, it was hoped to make Britain immune from bombing. When it failed, reliance was placed on having a superior bomber force than that of the enemy as a deterrent.

Group, Dowding gave a lecture, 'Fighter Command in Home Defence' to members of the RAF Staff College.[7] When compared with what later happened, his ideas and opinions proved to be remarkably prophetic. He first looked at how the war could most quickly be lost and decided this might possibly be caused by indiscriminate air attacks creating panic among the population of London; alternatively, an immediate paralysis of the food supply could have the same effect. If the country could be secured against a quick decision of this kind, the only defeat could come from the slower process of exhaustion of equipment, personnel, food, raw materials, sea transport and other resources. He thought London, in addition to being at the centre of the population, was also the focal point of the machinery of Government and the main centre for reception and distribution of imported food supplies, and concluded 'the defence of London is, therefore, the first and most important task in the defence of Great Britain', but he also had to be prepared for an alternative. Putting himself in the position of a Dictator of a European Country, his first objective would be to destroy the enemy's Air Force at his airfields, reserve storage depots and factories, etc. and, in so doing, paralyse his ability to retaliate; then, at leisure, adopt any measure likely to bring about a victory in the shortest possible time. He went on to say that unless, in the meantime while we were under attack, our bombers were systematically destroying the enemy's air force in a similar manner, we could never assure our own defence by the operations of Fighter Command and the Army associated with its work.

He continued,

'There is another possible form of attack which I think deserves closer study than it has received up to the present. I refer to the attacks on our food and supply ships at sea.'

He advocated, as a matter of the highest importance, arrangements for the diversion of shipping away from the vulnerable areas of the Port of London and its approaches, namely the Thames Estuary, to Western ports; his concern being the possibility of attacks against inland targets becoming unsustainable, and the bulk of the offensive power being turned against supply ships. He continued,

'It seems to me that our shipping will, broadly speaking, be as open to submarine attack as it was in the last war and it will now have to face the additional danger of attack from the air.'

A further possibility he thought, although not great at the time, was of invasion either by sea or on a smaller scale by parachute troops, and had to be kept in mind.

After a comprehensive preview of the future air defence system, he concluded,

'The main dangers to be guarded against are fire, bomb explosion and gas, probably in that order of importance.'

He considered incendiary attacks on property, enabling the enemy to utilise for purposes of destruction more than he actually carried in his aircraft, was at that time the greatest danger the civil population had to face. A single bomber might distribute a thousand small incendiary bombs and, with the building density in London being high, a single machine might initiate something like one hundred small fires. He went on,

'There is a serious danger that groups of individual fires, which are not properly dealt with, will unite and cause a conflagration which will be beyond the control of any fire fighting organisation which we are likely to be able to provide.'

Improvement of the fire fighting organisation was a necessity. Although unaware of it, those present at the lecture had been given an accurate glimpse of the future. Very few points Dowding made were wide of the mark. He had touched on the attempt to destroy the Air Force as an opening gambit in a subjugation policy, the possibility of increasing crippling shipping losses by U-boat and air attack, the destruction of British cities by fire using the incendiary bomb, with London being the principal target.

By the late summer of 1935, research at Orfordness of Radar had expanded to such a degree that further accommodation was required and Bawdsey Manor on the Suffolk coast near Felixstowe, was purchased. Although the research team was very small, the quality and variety of their inventiveness was remarkable. In April 1937, they were engaged in radar trials endeavouring to locate aircraft flying on pre-arranged courses over the North Sea. Results were confused and disappointing and Dowding thought the general standard of information was as yet unacceptable for use in his Operations Rooms. Nevertheless, by August a plan for the construction of coastal radar stations had already been agreed (See Appendix 3). They were each to have four receiver masts, 250 feet high, and four 350-foot masts for the transmitter; the reason for duplication was their vulnerability to air attack, and the likelihood that transmissions would be interfered with or 'jammed' by the Germans.

In the event of a mast or its aerials being damaged, or operating radio frequency becoming impaired, there were others ready to take over. To improve results they would be sited close enough together to form a chain where each station oversaw part of its neighbours' detection area.

Application of coastal radar was very much a combined effort of civilian scientists and Royal Air Force Signals specialists. Squadron Leader Raymund Hart, who originally was attached to Bawdsey in July 1936 to set up a radar school, became very influential in the methods adopted to improve and integrate the use of radar into the air defence system. After studying the results of the unsatisfactory April 1937 trials, the general opinion was that an improvement in tracking could be made if coastal radar stations were sited close enough to each other to permit an overlap of their respective fields of observation; this made it possible for every part of the area being watched to be covered by a minimum of two stations; an aircraft's position could be more accurately 'fixed' when using two or three independent readings (see diagram on page 15). This technique made things complicated, and required careful handling and correlation of readings from adjacent stations; they would now be linked in the form of a chain. To do this, a procedure was adopted whereby the readings, showing in the form of plots on a large grid map, were married together and from them a single accurate plot position was assumed. These were displayed in the shape of arrows on the gridded map, and from them the course of the aircraft could be seen. Officers aware of friendly aircraft movements identified friend from foe, thus extraneous information was filtered out.

At the outset, at Bawdsey a map table representing the area of the approaches to the Thames Estuary was set up by the scientists. Radar stations at Bawdsey, Dover and Canewdon supplied readings over direct telephone lines to a Filter Centre there. By the end of November 1937, information from the map was being passed by telephone to the experimental operations room at Bentley Priory, to the Headquarters of No. 11 (Fighter) Group at Uxbridge and Sector Headquarters at Biggin Hill. The Filter Centre was also receiving information from an experimental station at Dunkirk, near Canterbury, which was researching the possibility of radar being used to report aerial activity overland; the other stations faced seawards. From experience gained, a second filter centre was designed at Bawdsey covering a much larger coastal area from Dover to Norwich. In May 1937, the first Chain Home (CH) Radar Station, that at Bawdsey, had passed into the hands of the RAF; the two others, at Canewdon and Dover, were completed by August. All were given the name AMES (Air

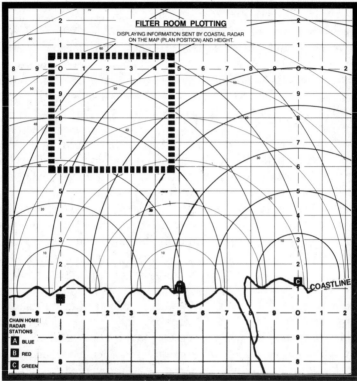

Using Radar to Track Aircraft Activity over the Sea

Tracks identified as friendly were discounted; others, when they reached the coast, were continued overland using Observer Corps Plots.

The 100 kilometre square (numbered 1–10) is divided into 100 squares; this is further sub-divided into 100 imaginary squares (British Modified grid). On this gridded map of the sea, plotters placed their coloured counters on grid references telephoned from radar stations. For ease of identification they have been more widely spaced on this diagram than was usual. Often they were so close that the counters would touch each other.

On the walls of the Filter Room, time indicators, divided into sections numbered 1–5, continuously worked in a 2½-minute cycle. Counters, commonly known as 'tiddlywinks', matching the appropriate radar station colour, were numbered on one side, with the equivalent number showing as dots on the reverse. When placed with a number showing, it indicated that the plot had been received from a C.H. Radar Station: when the dots were on view, it had come from a Chain Home Low Station. Plotters selected and placed counters to coincide with the figure currently illuminated for a half minute on the indicators. These were removed when the indicator cycle repeated the number and fresh ones were placed as the track progressed; therefore, no information on the table was more than two and a half minutes old.

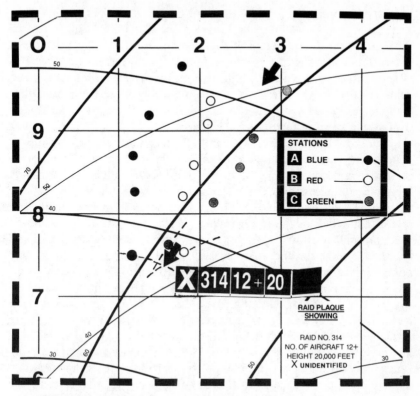

FACSIMILE SHOWING PART OF THE PLOTTING TABLE GRID (circa 1940) AND THE PROCESS OF "RANGE CUTTING"

The Process of 'Range Cutting' to Establish a True Plot

Range Arcs were drawn on the map in the colour of the Radar Station and extended outwards at 10 mile intervals. Assessment of range was a station's most accurate aspect. For accuracy, the Filterer relied on the position of plots from two or three adjoining stations. Using their positions in relation to the curve of the range arcs, by co-ordinating the three plots he estimated the position of the aircraft. Having calculated this, he placed an arrow with its tip resting on that point and indicating the direction the aircraft were going. The tip of the arrow now became a 'true' plot and this was broadcast as a grid reference by a Filter Room Teller to all Operations Rooms within the threatened Group. The tray placed at the head of the track carried other raid information.

On this diagram, the counters at the head of the track are 'A' 38 miles, 'B' 42 miles and 'C' 59 miles from their respective stations. The plot (tip of the arrow) given to Operations Rooms in this case would be W 1774. When busy, many tracks would be forming simultaneously.

15

Ministry Experimental Station), hopefully to disguise their true purpose. That same month the Treasury Inter-Service Committee sanctioned the expenditure for the full chain of twenty stations.

Development of Radar progressed under a shroud of great secrecy, although it was realised that in time the massive steel and wooden towers being constructed on the coast would inevitably be seen for what they really were. It was a surprise, however, that while on a visit to Britain with a high ranking German Air Mission, it is said that General Milch enquired how British experiments in radio location were progressing.

In the air, great technological changes were taking place. The biplane era was soon to come to an end; the day of the fast monoplane had arrived. It was now a necessity to have an instrument panel on which accurate flying aids were mounted, e.g. an artificial horizon, gyro compass and rate of climb/descent indicator. Where before navigation was achieved using prominent ground features, railway lines, woods, etc. which could be seen from the air and were marked on a four-miles-to-the-inch map not unlike a road map, now pilots were required to fly accurate courses given by a ground controller. Time was critical; enemy aircraft were also flying at greater speeds. No longer would time be wasted dodging around large build-ups of cloud with their restricted visibility; instruments were available for flying through them. The time in which a pilot was able to hold an enemy aircraft in the gunsight had also been greatly reduced, requiring heavier fire-power in a shorter time to destroy it. Generally speaking, fighter interception times had decreased by forty to fifty percent; the Gloster Gladiator biplane had a maximum speed reckoned to be 250 mph; by comparison the Spitfire was 112 mph faster. These great changes in the air inevitably soon led to a need for a change in air fighting tactics and few were in a position to advise. Staff Officers, in the main, were men who were experienced in flying biplanes and using tactics of that period, many of which were now becoming obsolete. Pilots with experience of the new aircraft types were few and far between, and with the prospect of war in the near future, they were necessarily left on flying duties. Much of the tactical side of air interception was learned by trial and error later on when German tactics became clear.

With Germany now seen as the biggest threat to peace, much effort was devoted to finding out their aircraft production figures and from these the desired strength of the British Home Defence Force was calculated. (The 1937 'Ideal' air defence assessment was part of this.) Over the years, as the intelligence estimates of increasing German production came in, readjustments to the size of the future British defence forces were made.

Starting with Scheme 'A' in 1933, by November 1938 Scheme 'M' providing for 800 fighters was under review (50 squadrons of 16 aircraft). From this figure, four squadrons were for the Field Force and four for Trade Defence, leaving 42 for Home Defence. Dowding now considered 41 'on whose presence he could rely' would be sufficient for Home Defence; to ask for more at the time, he said, would be an embarrassment, there were not enough airfields.[8]

While events in Germany were being closely watched, critical eyes were also observing the lack of progress in the creation of secure buildings for vital elements of Home Defence. The experimental Operations Room at Bentley Priory, conceived in the ballroom almost two years earlier continued in use; no plans for a permanent Operations Centre had been drawn up, much to the chagrin of the Air Ministry who, not surprisingly, were becoming concerned about safety. To get things moving, the Directorate of Communications Development was asked to liaise with a section of the Bawdsey Research Group and make a study of the likely requirements of Operations Centres generally.

By May 1938, sites for Nos 11, 12 and 13 Group Operations Centres were already chosen and on 2 June the Deputy Director of Plans recommended that all Group and the Command's Operations Rooms should be constructed underground and completed by March 1939 at the latest. There was a delay with the design of the latter, caused by Dowding's recommendation that final decisions on its layout could best be made at the conclusion and subsequent analysis of the results of the 1938 Home Defence Exercises in August. This reasoning was no doubt based on the alterations continuing in the experimental Centre; as new ideas were introduced and modifications suggested, carpenters and signals equipment people were frequently making changes to the layout of the Command Operations Centre. This was done with comparative ease in the ballroom, but if alterations became necessary after the equipment was transferred to the comparatively restricted area of the underground building, it would be an entirely different matter. The Air Ministry now regretted not having put a time limitation on the period of experimentation but realised that if they decided to proceed immediately, there was a likelihood that Dowding would refuse to accept responsibility for the centre, having made the recommendation for a delay until August. They suggested a small drafting committee should be set up to start preparatory work.

Wing Commander Whitworth-Jones of Fighter Operations wrote a Minute to Sholto Douglas, the Deputy Chief of the Air Staff, urging immediate action and proposed that a letter should be sent to Fighter

17

Command explaining they could 'no longer delay the design and construction of the Command Operations Room'.[9]

The August 1938 Home Defence Exercise showed that the radar early warning was working well, but the plotting at Bawdsey by inexperienced RAF men lacked the polish achieved by those who had developed the techniques with the scientists. Nevertheless, it was decided to move the entire filtering organisation from there to Bentley Priory. Other recommendations were for better communications and the need for more forward Direction Finding relay stations. These had been brought in to extend the poor range of the High Frequency radio system. It was envisaged that most interceptions of hostile aircraft would be effected over the coast and out to sea at which range, under conditions experienced during the exercises, the quality of the aircraft's radio signals was found to be poor when picked up by normal DF Stations. A greater priority was recommended for development and fitting of IFF (Identification Friend or Foe) to all home aircraft, a device which visually indicated on a radar screen the origins of the aircraft. On 7 March 1939, Lord Chatfield, then Minister for the Co-ordination of Defence, visited the Filter Room at the Priory when an exercise was in progress. By coincidence, A.F. Wilkins and R.H.A. Carter, the scientists at Bawdsey working on the IFF development, were down there having the apparatus flight tested and tracking the aircraft using Bawdsey CH Radar. Noting the good echoes coming from it, which classified it as 'friendly', Wilkins passed the plots to Bentley Priory Filter Room, confidently informing the plotter of the aircraft's identity. This was the first occasion on which identified radar plots were received, and Lord Chatfield was made aware of its historical significance.[10]

Bentley Priory was taking on a far greater importance than had hitherto been intended; now the central point in a massive network of communications in which information was digested and disseminated. With war threatening, the need to preserve it heightened. On 25 September 1938, building of the underground Operations Centre was sanctioned at a cost of £45,000, the impetus no doubt coming from the current Munich Crisis.

The euphoria created by the Prime Minister Neville Chamberlain's 'Peace in our time' pronouncement after signing the 30th September agreement with Hitler, had no effect on defence preparations. Six days later, Deputy Chief of the Air Staff, Sholto Douglas, held a meeting to discuss emergency measures to increase war readiness and it was agreed that the Radar Chain should be hastened and reach completion by 1 April 1939. To implement this, a meeting was arranged to discuss the

18

emergency measures required to meet this deadline; it was attended by those closely associated with the development programme, Robert Watson-Watt, Director of Communications Development, Squadron Leader J.A. MacDonald from Signals, R. Struthers, representing the Director of Works, and Wing Commander Whitworth-Jones FO 1 (Fighter Operations Section 1). In their judgement, fifteen stations could be completed on a semi-permanent basis plus three others if compulsory purchase of their sites was made. Manufacturers of the steel masts would need to work around the clock; the makers of electrical and technical equipment should do likewise. An excess of wooden masts was required in case production of those made of steel fell behind schedule. Personnel to man the stations would prove difficult. It was hoped that the high transmitter masts would make the stations difficult to attack from the air and much importance was placed on the interception of raiders over the sea.[11]

On 29 September, the day before the Munich agreement was signed, and with the international situation assuming grave proportions, work was pushed forward on the projected plan for the removal of the Filter Room from Bawdsey to Bentley Priory. A room in the basement which had previously only served as an office-cum-lumber room, was pressed into use; its basement location was thought to be an advantage from the safety point of view. The room was in the shape of a grand piano, and Squadron Leader Raymund Hart had to take this into consideration when he designed the layout and positioning of the table and installation of telephone equipment. The assembly was carried out at commendable speed and the room was able to assume control on 8 November using experienced members of Bawdsey staff.

Ten days later, at a conference at the Air Ministry which was discussing accommodation and administration of radar stations, Hart described how radar operators were now being trained by having them follow the movements of civil air traffic; at some stations, airmen were able to train almost continuously from 0900 hours until sometimes late at night. (This method of training had been suggested earlier by Sir Henry Tizard.) Hart later raised the question of who would do the filter plotting at Bentley Priory, asking if proposals would be considered to introduce the trade of 'Plotter', and whether it would be possible to consider ladies for permanent employment in that capacity. He had conducted research on ladies as plotters and 'they were entirely satisfactory'. It was agreed that this proposal should first gain the approval of the Air Ministry.[12]

During 1938, a fundamental change in air defence policy had occurred. The strength of the German Air Force was now thought to be numerically superior to that of the RAF and continuation of the policy of parity in numbers and its deterrent effect was beginning to look unsustainable, at least for the immediate future. Both financial and industrial resources, where the expansion programme was making heavy demands on skilled labour, were being fully stretched. To the chagrin of the Air Staff, Sir Thomas Inskip, Minister for Co-ordination of Defence applied pressure to alter the balance of aircraft production from the manufacture of the bomber to the fighter, a significant change which indicated he was placing reliance on a strong home defence system being able to withstand a German onslaught until such times as the heavy bomber strength could be built up to perform its intended counter offensive role.

The Entrance Hall. Taken from a painting by architect Sir John Soane which, like other works, was exhibited at the Royal Academy. 1799. *(Sir John Soane's Museum)*

Plan of part of the ground floor and gardens of Fighter Command Headquarters Bentley Priory. Produced for the proposed sale of the estate in 1895.

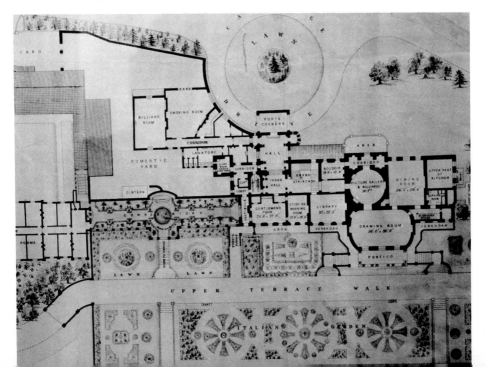

The building, with much of the original fabric still intact. The Conservatory (left centre) was removed at the outbreak of World War Two. *(Ministry of Defence)*

The Dowding Room – an earlier period. *(Crown Copyright)*

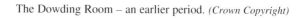

The Southern aspect of the house today. The room behind the Portico housed the experimental Operations Room. Next to it *(centre)* was Dowding's office, now a museum. Centre left, the lower section had its origins in the James Duberley house. *(Author)*

View of the Italian garden from the Dowding Room. *(Author)*

"Montrose", A.O.C.-in-C.'s Residence 1940. *(Sir Ivor Broom)*

Stanmore Hall, in Wood Lane off Stanmore Hill. Requisitioned and used for A.E.A.F. accommodation and Mess. 1944. *(Air Vice-Marshal "Sandy" Johnstone)*

The Gymnasium, when Bentley Priory was a Girls' School. *(Crown Copyright)*

"The Warren", Bushey Heath. W.A.A.F. Hostel.
(J. Clarke)

W.A.A.F. Joan Clarke (Née Crawford) at "The Warren" 1940.
(J. Clarke)

Sholto Douglas and U.S. President's wife, Mrs Eleanor Roosevelt, inspect the W.A.A.F. Dame Mary Welsh, Air Chief Commandant W.A.A.F., can be seen to the rear between them. 27 October 1942. *(I.W.M.)*

The Operations Room in the house. *(Crown Copyright)*

Early Operations Room in the house. In use until 9 March 1940. *(Crown Copyright)*

A scene of much innovation, the Operations Room in the house. Used until
9 March 1940. The plotting table can be seen below. Colour change clock used for
plotting is in the centre and the Air Raid Warning table bottom left. The lessons
learned here formed the basis of the system set up in the underground block.
(Crown Copyright)

The Command Operations Room in the Underground Block 1941. WAAFs used
the magnetic rods for plotting. WAAF June Clapperton (now Mrs Esau) can be
seen bottom right of picture. *(Crown Copyright)*

Chapter 2

1939 – Confrontation

Progress in the construction of the Fighter Command Headquarters underground block at Bentley Priory was very slow, so much so that by the end of 1938 requests were made for a temporary training room elsewhere by Air Commodore Maund at the Air Ministry. The entire construction period was one of frustrating delays. Estimated completion dates came and went. In reply to a critical Minute in July 1939 from the Deputy Director of Operations (Home), the Director of Works replied,

> 'This particular job has not been one of the happiest which we have been called upon to carry out; from the start we have been dogged by bad weather, we have had a landslide of serious dimension; we have had the stop and start orders of the Commander-in-Chief.'

At that time he was already saying that the structural work would not be completed by the estimated 15 September. The contractor's men had been working twenty-four hours a day, seven days a week since 10 January attempting to complete the project as soon as possible. Seventy men were engaged during the daylight hours and, under dim illumination which incidentally had to be sanctioned by the Home Office, twenty-five men continued working throughout the night, this labour force being what was thought to be the maximum number able to be usefully employed.[13] The original design was calculated to give total protection, but the specifications were changed to give structural strength to withstand a direct hit from a 500-lb General Purpose bomb or 250-lb SAP (Semi Armour Piercing). Because of the amount of water expected to be at the proposed depth, it was advised that it should be reduced. The estimated cost of the project was £60,000, plus a further £7,000 for Post Office work. Dowding was not satisfied, enquiring whether extra concrete could be put over the top or, as an alternative, if old battleship armour plating could be used.[14] The enormous excavation, said to be at an average depth of forty-two feet, required the removal of 58,270 tons of earth. The basic

21

structure took 23,500 tons of concrete, a high percentage of which was reinforced with steel. Later, further delays were caused by concern over the delicate signalling equipment becoming corroded by the dampness exuding from the drying concrete. There was a fear that wire insulation would deteriorate and soldered joints might corrode; it was estimated that in the air raid warning apparatus alone there were 4,000 joints. It was not until six months after the outbreak of war that the Operations Centre came into use.

In early February 1939, the Air Ministry were discussing with the GPO the provision of a standby Operations Room which could take over from Fighter Command Headquarters at Bentley Priory in the event of it being destroyed. Making a decision about its location was not easy and it rested largely on advice from the GPO. Close collaboration with them was indispensable; the entire raid reporting and most of the interception organisation was reliant on the civilian telecommunications system. The Air Ministry suggested Hendon, but the GPO favoured Leighton Buzzard where the Air Ministry's central telephone/teleprinter exchange was near completion; it was also where the necessary GPO connections converged. In the long term, they advised that a new centre should be established near Liscombe Park, two miles West of Leighton Buzzard. The standby Operations Centre was ready for occupation in July 1939 and it soon gained importance more for its secondary role, that of being a training centre for Operations and Filter Room personnel. Until the end of 1939, the training was done there by scientists from the Operational Research Section. It was a duplication of the layout and system currently in use at the Priory. The original policy was for it to be a temporary arrangement but Fighter Command were still insisting that all new lines be duplicated there as late as the middle of 1940.

On 20 May filtering ceased in the basement at Bentley Priory and was relocated in a more convenient, though far from safe, room upstairs next to the Operations Room where it stayed until nearly six months after the outbreak of war. It was of similar construction and materials to that of its neighbour, basically wooden scaffolding supporting a balcony for overseeing a large table map below. The balconies arranged on each side of the intersecting wall and at the same height allowed for a hole to be knocked through so that people could walk from one room to the other. The ornate decor, dating from a much earlier age, provided a bizarre backdrop to the crude wooden structures supporting the conglomeration of air defence equipment. Paintings and gildings, embellishments of the frieze, were in strange contradiction to the scene of electrical gadgetry and apparatus. The technology which was eventually transferred to the underground block was the product of years of development. Keith Park, then an Air Commodore and Senior Air Staff Officer (SASO) at Bentley Priory, had devoted much of his time to furthering its progress, as had Dowding.

An event which caused amusement in the usual mundane affairs of the Filter Room occurred in late May 1939 when the East coast radar stations began locating the presence of a very large craft flying slowly offshore. It was established that this was the giant German airship *Graf Zeppelin* and it was correctly thought to be interrogating the British radar defences. When navigating in thick cloud, it broke radio silence and reported its position to Germany as being a few miles off the Yorkshire coast; the radar track on the Filter Room table clearly showed it as being over Hull. Squadron Leader Walter Pretty (later Air Vice-Marshal Sir Walter Pretty) relished the situation, later recalling how greatly they were amused by the thought of transmitting a correction signal. This, of course, would have confirmed to the crew that they were under radar surveillance and given the game away.[15] Similarly, on 7 and 26 June, reconnaissance aircraft were tracked and it was thought likely that a complete series of photographs could have been obtained of the East and Southeast coast. Caution was urged should a protest be made to the German Air Attaché; divulging accurate positions of territorial infringements might arouse interest in how they were obtained. Radar and the 'Y' Service, who were monitoring German wireless transmissions could be exposed, the latter nullified by aircraft observing wireless silence.

Squadron Leader Walter Pretty had a close association with the Filter Room and came from a purely Service background, training at Cranwell and being commissioned as a Pilot Officer. (He later returned there and took a Long Signals Course at the Electrical and Wireless School.)

He first met Dowding during the 1936/7 Biggin Hill Experiments when he was Biggin Hill Sector Signals Officer and member of the experimental team, which established very important interception techniques for future application of Radar into the air defence organisation. After a two year spell in Canada on an interchange arrangement, he returned in 1939 to Fighter Command Headquarters at Bentley Priory. He later said,

'A fantastic metamorphosis had occurred during the two years I was away. From one experimental radar station at Bawdsey there now existed a completely integrated Chain of Stations stretching from Ventnor, along the South Coast, up the East Coast past Bawdsey and on to the Firth of Forth. Further North there was an additional Station to help protect the Fleet at Scapa Flow. This complex organisation was splendid and generally adequate for the day war as it evolved. "Stuffy" understood radar and its shortcomings. In October 1939 "Stuffy" sent for me and I can remember his exact words. He said, "Whether or not we win the day war depends on the success or failure of the eight-gun fighters, but I know we cannot win the night war". By this he meant with the weapons then in our armoury.

The stage was set for the daylight Battle of Britain, but this he relied largely on his good Commanders to win. All through that battle his striving to solve the problems of the night war never flagged. The more specially equipped Beaufighters, which "Stuffy" fought so hard to get to win the night war, arrived too late for him to be given the credit for his untiring work. Much of this went later on to his successor, but I'm sure "Stuffy" didn't begrudge it.'[16]

Walter Pretty was dedicated to his work, spending long periods away at Bawdsey and other radar locations, but he was also managing a small amount of social life, much of which was spent in the company of a member of the ATS. (They were, incidentally, the first women's Service at the Priory, and well ahead of the arrival of the WAAF.) The couple were married the following year in June 1940, at a time when the war and the country's future were entering a critical stage, and a honeymoon was arranged away from Bentley Priory, not, as can be imagined, a holiday by the seaside, but visiting the radar establishments at Hawks Tor, near Plymouth, and Worthy Down. He was deeply engrossed in the improvement of operational efficiency and development of radar night fighting equipment and techniques. Home life was very irregular; often after working throughout the night, he went home for a shave and change of clothes, then departed. The pressure to perfect the interception of night bombers was intense. Because a shroud of secrecy covered everything remotely connected with his job, it was essential for him to suppress his natural gift for communication when at home; for some time after they first met, his wife Betty harboured the notion that perhaps he was working in Intelligence. They had settled nearby in Manor Cottage, once the Hartsbourne Golf Course greenkeeper's residence and, when their first child was born, Betty Pretty could regularly be seen pushing the pram up the Bentley Priory drive on her way to shop at the NAAFI, occasionally taking the opportunity to have a quick word with her husband while *en route*. Later she was very amused to hear her young daughter telling a friend that her Daddy was 'working in the NAAFI'.

Squadron Leader Raymund Hart (later Air Marshal) graduated from the Royal College of Science as a physicist and studied radio at the École Supérieur d'Électricité in Paris: a scientist in the truest sense of the word. During the First World War he became an operational pilot winning the Military Cross, and in 1935 qualified as a Flying Instructor. The following year, when a Flight Lieutenant, and at the formation of Fighter Command, he was attached to the Staff of No. 11 (Fighter) Group at Uxbridge as Deputy Chief Signals Officer to Squadron Leader A.F. Lang. When radar was in its infancy, Raymund Hart was well placed to assist with integrating it into the existing raid reporting system and he was responsible for devising the working procedure of the Filter Room. In the field of radar he was influential in creating the close relationship that existed between Fighter Command Signals and the Bawdsey scientists, from which enormous benefit was gained.

Since the 1938 Air Exercises, two small groups of civilian scientists at Bawdsey were researching ways of gaining the maximum benefit from the information supplied by coastal radar, by studying operational procedures. E.C. Williams' group was concerning itself with improving rapid analysis and relaying of the information to the control centres; the other group, Messrs G.A. Roberts, I.H. Cole and J. Woodforde, was applying itself to the study of ground control of intercepting aircraft and was working in Group and Sector Operations Rooms, observing procedures used by Controllers. After the first major test of the radar chain during the 1939 Air Exercises, in which interceptions were carefully monitored by the Bawdsey scientists who were serving as observers in the Filter Room and Operations Rooms of Fighter Command, Dowding recognised the great value of their reports and recommendations and asked that a section should be permanently established at Bentley Priory. Once there, they would remain close to the centre of activity. This suggestion was no doubt precipitated by an earlier informal agreement between Raymund Hart and the Superintendent at Bawdsey, A.P. Rowe. They had realised the disadvantages inherent in a plan to have the entire research team at Bawdsey relocated hundreds of miles away at Dundee in the event of war, the thinking behind the move being that Bawdsey would almost certainly be an early target for air attack. Keith Park, SASO at Fighter Command was also thinking along similar lines and he too pressed for G.A. Roberts and his colleagues to remain at Stanmore.

Both groups combined to form what came to be known as the Radar Research Section, later renamed the Stanmore Research Section. It was put under the direction of H. Larnder, an engineer with technical experience in communications throughout the world and one-time employee of the International Standard Electric Corporation.

A third group of Bawdsey scientists moved to Leighton Buzzard and continued its allegiance to Bawdsey Research Station; by February 1940, it had grown to such a degree that it was used to form the base from which the Headquarters Unit of a new No. 60 Group (Signals) was created, which, under Air Commodore A.L. Gregory, was given responsibility for the technical and administrative control of the Chain Home radar, and for assisting in the introduction of all new radar equipment into the Air Force.

Meanwhile the Stanmore Research Section carefully monitored the performance of each radar station. They watched Operations and Filter Room working, taking notes for analysis and compiling reports, and suggested improvements which were tried and implemented into the system. These scientists added a new dimension to the prosecution of war; soon many other equipments and technical procedures were to be scrutinised by scientific minds. Realising the benefits of this arrangement, Bomber and Coastal Commands asked for similar Sections to be attached to them, and General Pile of Anti-Aircraft Command demanded one for his Headquarters at Glenthorn. What became known as Operational Research became firmly established.

The early sporadic German raids against Britain provided much valuable material for improving the efficiency of the raid reporting and interception procedures. By studying the occurrences of raids that failed to be intercepted, detailed examination of the statistics revealed whether faults at individual radar stations originated from engineering problems or from poor operational efficiency of the staff, and the required corrections were made. A measure of the value attributed to Operational Research at Fighter Command can perhaps best be shown by the number of scientists employed; by 1943 the section had grown to there being one Principal Scientific Officer, four Senior Scientific Officers and no less than fifty-eight other scientists.

Henry Tizard had reasoned, as early as 1936, that the future air defence system and its interception techniques would be insurmountable by day and compel the German Air Force to turn to night bombing. How to find and shoot down an enemy raider during the hours of darkness was to become the major problem in the succeeding years. At Bawdsey Manor the small group of scientists then working on the development of the radar chain made a decision to diversify their research. A. Wilkins was to continue with the coastal radar chain project and E.G. Bowen would take on a new line of radar research and development, that of airborne radar. Where the equipment for the coastal chain was of gigantic proportions with a range in exceptional conditions of nearly 200 miles, the new apparatus would, out of necessity, be in a miniaturised form to fit into a small aircraft and this requirement allowed for a set of only very short range; it used a narrow beam. Airborne radar proceeded along lines of development which would benefit two similar projects, one, the detection of surface ships, later known as Air-to-Surface Vessel (ASV), the other, Air Interception (AI) for air-to-air detection, the former taking precedence. The coming months were very productive, and output from the Bawdsey group, which by now had steadily increased in number to ten scientists, was impressive in its conception and advancement of equipment. Flight demonstrations were organised for the C-in-Cs of all the RAF Commands and other VIPs of known interest, using twin-engined Avro Ansons and single-engined Fairey Battles. It was in an aircraft of the latter type that a demonstration for Dowding was conducted in early July 1939. Squeezed tightly into the space intended for one person, E.G. Bowen, by using the information displayed on the cathode ray tubes as his sole means of detection, successfully guided the pilot into an interception position with the target aircraft. Dowding was clearly very pleased. In his book, *Radar Days*, Dr Bowen describes how, after an extremely poor landing at Martlesham, he was prompted to apologise for the indifferent touchdown. He relates, 'Stuffy took a deep breath and said, "I always say, the most important thing is to land the right way up", and he said no more about it.' After lunch the two men were left alone to discuss the night interception problem and the scientist was impressed by Dowding's grasp of the difficulties involved. He wrote, 'He covered the whole field . . . I had never heard such a clear and definitive analysis of the fundamentals of night fighting.'[17]

In a letter to the Air Ministry on 10 July, Dowding wrote,

'I was very much impressed with the potentialities of the apparatus (although of course it was installed only in a "lash up" form). The range and approximate position of the target aircraft were clearly indicated and I formed the opinion that an approach in the dark could be easily effected after a small amount of training and practise, provided a stern position with range of target could be attained.'

He made out a strong case for the use of a twin-engined fighter with a two-man crew and suggested the Blenheim as an admirable 'test bench'.[18] In the succeeding weeks he appears to have had a change of heart about how easy an interception was likely to be and became anxious about getting the right kind of man to operate the radar set installed in the Blenheim, by now perhaps realising how much the success of the demonstration had been due to the expertise of the scientist. He asked the Director of Signals at the Air Ministry if it was possible to use Voluntary Wireless Corps personnel. He continued to study the AI radar development programme very closely, through regular reports on operational tests and making occasional visits to Bawdsey.

On 14 July, as a result of Dowding's enthusiastic report about AI development at Martlesham, Sholto Douglas, Deputy Chief of the Air Staff (DCAS), who was fully aware of the deficiencies of the night defences, pushed forward a scheme in which a Blenheim was fitted with AI Radar so that tactics for its use could be devised; this was to be given the highest priority. He also instructed that twenty-one AI sets were to be manufactured by hand, six of which were to be given to Fighter Command, the others to be held in case of emergency; four Blenheims were to be prepared to receive the sets.[19] By 30 August, four experimental aircraft equipped with Mk IV AI Radar were attached to a special Flight of 25 Squadron, under Flight Lieutenant J.G. Cave.

The Home Defence Exercise carried out between 8 and 11 August 1939, was to be the final peacetime test of the system; less than a month later, Britain was at war.

When analysing the results, Dowding commented on how previously confusion had arisen when Observer Corps Centres were passing information to Group and Sector Operations Rooms on every raid showing on their map tables, some of which had not originated from radar tracks over the sea. To improve the situation Dowding insisted that only the radar tracks should be followed up; the others would be integrated into the system via other means. This new procedure, he noted in his report, was working well.

At this time, the only underground Operations Centre in use was at No. 11 Group Headquarters, and Dowding expressed concern about the safety of the somewhat flimsily constructed Sector Operations Rooms in exposed positions on airfields. (At an earlier meeting Air Vice-Marshal E.L. Gossage, commanding No. 11 Group, asked for them to be duplicated elsewhere; alternatively Leigh-Mallory of No. 12 Group suggested that they should be bomb proofed.) The Filter Room at Bentley Priory was working well but having difficulty in estimating the number of aircraft in a raid. (This problem was never adequately solved.) The radar chain during the Exercise had operated on a limited front from Bawdsey to Dover. RAFVR plotters in Operations Rooms were said to be extremely satisfactory. Bouquets were also given to the Observer Corps, and the GPO for their telephone communications; the brickbats went to the searchlight organisation for inadequate performance, and also to the Air Ministry for not pursuing his idea that a section should be set up which would collect and disseminate future Intelligence information about the enemy's choice of objectives, tactics, habitual formations and the effects of his projectiles. Referring to nightfighting, Dowding commented, 'I believe the eventual solution of nightfighting will be found in air-to-air RDF (AI) and that a specialised type of nightfighter will be required for this purpose.' The report encompassed the entire working of the air defence, raid reporting, fighter control, AA guns, searchlights, etc. and passive defence measures, civil air raid warnings. Moving outside the results of the Exercise, he also recorded how, during the Exercise, only about half the Fighter Stations had a week's supply of belted ammunition, and how the armour plating of Spitfires was not progressing well, comparing them unfavourably with the work on the Hurricanes; fitting the aircraft with Reflector Gunsights was very slow as was the arrival of new muzzle attachments for their guns which reduced a squadron's re-arming time from about two hours to roughly fifteen minutes. On aircraft interception, Dowding concluded,

'While I am far from implying that the present system is perfect, I feel that a very great advance has been made during the past year in the mechanism of intercepting raids in daylight.'[20]

This quiet air of optimism he had conveyed to the nation on BBC radio on the 12 August. He had also spoken in a similar manner at an Observer Corps dinner at Coventry, and on that occasion made comments construed as being of a political nature and which were quoted by the press the following day. The upshot was that Sir Cyril Newall, Chief of the Air Staff, thought it necessary to ask for an explanation. In reply, Dowding wrote of how he told the Observer Corps how important their duties were to the defence of the country, and went on,

'I said that I always took every opportunity to combat the general attitude of pessimism in the country as regards the effectiveness of air defence. I did not refer in words to Lord Baldwin and his dictum "The bomber will always get through",* but that was in my mind in any reference which I may have made to politicians. I most certainly did say that salvation would not come from hiding in holes and cellars. [He ended,] 'I said there was no greater pacifist in the country than myself, and I prayed from the bottom of my heart that no war might come; but if it did come it would be a good one from the Home Defence point of view. I could perhaps sum up the substance of my speech as follows: People in this country have an exaggerated fear of the effects of air raids. They must be prepared to suffer some loss and damage in the first stages of a war, but the attacks will very soon be brought to a standstill. You are contributing to this result. Take comfort to yourself and tell your friends.'[21]

It now seems ironic that one of the most devastating raids on Britain fell on Coventry.

On 1 September 1939, Germany invaded Poland, an action which decided the course of global affairs for generations by instigating events which, within two days, were to lead to the beginning of the Second World War. Home defences had changed very little since the recent exercise; there had been little time for improvements, in spite of many shortcomings, particularly in the provision of AA guns; the whole was based on a reasonably firm foundation which withstood the demands of a rapid and very large influx of personnel, as it moved from peace to wartime footing.

Responsibility for the air defence system was placed with Fighter

* From a speech he made in 1932, when Lord President of the Council for the National Government, in which he said, '. . . I think it is well also for the man in the street to realise that there is no power on earth that can protect him from being bombed. Whatever people may tell him, the bomber will always get through.' (This axiom remained in the minds of many people. There was much misinformed opinion in the media.)

30

Command; in a letter of 19 September 1939, A.W. Street, wrote to Dowding on behalf of the Air Council:

'I am to confirm that full operational Control of the active air defences of Great Britain, consisting of the Observer Corps, Fighter and Balloon units of the Royal Air Force and gun and searchlight units of the Army, is vested in yourself as A.O.C.-in-C. Fighter Command.'[22]

Guarding against attack from the air, there was now in place a unique fully-integrated network for identifying and reporting raiding aircraft and a reliable procedure whereby defending fighters and guns supported by other sections of the active defences could be given as much time as possible to react, and their destructive power brought to bear. Reasonable warning could also be given to those concerned with civil defences. The initial stage of raid reporting came from the chain of radar stations, sited at appropriate places in the east and southeast coastal areas. On the southeast corner of England these were more closely spaced and were roughly at thirty to forty mile intervals. They detected the presence of aircraft over the sea and the land beyond, at ranges within an average radius of between eighty and one hundred miles, but occasionally, in favourable conditions, up to two hundred. Greatest protection had been afforded to areas assumed to be vulnerable to bombers flying directly from Germany and approaching the southeast corner of England. On the northeast and southwest coasts the stations were more widely spaced. The Radar Chain indicated the position of aircraft and the direction they were flying, giving a useful guide as to the number of aircraft and their height. A station's most accurate measurement was of range and, by co-ordinating readings of two or more sited close to each other, the location of the aircraft could be accurately 'fixed' on a map. The coastal radar was of great benefit to the defenders; by giving a good indication of where enemy aircraft were, it made it possible to position fighters for an interception, and by giving an early warning they could be put in that position at the right time and also allow them to remain on the ground until required, saving fuel and engine wear, as well as reducing the work load of pilots. The eighteen coastal stations then in use were linked to the Filter Room by direct telephone lines, and filtered plot positions showing on the table were telephoned simultaneously on a multiphone linkup to the Command Operations Room next door, to the appropriate Group Headquarters and all their subordinate Sector Stations Operations Rooms who were responsible for the ground direction of fighters. Every track was given a raid number which was carried on a plaque together with other raid information. At

Group Headquarters liaison officers passed the information to Observer Corps Centres. Uniform scale grid maps were used throughout the entire system and these being identical ensured that they all showed the same picture of the activity in their area thus making it possible for a Group Controller to discuss a particular raid over the telephone with a Sector Controller, and by using the raid's number they knew they were seeing the same raid and could plan its interception.

The next stage in the raid reporting network was performed by the Observer Corps. In tiny observation posts usually positioned between six and ten miles apart, observers watched the sky and reported the position and details of all overland activity to a parent Observer Corps Centre. Their sight or sound observations were processed and plotted on the standard grid maps. These were linked to the Filter Room's radar track, plots of which had been passed to them via their local Group Headquarters. This had the additional benefit of maintaining the original track number and details. To ensure that the fighter controllers were informed first, the Observer Centres relayed their overland plots to Sector Stations and Group Headquarters, the latter passing it to gun operations rooms and Bentley Priory. (From 25 September 1940, No. 11 Group Centres used direct teleplotting links with the Command Operations Room to avoid delay in issuing raid warnings to London and the Home Counties.

The function of the Command Operations Room at the Priory was almost purely executive; the Controller would usually become involved with operational affairs only on occasions when a raid appeared to be approaching the boundary between two Groups and it became necessary to delegate which of them would effect the interception. He was, however, able to speak to any Group and ask for information on current activity, e.g. which Units were in action. He was also responsible for the issuing of civilian air raid warnings throughout the country; this was regarded as being the Operations Room's prime task. A Home Office representative assisted.

Tactical deployment of fighters rested with Group Headquarters who could see the state of 'readiness'* (preparedness) of Squadrons on the Sector airfields by looking at a large display panel, commonly known as the 'Tote', on the wall of their Operations Room, and could decide which of them were available to be sent off to intercept a raid or, if desirable,

---

* A system whereby pilots were on standby at given periods of notice to prevent many wasted hours sitting in their aircraft. The squadrons were organised on the ground in preparation for commitment into battle.

be put on patrol in an advantageous position. By carefully watching the progress and direction of raids on the Operations Room table and noting the estimated heights and strength showing on the plaques, the Group Controller deployed his forces. An instruction identifying a particular raid and whether a section, squadron or squadrons were to intercept it would be given to the appropriate Sector and it 'scrambled' the aircraft. Once in the air, the Sector Controller would endeavour to direct his fighters by radio to within sight of their prey, which in good conditions would be roughly three miles, but this naturally depended greatly on cloud and weather. He knew where his aircraft were from plots showing on the table. These plots were provided by the radio direction finding system known as 'Pip Squeak'.*

This worked as follows. One aircraft in each of four formations transmitted a signal for an allotted fifteen seconds on a one-minute Operations Room Clock – 'Pip Squeak'. These signals were picked up by three Radio Direction Finding (RDF) stations which immediately reported these by direct landline to their associated Sector Operations Room. There, by relating the transmission time to a section of the clock, the squadron could be identified.

On sighting the enemy, the fighter leader would call 'Tally Ho'. This signified that he was taking control of the interception and that the Sector Controller should maintain radio silence until the engagement was complete.

* On a table map a string was attached through a hole at the location of each station and when that station reported the direction from which it had picked up the aircraft's signal, the operator of the string aligned it with that direction. Thus when three strings were aligned in unison, where they crossed was the position of the aircraft. The magnitude and complexity of the aircraft control system can best be seen by studying No. 11 Group. Seven Sectors each had three D/F Stations for 'Pip Squeak' speech transmissions.

Chapter 3

Expansion—The Role of Women

A t 1806 hours on 24 August, the code message ACTION AOGAYOR was sent to Dowding by the Air Ministry and an instruction was immediately sent to the GPO London Trunk Exchange directing them to switch through Air Defence and Anti-Aircraft landline circuits by 2030 hours. Another message was sent out to all Chief Constables and Officers of the Observer Corps directing that a state of 'Readiness' be achieved by the same hour. Within two hours, all members had reported and the Post Office engineers had switched over 2,330 circuits to put the system on to a war footing.[23] The following day, heavy Anti-Aircraft guns moved into the Priory grounds for Station defence; the men were to live under canvas. Lieutenant-General Sir Frederick Pile had made Headquarters Anti-Aircraft Command at 'Glenthorn', a large house on the estate, some time earlier.

Deeply rooted in the minds of RAF leaders the thought remained that German bomber strength was sufficient for an attempt at a decisive early 'knock-out' blow against London to be made as the opening gambit of their war strategy. In a letter dated 28 August sent to all the Controllers in Fighter Command's Operations Rooms, Group Captain Howard-Williams instructed them as follows.

'In the event of a "Mass Attack" on London, the executive order "Concentrate on London" will be issued by the Controller (at Bentley Priory) to Groups. The effect of the order will be that the Controllers of 11 Group will order all available aircraft into the air to patrol off the East of London and will bring up the Tangmere Squadrons to the South. The Controller of 12 Group will send all available Squadrons from Debden and Duxford to patrol off the North East boundary of the Inner Artillery zone.' [This zone was roughly speaking the London Area.][24]

At 11.15 a.m. on 3 September, the voice of Prime Minister Neville Chamberlain announcing the outbreak of war was heard on the wireless set in the Officers' Mess. Very soon the wailing of the public air raid warning siren could be heard throughout the area; the result of a false alarm emanating from a report received by the Canterbury Observer Corps telling of an unidentified formation of aircraft off the coast. Before they had been classified as friendly, someone had arranged for a warning to be sounded throughout a large part of Southeast England. (The aircraft were later found to be of French origin and bringing officers to a military mission.) About the same time, another misinterpretation of events caused a 'Red alert' in the North; on this occasion unidentified aircraft appeared in one of the 'Bomber Lanes'. These were air corridors along which friendly aircraft were directed to fly when sent out and returning from activities over the Continent. In the Filter Room, Bomber Liaison Officers, who were informed of all Bomber Command aircraft movements, assisted in the identification of tracks appearing on the table map. Two such people were later to become well known figures, Squadron Leader Tom Gleave and the then Acting Sergeant (unpaid), F.F.E. Yeo-Thomas (The White Rabbit), who was later parachuted into occupied France and served with the Resistance. (It was during his time in the Filter Room that Yeo-Thomas met his future wife, Barbara, a pretty twenty-four-year-old member of the WAAF. Signs of edginess and inexperience were apparent in the defences. A more serious error occurred on 6 September when poor aircraft recognition led to two Hurricanes being shot down by Spitfires, causing the death of a pilot. On that day AA Command also admitted shooting at friendly fighters.

An unnecessary number of public air raid warnings were anticipated in the light of recent experience, and were expected to create major disruption and loss of output in industry. Immediate steps were taken in the Command Operations Room to tighten up the procedure.

In the grounds of Bentley Priory barbed wire fences and barriers were placed to thwart the progress of any would-be infiltrator. Sandbags were used to form protective walls for the gun emplacements and other points likely to be at risk from bomb blast or bullet; all personnel were carrying gas masks, tin helmets were becoming commonplace and identity cards showing a photograph of the owner were issued. The windows of the buildings were draped with blankets at night, a practice which soon changed in favour of a coating of black paint, and the house was camouflaged overall with dull green paint. Private cars were parked out of sight under trees; their owners, incidentally, were required to fill in a form to avoid them being requisitioned for Service use and also to gain a petrol allowance for journeys when used for RAF duties.

35

Many amenities were affected by a 'quart-into-a-pint-pot' existence as peacetime capacity expanded to make room for the great influx of staff, much of which was now working on an around-the-clock shift basis. The Officers' Mess soon became overcrowded and to speed up service it became necessary to employ extra people as waiters; the ATS helped by permitting the use of their girls as waitresses and cooks. The problem of lack of space was overcome by constructing large huts in the grounds which coped with the need for messing facilities and accommodation for Officers, airmen, soldiers and the women auxiliaries. By the end of the year no less than fifteen such buildings were in use catering for the overspill and the expansion of old, and development of new, departments; this mushrooming continued well into 1940, by which time the grounds were resembling a small hutted village. While the new people were being settled in, the volume of work in the Signals Section was increasing and a stop-gap measure of June 1938 origin, where Officers' wives could be trained for cypher work, was introduced. (The policy was for them to train and work without remuneration and be used in emergencies.)

E.A. Barnett was a Volunteer Reservist and taken into the RAF as an Aircrafthand/General Duties. He was put into the Code and Cypher Section, a province which had until then been restricted to Officers only employment. This special dispensation was granted on account of his previous experience in the Air Ministry's Code and Cypher Section, something which later was, on several occasions, instrumental in preventing his posting to another job; it is difficult to grasp why someone with such experience could have ever been considered for anything else. His new Service colleagues required training, as did the Officers' wives. (By early October, eight wives were being employed full-time.) It was then that, in a civilian capacity, Mrs Nicholl, the AOA's wife, Mrs Park, the SASO's wife, Mrs Aitken, the CSO's* wife and the Unit Signals Officer's wife, Mrs Coe, became impressed into serving in the daily working of Fighter Command. The Command Cypher Officer at the time was Major Franks, a retired Royal Marine Officer, who had fought in the First World War at the Battle of Jutland; his deputy was a Flight Lieutenant Daly, a Southern Irishman from Cork, another veteran of the earlier war. This largely improvised section, made up of civilians, Reservists and World War One veterans, was given an office in a hut on the East side of the house. Having joined the Volunteer Reserve in June 1939, E.A. Barnett

* AOA, Air Officer Administration; SASO, Senior Air Staff Officer; CSO, Chief Signals Officer.

had not had time to do any recruitment training before being 'called up' and, being on shift, there was no requirement that he should train to do drill or parade duty. This became embarrassing when later, as a Corporal, he was directed to attend a unit course that involved rifle drill. However, the solution was close at hand in the person of a civilian clerk, who was a member of the Home Guard. A hastily contrived off-duty course of instruction avoided further discomfiture.

Mrs Brenda Rintoul (née Vancourt), Sir Hugh Dowding's step-daughter, also served in the Code and Cypher Section during the early days of the war:

'Before Fighter Command came into being, Dad was working at the Air Ministry as Air Member for Research and Development. When he was posted to Stanmore, initially, he was actually working some of the time from home at Wimbledon Hill and travelling to and from Stanmore each day. The reason for this was that the Air Ministry had not yet found an official residence for the Commander-in-Chief but, as soon as that happened, he moved there together with my Aunt Hilda. The house they chose was "Montrose", in Gordon Avenue in Stanmore Village.

'There were the social occasions; dances, tennis parties and, of course, the interminable cocktail parties, but these were never lavish affairs, laid on at immense expenditure. What he did like at Bentley was having the lovely Christmas parties for the children of officers and other ranks, which were held in the Billiard Room at "Montrose". He liked these very much and, even when I was living away, I would come up for them. I recall on one occasion a little girl, no more than three or four years old and prettily dressed in a little pink frock, having got a sixpenny piece out of a cake or something, she turned to him and said, "I collects money", and he said to her very gently, "That's very sensible, continue to do it all your life."

'He didn't care much for all the other socialising, sometimes used by others to gain favour and worm their way up; he believed that progress should be won by work and competence. If Mother had lived, I believe he would have enjoyed the social side of life associated with his job, because she was always so full of fun and wanted to be involved. My Aunt Hilda brought Derek and me up and, being the hostess at "Montrose", it became her lot to entertain some very distinguished guests, some rather daunting. When I learned that Prime Minister Neville Chamberlain was coming to dinner, I was rather apprehensive and viewed the prospect with some trepidation, so much so that I said to Dad, "I'm terrified of these people", to which he replied, "You must never forget that they all wet their nappies the same as you did." This philosophy is something I have practised ever since. I can recall the earlier visits of Sir Henry Tizard when he used to come and discuss things with Dad, who was at that time planning the Operations Room table using a layout on the sitting room floor at "Montrose". Tizard would say things like, "I think we should have an R.D.F. (radar) station sited here, you know." He was the real brain behind it all, certainly from the radar point of view. It was quite fascinating in those days; little did we know what we were in for.

'Occasionally I went on visits with my father to the RAF Stations. He didn't give them a day's notice, but would ring up from Command and say, "I shall be down in an hour", or perhaps, "I will be down in two hours", just to warn them. He told me, "I want to see how things really are and how the men are being looked after; I don't want the C.O. to go and clean everything up." He really was strict, even with the officers. He would just open up the odd cupboard and look in. I went with him on one occasion to Tangmere, where they were all very nice to me. I think it was "Batchy" Atcherly who said to me, "For goodness sake keep the Old Man away", I said, "I can't do that; I'm afraid it's quite impossible."

'In 1938/39, I was working at Bexhill but came up quite a lot to Bentley to see them, but in July '39 I returned home to live at "Montrose" because my Father said he felt that war was going to be declared pretty soon and I was to prepare myself to do something when it came. He originally wanted me to be a plotter on his Operations Room table. With the WAAF literally only a few days old, and none of them, as yet, serving full-time, there was a big shortage of people in the Code and Cypher Section and they recruited and began training some of the Officers' wives; I was allowed to become a "wife" on condition that I didn't claim any payment. It was thought that the wives were very sound from the security point of view and they were paid as civilian staff. I think there were about a dozen or so who had volunteered or were pushed into doing it. Being unmarried, I was not regarded as being in quite the same category, and I also think my father wished me to be an unpaid Auxiliary, like the WAAF. They were getting overloaded with signals and couldn't cope, which is why we were called in. Information was flooding from the various RAF Stations and other sources, and everything was received in code; of course, you couldn't say anything over the telephone because you never knew who might be listening. To start with we were taught only two cyphers, one was figures, the other was teleprinter (later in the war, we were using thirty-six codes). Signals were pouring in throughout the day and night and this had to be attended to by working in shifts throughout the twenty-four hours.

'At the outset the Section was housed in a room in the house next to the old Operations and Filter Rooms, then it moved to a hut outside, and finally went underground.

'When they were excavating the hole for the Underground Operations block, we all went along to see what was going on. It was an enormous hole, the bottom of which was covered by a deep layer of sticky mud. The workmen were lowered down by a sort of crane affair. There was a story current at the time, which later became embroidered with the telling, of the Irishman who became stuck and was heaved out leaving behind his gum boots in situ. The joke was that they said it was his trousers that were left behind.

'The administration side of the Priory seemed to have a much cushier time than us; no night work or shifts or anything like that. At the beginning of the war I found working at night very wearing; every third night was spent on duty. When you did a night on, you would have to come back that afternoon, two till nine, having come off at eight, so you had to snatch some sleep when you could. Sometimes in the Cyphers you had a pretty good night, but on others you would never cease work.

'The material originated from "Signals" on pieces of paper, and they delivered it to us by hand. Eventually, when the system was finalised, it was transported into the department through the Lamson Tube. We removed the papers from their containers and de-cyphered them; from these a number of copies were made which were passed out for distribution to the C.-in-C. or Admin., or whoever. We always kept one copy, but you never kept the cypher and the English copy together in case we had a spy among us. As part of the security, we also changed the beginning of the code very often, usually once or twice a week, and this had to be done at an arranged time, which was also changed at irregular intervals. All outgoing signals were put into code, nothing went out in English.

'Eventually the Air Ministry said that we wives, and daughter, could put on WAAF uniforms and become WAAF Officers, but Dad wouldn't have me becoming an Officer; he said, "No, you will go through the ranks, you're not just going to become an Officer without knowing what you are doing." He was very correct about such things, and when my brother Derek and I discuss it now I don't think we regret it a bit. So I went through the ranks and all the wives who wished to continue automatically became Officers, just like that. Dad thought this was very bad and they should have set an example. After my training away from the Priory, I put down that I wished to be posted to somewhere in the South. Dad was at Bentley, Derek was a fighter pilot at Hornchurch, and I felt that it was not a good idea for me to be posted to somewhere like Wick in Scotland if there was ever an emergency. Luckily, I was posted back to Fighter Command which was all very nice but not without its problems, the main one being that I had to try to get through to Dad that our relationship when on duty had to be different from that of home life: we were now playing soldiers. The signals which were addressed to him personally I would sometimes take to his office, whereupon I had to salute. This was about the time that the Battle of Britain was blowing up and we had a tremendous lot of work coming through, much of it top secret stuff which had to be delivered to him personally. On one occasion I arrived when General Wavell was talking to him in the office; I saluted and said, "I have a message for you, Sir", and handed him the book in which we recorded the delivery and he signed for it. He then turned to General Wavell and said, "Oh, by the way, this is my daughter, Brenda." Having gone through the correct formal procedure, I was very cross with him and said, "Look, Dad, we're playing soldiers now; you can't talk like that, you must remember this." This sort of thing was always a bit of a strain and one didn't wish to emphasise any familiarity otherwise people could be saying something like, "Oh, she is the C.-in-C.'s daughter and gets preferential treatment." He was very conscious of this, and I think Derek and I had a harder time than the others because of it. The situation was further exacerbated when Derek, at one stage, was off flying for a bit (he had been shot or had broken something), anyway, he too was posted to Fighter Command Headquarters, and so the three of us were there all saluting each other; it seemed like a game we were playing.

'Derek had finished his training at Cranwell in August 1939, and was put straight on Spitfires with No. 74 Squadron, and it was always very worrying because on the Operations Room table we knew when he was in the air and Dad used to sit there and watch. He also used to come and see me in the Cypher Office occasionally when I was on duty. He became awfully upset when his boys were being killed; he called them his "boys", and I think he tended to regard them all as his sons. He also had the welfare of the WAAF at heart; regularly once a week he asked our Senior WAAF Officer, Section Officer Bessie McLeod, if she had enough soap and the usual requisites for the girls. This so impressed her that to her dying day she always said that she had never met another Commanding Officer who asked such thoughtful questions. Until that time, no Commander-in-Chief had ever had to cope with such a sudden big intake of women into his Command. Section Officer McLeod was a wonderful Commanding Officer.

'After Dad had been gone from the Priory for some time, I asked for a posting and I was sent to Oxford to instruct the Americans, who were just coming into the war at that time; this I was very unhappy about because I had long thought that instructing was not my forte. So I rang Dad up at Wimbledon and said, "Dad, can you use some influence and get me posted somewhere else?" He replied, "You are in the Service now; you go where you are sent", and that was that. By now he had taken on the job of Air Raid Warden at Wimbledon.'

Charles 'Chic' Willett volunteered for the RAF at the outbreak of war and as he could type was immediately accepted for administration duties in the RAFVR:

'I passed the medical and three days later received instructions to report to RAF Uxbridge. There were about two thousand of us; some, including myself, were accommodated in tents. After initial formalities – attested, vaccinated, inoculated and kitted out, about six hundred of us entrained to RAF Northcotes on the Lincolnshire coast. After completing a few weeks' basic recruits training, I was posted to Bentley Priory with five other airmen.

'We arrived at 3.30 p.m. on a Friday at the beginning of October. The Flight Sergeant i/c the unit Orderly Room was dressed in the old style uniform (Dog collar) being an "E" reservist; in fact the Unit Headquarters staff were mostly reservists.

The Flight Sergeant asked who we were and I explained that we were posted in from Northcotes, to which he replied, "Well I don't want to see you now – we are off for the weekend." I noticed that one of the Corporals was looking at me with a rather quizzical expression. He said, "Your name is Willett isn't it?", and to my surprise I recognised him as the chap I had bought my furniture from at Canterbury after my marriage in 1938. He said, "I am going home to Canterbury at five o'clock. You had better come with me." Everyone in our party from Northcotes was given a railway voucher and we all went our separate ways for the weekend, returning to the Priory by 12 noon on the Monday.

'When I arrived back, I found out that there was very little accommodation available; just enough for about thirty regular airmen who slept in a building within the Priory grounds. We newcomers had to bed down in the gymnasium with about three hundred Army personnel (mostly A.A. Gunners); each had a palliasse and a blanket, and all were crammed on the floor like sardines. At the far end of the Gym was a small stage lit by a dim blue lamp. Periodically a bell rang and bods clambered all over you as they made their way out; mostly they were going on duty, manning the guns on Stanmore Common.

'The difference in atmosphere from that which I had recently endured at Northcotes recruit training was very marked indeed. Here at the Priory in these early days there was very much a 9 to 5 feeling; unless on duty, weekends off varied, either Friday to Monday (long) or midday Saturday to Monday (short); you would never have thought you were in a Service establishment: it could quite easily have been a large insurance company like the Prudential. There was, however, a positive air of war preparation and everything was conducted in a smooth and controlled manner. Fighter Command Filter and Operations Rooms were manned round the clock and the Signals Traffic Office also. By five or six in the late afternoon most administrative people finished duty leaving a few essential posts covered, i.e. the Duty Staff Officer who had a bedroom in the Priory, and the duty clerk in the Central Registry who was in direct contact with the Traffic Office using the Lamson Tubes to pass messages. At night about ninety-five per cent of incoming signals were routine items, however, operational messages would be received such as a signal from the Admiralty asking for fighter protection for a convoy leaving a northern port. This decoded signal would be sent by the duty clerk to the Duty Air Commodore in the Operations Room with a copy to the Duty Staff Officer. The Duty Air Commodore would immediately make the arrangements for continual fighter cover as the ships made their passage through the sea area protected by squadrons from 13, 12, 11 and 10 Groups, each of whom passed on their charges to the neighbouring Group. Most Duty Clerks found the work interesting as when on duty away from their normal work, they felt that they were at the centre of things and had some idea of what was going on in other departments of the Command. Nobody discussed their work;

if you did not need to know, you were not told. Most staff personnel lived out of camp and went home after duty.

'We were encouraged to bring our wives and children to live near the Priory; my wife and baby son had a bed-sitter with shared kitchen in Bushey Heath. Those who lived in Camp were accommodated in hastily erected prefabricated huts within the Priory grounds. Other ranks were on duty at 8 a.m. when the colour hoisting parade was held, each department providing a number of parade personnel.

'When I first arrived at the Priory, there were about thirty Aircrafthands who were regular serving airmen. They were classified as non-tradesmen; their duties included keeping the Station clean, guard and fire picquet etc. They were a rather shrewd lot and later some became expert plotters in the Operations and Filter Rooms. These men were remustered to the new trade of Clerk Special Duties. One memorable incident in which some of these characters were involved occurred shortly after I arrived at the Priory. The Station Camp Commandant lived in a house which had been in earlier days a lodge near the Harrow Road entrance to the estate. At the time, there was anxiety about saboteurs and worries about the A.O.C.-in-C.'s safety; the Irish problem was of additional concern. One of the security measures taken included an In-lying Picquet, a Corporal and four men, who occupied a room off the tunnel under the Priory building. To mobilise the picquet each entrance had an alarm bell wired direct to their room, and when this sounded, standing orders were that they were to fix bayonets, put "one up the spout" with safety catch on and run to the entrance in question. One evening the Station's Camp Commandant's car caught fire at his residence and he could not raise the fire picquet, which was not altogether surprising because they were at the nearby "Windmill" public house, in desperation he pressed the bell for the In-lying Picquet. Out they rushed with fixed bayonets and full of purpose; they had incidentally left the ammunition behind; and arrived on the scene. There was nothing they could do about it; it was not their type of emergency and we are left with the amusing picture of them watching like solemn Indians the Camp Commandant's burning carriage.

'Expansion of the RAF was going on at a phenomenal rate bringing in people right, left and centre; being such a small service, promotion was rapid and literally a bright person could become NCO within a few months. Our regular aircrafthands were non-tradesmen (Group 5), some however were employed as plotters in the Operations and

Filter Rooms and became very experienced in these skilled duties. The Signals branch, in fairness to them, had them remustered to a Signals trade at a higher rate of pay, this however caused confusion and a new trade of Clerk Special Duties (Group 4) was brought into the RAF.

'From the early days of the war until "Dunkirk" I worked in the Unit Orderly Room under the Station Camp Commandant, Major Ward (Rtd.). He was a civilian; in fact at this time civil servants occupied many executive positions in the Command Headquarters. It was not until 1940 that Ward was commissioned in the rank of Squadron Leader. In June 1940, I left Station headquarters and worked in 'P' Staff of Command headquarters under Squadron Leader Daniels (who, like Ward, had been Major Rtd.). He was the Senior Personnel Staff Officer of Fighter Command. Postings, Promotions, Honours and Awards, Courts Martial, etc. passed through his hands. It seems in retrospect astonishing that "P" Staff was run by just this one officer. It was not until Sholto Douglas arrived after the Battle of Britain that "P" Staff became a much larger department. By now I was a Corporal and a part of my duties was to stand in for the NCO who was Dowding's clerk, and when he went on leave or day off, etc., I took over. The work was straightforward – typing, In and Out trays of files, recording and passing on correspondence and telephone. The same applied to Dowding's Personal Assistant (P.A.).

'Later I was promoted to Sergeant and, when Sholto Douglas took over from Dowding, I became NCO i/c the Secret Registry. Here, together with the Central Registry was received all correspondence to the Command; we were the receiving and despatch centre for all communications. It came by post, despatch rider and teleprinter signals. Items were recorded, appropriate files found and distributed to the offices concerned. Distribution throughout the headquarters was done by Air Ministry Wardens who, in their Navy blue uniform, acted as messengers. The Secret Registry was staffed by seven RAF/WAAF and the Central Registry which dealt with masses of non-classified items and all outgoing mail had about twenty working there; this included four civilians. I also was responsible for maintaining the Archives which contained past secret files of historic interest and importance.

'After Dunkirk, all Airmen were made to attend a battle course and became part of the defences under a "Backers Up" title. Patrols were carried out in and outside the Priory grounds. Exercises in stealth at night, when patrols creeping in from Watford or Stanmore tried to enter the Priory grounds unseen, were carried out; no one succeeded in this. The next step from the "Backers Up" formation was Defence Squadrons being formed. These squadrons were trained by NCOs from the Guards Brigade and later the squadrons became the RAF Regiment. Part of the Priory defences included a holding battalion of the Guards under training at the Priory.

'Most of the Duty Air Commodores overseeing the Operations and Filter Rooms returned to active service after years in retirement and dropped rank to Air Commodore to be serving again. T.L. Webb-Bowen and I.M. Bonham-Carter were formidable characters, the latter having at some stage in his career lost a leg. I recall he owned a mongrel that had a habit of chasing airmen who were passing on their bicycles; the dog would snarl and snap at their heels. When seeing this, Bonham-Carter would shout, "Kick him! Kick him!" As soon as it heard its master's voice, the dog, now being well accustomed to this, knew exactly what would happen, and what alternative tactics to apply. This was the usual course of events, but Heaven help the airman who kicked out at the dog without the old man shouting so.

'During the dark days of 1940, the atmosphere at the Priory was most extraordinary; no one really thought that an invasion was likely to happen; it was simply unthinkable; it just couldn't happen. No one realised the great historical events being played out at the time; everyone simply got on with the job, the place was a veritable hive of activity.

'The occasions I spent working in Dowding's office were most interesting. Sir Hugh was a very reserved man. He was not at all socially inclined (the complete opposite of Sholto Douglas, his successor) and apart from duty functions, rarely went out of an evening. He lived with his sister in "Montrose", his house in Stanmore, from which he normally arrived at the Priory at 9 a.m. and returned home between 5 and 6 p.m., the same hours as most of the headquarters staff. Each morning General Pile, the Commander-in-Chief of Anti-Aircraft Command, came over from his headquarters at "Glenthorne", a mansion in the Priory grounds near the Harrow road. Their talks were not only confined to the war but covered many other subjects; they were firm friends. Dowding rarely visited other Stations in Fighter Command, he was so occupied in his office. His Staff Officers did the visits to Stations and Squadrons, reporting back to him on the subject of their visits. The atmosphere throughout the headquarters was very calm, and it seemed to me that this reflected Dowding's personality; he was even-tempered, always calm although under great pressure. A complete gentleman, meticulous in dress and when he left his office always wore his hat – the only officer in the headquarters to do so. Only when an officer wore his hat was it necessary for junior ranks to salute; in all the departments they left them off, thus doing away with constant saluting. I think that Dowding felt that being the A.O.C.-in-C. he had to be fully dressed. The files in the "Out" tray in his office carried a well-defined feature, the distinctive writing produced from the broad nib of Dowding's fountain pen. At times he produced such a wide scrawl that a single sentence could fill a foolscap page.

'There were times when the A.O.C.-in-C. seemed totally preoccupied with a particular matter, giving it very deep thought. After Dunkirk he began to spend more and more time on duty and during the Battle of Britain worked very long hours. When the night raids started in earnest in September, he would regularly go off to see the working of the night defences around London. Consequently he became very, very tired – he was carrying the burden of the daylight battle at the same time. Churchill once phoned him and wanted to see him at "Chequers" over the weekend; Dowding was emphatic in his refusal, telling Churchill that his duty was to be at his post and not at "Chequers"; I imagine Churchill was not pleased. It would have been easy to have said something like, "Sorry, Prime Minister, but I have rather a lot on at present, please excuse me", but that was not his way.'

Chapter 4

Force Requirements – Day and Night Fighters and Radar

T he quick subjugation of Poland had come as a shock. The news filtering through from there gave a clear indication of the German strategy; one outstanding feature was the air attacks on Polish industry. This knowledge was to have a very profound effect on British thinking; in France it amounted to something more. In a series of heavy blows against the Polish Air Force and its supporting industry, much of it had been destroyed within days, making it possible for German air power to be concentrated on supporting the ground forces. Little consideration had been given to the morality of bombing factories in residential areas; the principle of total war was being applied from the beginning. The very successful tactics they employed were carefully analysed and it was plain to see that the opening gambit was to attain dominance in the air.

On the first day of the war, Fighter Command's strength was twenty-five Squadrons of Regular airmen and fourteen Auxiliary Squadrons in various stages of efficiency, in all considered to be roughly the equivalent of thirty-four operational units. By this time, the Air Council's estimate of the number of fighter squadrons necessary for Home Defence had risen to fifty-two. To Dowding's consternation, four of his Hurricane Squadrons, due to a long-standing arrangement, had already been earmarked to go to France with the Field Force within ten days and without any threat being imposed there. He had been given assurances that while Fighter Command was below strength, this would not be allowed to occur. Further plans to employ his home units over France were also being made which would, Dowding estimated, leave him with only twenty-six squadrons. Noting the factory output of Hurricanes was reaching a little less than two a day, he was moved to envisaging the situation which would arise if France became involved in early fighting. His conclusion was that the output of all new Hurricanes would be taken up in making good the losses over there and this would also soon be eating into, and preventing the build-up of, his aircraft strength at home. In a letter to the Air Ministry on 16 September, thirteen days after the declaration of war, he wrote,

'It is clear, therefore, that the dispatch of 4 Field Force Squadrons has opened a tap through which will run the total Hurricane output, and that the Hurricane Squadrons at home would become a diminishing force . . . Finally, I must entreat with all the force at my command that the Air Council will take this matter seriously. They have laid down a strength of 52 Squadrons as necessary for the defence of this country. They apparently contemplate with equanimity a reduction of the fighter strength to exactly half that figure . . .'[25]

The warning had been given; as yet the whole thing was but a paper exercise; as will be seen, very soon the reality would become a nightmare.

Earlier, the Air Staff instigated research into how best the offensive power of the long-range bomber could be used to reduce the scale of any likely air attack against Britain and a review of German industry was conducted to decide which of their companies contributed most to their air potential and were, therefore, most worthy of early destruction. When the report was produced in June 1939, it was realised that, no doubt, the *Luftwaffe* was engaged in a similar exercise and looking at British industry with the same object in mind. As a consequence, the Air Staff conducted their own survey and some 7,000 factories were listed with a final selection of 116 being singled out for protection against low-flying attack, these being considered to be vital in sustaining British air strength. The current distribution of balloons and light Anti-Aircraft artillery was re-appraised and altered where necessary.

With the experience gained from the Polish front, the Chief of the Air Staff (RAF's most Senior Officer), Sir Cyril Newall, wrote a very important note on 15 September 1939, on its implications for the Royal Air Force:

'Information at my disposal with regard to the considered views of the German Air Staff as to the most effective method of employment to their air striking force in a war against another air power is to the effect that they regard the destruction or neutralization of the opposing air force as the primary aim at the outset . . .

Hitler's initial order on the outbreak of war to the effect that the Polish Air Force was to be wiped out, and the subsequent course of events in Poland during which the Polish Air Force and aircraft industry have in fact been destroyed, both, in my opinion, considerably strengthen the view that if, and when, the enemy directs his air attacks against this country, his first and primary objectives may well be the key factories in our aircraft industry as well as our airfields . . . If he succeeded in this he would, however heavy the losses he incurred in the process, establish air superiority over this country and retain a margin of air strength to turn virtually unopposed against any vital objectives in Great Britain which he might select.'

In his note he then named key areas in the country which he considered most vulnerable, and concluded,

'In view of the situation outlined above, I propose, if my colleagues agree, to issue a general directive to the Air Officer Commanding-in-Chief, Fighter Command indicating that our aircraft industry is to be regarded as a very probable first objective for enemy air attacks against this country, instructing him to re-examine the defence situation on that basis, and requesting him to undertake, with particular reference to the areas mentioned, any modification to the present deployment of our defences which may consequently appear desirable.'[26]

The Directive was approved by the Chiefs of Staff Committee of the War Cabinet the following day, and arrived on Dowding's desk at the Priory, signed by Deputy Chief of the Air Staff, Air-Vice Marshal R.E.C. Peirse, on 18 September. Included in it was a list of ten factories and sensitive areas regarded as vital points in the aircraft industry who were to be provided with special protection.[27] (See Appendix 4.) After a War Cabinet Meeting on 22 September, Peirse sent a further letter which had also been endorsed by the Chiefs of Staff. It indicated in general terms the areas from which defence weapons were to be withdrawn to implement the now changed defence emphasis. It said,

'In the light of circumstances today, the threat of air attack on London as an initial act has receded. The emphasis instead is on the Air Force as such, including the aircraft industry.

'Therefore, as a general guide, it can be assumed that the Central London area together with areas such as Cardiff, Swansea, Leeds, Liverpool and Manchester (less the Widnes-Runcorn area) which receive protection from the general air defence of the Country, can be regarded as reservoirs from which limited withdrawal can be made in favour of those key factories indicated to you in the Air Ministry Directif of 17 September . . .'[28]

This re-distribution of the air defence resources had been strongly advocated by Winston Churchill, then First Lord of the Admiralty, in a letter to Sir Kingsley Wood, Secretary of State for Air, on 18 September.

At a conference at the Priory on 10 October to review urgently the problem of providing some measure of protection for shipping against air attacks, the question arose whether a change in fighter employment could be made. Dowding asked that Chief of the Air Staff Sir Cyril Newall should be asked for a ruling. Air Vice-Marshal R. Peck, Director-General of Operations, replying on his behalf, wrote,

> 'I am to state that in accordance with the Directif issued under D.C.A.S. on the 17 September the defence of Great Britain and, in particular, the provision of protection of vital points in the aircraft industry, remain the primary commitment of your Command.'

He did, however, make one concession;

> 'in order to afford a measure of protection to convoys on the East Coast, it would be necessary to move certain of your forces to other aerodromes nearer the coast.'[29]

In earlier discussions, Dowding explained to him how radar could not detect low-flying aircraft. If heavy attacks on East Coast shipping developed, heavy losses could best be avoided by transferring it elsewhere. This view was passed to the War Cabinet. The fact remained that he was still expected to offer some protection using an already understrength fighter force.

As can be seen, Dowding's orders were clear. He was to organise and use the weapons of home air defence with a primary commitment to protection of the aircraft industry on which the survival of the air force was dependent. For the moment, complying with the Directif meant a redeployment of guns, balloons, searchlights, etc. Preservation of the civilian population, defence of the general industrial base of the country and protection of ports and most shipping were of lesser importance. The Directif of 17 September 1939, approved by the Chiefs of Staff Committee of the War Cabinet, which ordered the AOC-in-C Fighter Command to preserve vital factories in the aircraft industry, remained in force throughout 1940. Its influence on tactics should be remembered when assessing events and criticisms of this period. The factories, from which the British would make good their fighter losses, would ultimately decide how long air resistance could be sustained; in a war of attrition it was thought the *Luftwaffe* could win by virtue of their numerical superiority. Losing the factories would also directly affect Bomber Command's ability to continue raids on Germany. (The only permissible deviation from the September Directif came later when it was accepted that fighters would be sent to give protection to defending naval units if invasion was in progress.)

For the British, events in Poland had brought about a shift in policy and some reorganisation of gun, searchlight and balloon defences; in France, on the other hand, they realised how vulnerable they were to the tactics the Germans had employed and strong air cover for their ground forces would be needed. It is not surprising then that almost from the beginning the cry from them was for more RAF fighter support. The British Air Mission over there had already communicated their concern about the French Air Force's weakness in bombers, in both quantity and quality. As early as 16 September, General Gamelin was already indicating that, if an air war was started, he would ask for British fighter and AA gun reinforcements. At a meeting at General Gamelin's Headquarters near Paris on 21 September 1939, Sir Cyril Newall explained how fifty squadrons were needed for the defence of England; he had only thirty-one; there was none available for defending the Grand Fleet at Scapa Flow.[30] General Vuillemin, head of the French Air Force, said they had only thirty-two Fighter Squadrons altogether, including those for the protection of the army zone and for the rest of the country. Newall further emphasised the difficulty which he would have in securing Fighter Squadrons for use in France in the face of urgent demands that would certainly be made on the Home Front.

Once more pressure was applied at the beginning of October, this time on the political front; the French Ambassador took General Armengaud to see Lord Chatfield, the Minister for the Co-ordination of Defence and he also visited Sir Kingsley Wood, Secretary of State for Air. The theme was familiar, overstatement of the number of German aircraft thought likely to be employed, understatement of their own resources. With hindsight, it seems surprising that no-one in Britain had any accurate figures on the strength of the French Air Force. A Staff Officer at the Air Ministry, asked to report on the French request, wrote, 'It is always difficult to get at French figures but we believe their total establishment is something in the nature of 600 (Fighters).' He then added this figure to the number of British Hurricanes sent over there and concluded that a total of 664 machines were available against 544 for home defence. He further commented, 'One of their troubles is that their fighter defence is so badly organised.'[31]

Dowding attended a conference at the Air Ministry on 2 October which dealt with the formation of new fighter squadrons and the future dispatch of fighter units to France. Initially the conversation centred on the forming of new Blenheim Squadrons; it then moved on to the provision of operational training for pilots. He was in disagreement with Sholto Douglas about the final training of men leaving the Flying Training Schools and suggested that those to be employed in home defence operations could receive their operational training in the Squadrons once intensive operations started. He wished to use the aircraft and personnel of No. 12 Group Pool as a basis on which to form two new fighter squadrons; these resources were required for this more important purpose. In his view, intensive operations would not be continuous and it should be possible to train them effectively in operational conditions: he would prefer at any rate to attempt to do this. Sholto Douglas favoured their final training being completed in a Group Pool, arguing that if the C-in-C's view was accepted, 'we faced the risk of a shortage of operational pilots at a critical time, without arrangements having been made for their training', and added, 'It would not be possible under intensive air raid conditions for satisfactory training to be carried out.' Dowding replied that at present Fighter Command's pilot strength was nearly double its essential minimum and went on, 'In home defence fighting, casualties in pilots would not be heavy.' (He later explained how this judgement was made at the time on the premise that interceptions would be effected beyond the operational range of German fighters.)[32] If his proposals did not work, he would improvise arrangements within his Command. His views were accepted and it was agreed that additional Squadrons should be formed at the expense of No. 12 Group Pool. Dowding was concerned about the surplus of pilots, fearing a falling off of standards; his opinion was that it was impossible to keep more than twenty pilots per squadron in flying training; Sholto Douglas assured him that plans were in hand for forming reservoirs for any pilot surplus. The conclusion of the discussion was for the bulk of the Pool to be made into half squadrons operating Blenheims, meanwhile the No. 12 Group Pool would continue on a much reduced level. At the time of the Battle of Britain, three Pools, or Operational Training Units, were in existence.

The question of dispatching more fighters to France was discussed, and Sholto Douglas said that 'we might be forced to send more'. He asked Dowding what would be the best course to adopt if it was necessary to dispatch two fighter squadrons to France. If they were requested immediately, it was agreed for the two Gladiator Squadrons Nos 615 and 607 to be sent. Air Vice-Marshal Peck, who had recently returned from there, remarked on the weakness of their fighter organisation. In

Dowding's view 'the likely course which the war would take might well demand the use of all possible resources at home'. He later added how 'we had known for many months of the inadequacy of the French fighter organisation'; they were given ample opportunities to study ours and it was still not too late for them to achieve something better.[33]

Three days later, on 5 October, Newall wrote to Dowding, making it clear that he felt that the war could be lost in France. The letter, in part, said,

'You may rely on me to resist to the utmost any pressure that may be exercised by the War Cabinet to send more fighters . . . But we must face facts, one of which is that we could possibly lose the war in France as much as in England . . . What I am asking you to do, therefore, is to do your part in making such preliminary plans as will reduce the confusion and loss of efficiency that is in any case bound to arise if the time should come that we cannot refuse to send further fighters to France'.

He then went on to suggest how extra support could be given and finished by saying,

'Finally let me repeat – I am not preparing to sell Fighter Command to the French. I am merely asking you to take the necessary steps to ensure that if we are really in danger of losing the war in France through lack of fighters (a situation which I do not think is likely to arise), we shall not find ourselves caught unprepared.'[34]

Dowding, not sharing the view that, if the French were defeated, it necessarily followed that Britain's war would end there, and now very concerned about the possible frittering away of the most important part of the defence system he had so painstakingly been building over the years, replied:

'The first point, which I mention in passing, is the French difficulties are largely due to the pathetic inefficiency of their Interception System. I have not been told what steps they are taking to set their house in order, even at this late date.'

He then outlined what preparations would be made to comply with Newall's proposals; two Hurricane Squadrons would be prepared for possible dispatch; they could be used as complete squadrons or divided between the four already in France, becoming an additional Flight to each. On an idea of Newall's that Spitfires based in Kent could be used over the Low Countries, Dowding made no comment at all. He finished by saying,

'Before I deal with the rest of your letter, I want to ask you two questions: What are *your own* figures for wastage in Fighter Units when they get into action in France? Have you told the War Cabinet that the output of Hurricanes is about 2 per diem, and that three quarters of this is at present earmarked for Home Units?

'I hope that you will not think that these are otherwise than pertinent questions, since the amount of pressure which the War Cabinet will put on you to send more and more Squadrons to France must be conditioned by their knowledge as to the ultimate effects of such pressure.'[35]

On the day Dowding was drafting this reply, the British met the French for further discussions at Gamelin's Headquarters near Paris, and the question of fighters and AA gun support arose again. Newall was once more emphatic that everything possible was being done and pointed out that more fighters to France was a matter for Government decision at the time. Speaking quite frankly, he said that they (the British) had prepared a good plan for the defence of England and were not quite sure that the French had made a good plan for the defence of France. General Vuillemin replied that they had, but that France's plan for air defence was to have been ready for the middle of 1940. General Gamelin remarked on how the French 'had had to concentrate chiefly on their army.'[36] Their insistence on additional fighters being sent in spite of what they had been told led to bitter controversy later.

Commenting on an Air Council's statement that any extra fighter expansion could only be achieved by sacrificing production of aircraft for other operational Commands who also had a part to play in the general field of air defence, Dowding wrote:

'The best defence of the Country is the fear of the fighter. If we are strong in fighters we should probably never be attacked in force. If we are moderately strong we shall probably be attacked and the attacks will gradually be brought to a standstill. During this period considerable damage will have been caused. If we are weak in fighter strength, the attacks will not be brought to a standstill and the productive capacity of the country will be virtually destroyed.'

He went on to add that other components of the air force would then become 'wasting assets'; keeping them at full strength at the present time would 'prove to have been a fruitless sacrifice'. He argued that the Home defence organisation should not be treated as co-equals but 'should receive priority to all other claims until it is firmly secured, since the continued existence of the nation, and all its services, depends upon the Royal Navy and the Fighter Command'. He also pointed out that the threat would be increased if the neutrality of Holland and Belgium were violated.[37]

The Chain Home radar stations adequately detected aircraft from 25,000 to 2,000 feet; below this their very wide 'floodlight' type of transmission failed, leaving a gap through which low-level raiders could approach (See diagram). On 18 November a new type of radar station, the Chain Home

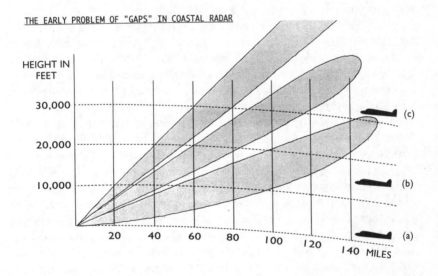

THE EARLY PROBLEM OF "GAPS" IN COASTAL RADAR

Diagram showing the limitations of a Chain Home Radar Station at various heights. Great lobes of radio waves were projected outwards and upwards from the station. Between these were gaps through which an aircraft could fly undetected.

(a) is beneath the lowest lobe and remains undetected until it is within 10 miles. (Chain Home Low Stations were set up to cover this area.)

(b) is flying through the lobes with the least gap area.

(c) is high, where the gap area is greatest and the radio waves are at their weakest. Detection at this height was particularly difficult. Special gap filling aerials were introduced to cover these areas; even so, it was not unknown for raids to find their way in undetected.

Every station required tailoring to accommodate the effects of the local topography on its transmission; it also needed to be accurately calibrated.

Low (CHL), which, as the name suggests, was for low-level detection, was brought into service at Fifeness in Scotland. It was conceived by John Cockcroft (later Sir John) with a small group of scientists at the Research Establishment at Christchurch, Hampshire and was based on the principle of using a narrow 'lighthouse' rotating beam, unlike its static counterpart. General height reading was poor, but of great merit was its ability to scan the gap beneath the CH stations and the sea. Being considerably smaller and not reliant on massive steel and wooden masts, it was comparatively easy to construct and within weeks many had been installed. In the days prior to their introduction a trawler screen placed out in the North Sea was used as advanced Observer Posts reporting by radio to Stoke Holy Cross and Stenigot CH Stations.

Installation of many CHL Stations would have required many additional plotters in the Filter Room, which was impractical within the limits of the plotting table and room. The anticipated problem was solved by having their plots sent in via a parent CH station, and in this way there was no need for extra staff. The CH stations were themselves being improved with the addition of anti-jamming gear and better transmitters.

At the end of August, prior to the outbreak of war, an experimental Flight of AI radar-equipped Mk IV Blenheims of No. 25 Squadron was sent to Northolt under Flight Lieutenant J.G. Cave; after five days he was succeeded by Flying Officer G. Drew. A young civilian scientist, Robert Hanbury Brown, a leading figure in radar research and member of the Bawdsey research team, and his assistant R. Mills, were attached to the Flight. They were given the almost insurmountable task of launching night fighting AI Radar sets into service with the RAF. Hanbury Brown was the only person able to operate the equipment and, in the capacity of tutor and technical adviser, gave both instruction and support. (Professor Hanbury Brown later pointed out that it was a basic mistake to send such a complicated, novel, operationally untried equipment to an operational squadron.)[38]

Four long-nosed Mk IV Blenheims had arrived at Northolt fully equipped with the AI sets in the glazed nose section of the aircraft, but Dowding had asked for the short-nosed version of the aircraft. Moreover, the positioning of the sets was incorrect; when installed next to the pilot in the nose section, it was seen that the intensity of the light emitted by the apparatus would attract the attention of hostile aircraft. Their relocation in the back, which incidentally had also been advised by the scientists, required a redesign of fittings and many alterations; the lack of facilities at Northolt greatly delayed completion of the job.

56

Very early on in the introductory programme, a fundamental point became clear to Hanbury Brown as he observed the operational efficiency of the AI trials, and it was that if the equipment were to be of real value, there was a vital requirement for an accurate and immediate source which visually showed the position of both raider and interceptor. From it a ground controller could then, by seeing their relative positions, be able to direct his fighter pilot by radio and bring him to within the very short range of his AI set. He suggested that this could best be accomplished by a radar set being specifically designed for such a purpose. (Why others closely involved with the interception problems had not thought of this before puzzled Hanbury Brown.) He wrote a memo conveying his idea to Dr E.G. Bowen who, realising its value, passed it on to the Air Ministry Research Establishment. There the matter rested.

The RAF Wireless Intelligence 'Y' Service at Cheadle began sending to Fighter Command decoded German low-grade wireless intercepts which they had picked up from German aircraft. They were also able to pinpoint the positions of a chain of wireless stations being used by German aircraft when making their way towards the British Isles, and in particular those assisting German seaplanes who were laying mines in the mouth of the Thames Estuary at night. To do this, the aircraft had either to fly very low or alight on the water. Either way, their track disappeared from the table in the Filter Room as they dropped beneath the level of the radar. Scientific observers drew attention to the possibility that it was at this point that mine-laying was in progress and the Naval Liaison Officer relayed this information to the Admiralty who sent minesweepers to clear the indicated area. A Flight of three AI-equipped Blenheims from No. 600 Squadron was sent from Hornchurch to Manston on 27 November hoping they would be able to disrupt mine-laying operations; shipping losses to magnetic mines were becoming very serious. An effort was made by Squadron Leader Walter Pretty to control these aircraft directly from the cathode ray screens of Dover and Dunkirk CH stations which achieved little success; a similar experiment had been carried out earlier at Martlesham by Squadron Leader Tester, using the Bawdsey CH Station. At the beginning of January 1940, interest became centred on the new CHL station at Foreness which had been rushed into service to detect mine-laying aircraft. Flight Lieutenant Hiscox and Walter Pretty were experimenting with an interception technique which was showing promise and claiming the attention of H. Larnder and J.H. Cole, scientists of the Stanmore research section, also the interest of Robert Watson-Watt and John Cockcroft.

Using a CHL station in this manner greatly highlighted its inadequate range and height reading performance, the former deciding the amount of time during which a ground Controller could bring about an interception. To improve this, Dowding suggested the stations should be directly linked to a nearby CH station which benefitted from commencing plotting at greater range and which also had a better height reading capability. Their detection of activity much earlier allowed the Controller at the CHL station more freedom to position his fighter by radio into the vicinity of a raider; eventually both to appear at the same time as luminous blips on his screen. Dowding was also pressing for the introduction of IFF (Identification Friend or Foe), a device which, when carried by friendly aircraft, altered the shape of the blip showing on a radar screen. When conducting an interception and both aircraft were indicated, this could identify the fighter.[39] In a matter of weeks an improved IFF device had been made and was being used in interception experiments.

Analysis of results using the CHL station at Foreness assisted with the development of a much modified CHL radar apparatus with a height reading capability which was later produced in a remarkably short time by the combined effort of scientists and manufacturers. Use of the rotating beam principle, referred to earlier as a radar 'Lighthouse', had been proposed by E.G. Bowen in July 1938 but Watson-Watt had informed his successor at Bawdsey, A.P. Rowe, that he did 'not require any work to be done on the RDF Lighthouse in the very near future', and the idea had been shelved.[40] The new station was termed GCI (Ground Control Interception), and was the result of close collaboration between the Stanmore Research Section and signals staff at Bentley Priory who laid down the specification, and a small team of scientists under Dr Denis Taylor at the Air Ministry Research Establishment at Swanage. Part of the system was the marriage of some major components in use elsewhere, which were the products of other scientific teams.

Progress with AI radar was earlier hampered by the decision to move research away from Bawdsey at the outbreak of war; it also fragmented a highly successful scientific team. Watson-Watt had chosen a location at Dundee which, unfortunately, was found to be lacking in facilities for research and development. The airfield at Perth was no better when it came to installation of the sets into the Blenheims. After several irksome weeks, the Unit was transferred to St Athan in South Wales, the home of No. 32 Maintenance Unit. The Unit was mostly engaged in training personnel on the installation and testing of AI equipment in Fighter Command Blenheims and ASV (Air-to-Surface Vessel) shipping detection sets into Coastal Command Lockheed Hudsons. Scientific research and development was reduced to a secondary role. Dr E.G. Bowen, who originated the AI and ASV radar while at Bawdsey, was given the task of administering the unit. Responding to a request in a letter of 6 November 1939 from A.P. Rowe, who had taken over as Superintendent at Bawdsey Research Station from R. Watson-Watt, Bowen described the layout and accommodation being provided at St Athan. In further correspondence Rowe, in true bureaucratic fashion, asked that all future reports should be in triplicate, the final paragraph saying,

'I hope an organisation can soon be set up which will not involve my being responsible for work in another country, but meanwhile I should be glad if you would give me a clear and broad picture weekly of what you are doing, and I'm afraid the last report is not up to your usual standard.'[41]

Indication of Bowen's growing frustration showed in a report for the period ending 31 January 1940 in which he wrote:

'The research was not pressed through to its conclusion, development was non-existent, there were; no Service trials, installation has been hurried, training of personnel to use the equipment has been sketchy in the extreme, and there has been little or no provision for maintenance. Under the circumstances, it would have been remarkable had any of the applications gone through to the stage of utility in war operation without any hitch.'[42]

Perhaps not the most favourable environment for high technology and in such desperate times. This poor state of affairs made its own contribution to the delays and difficulties encountered in the months ahead.

At the instigation of Dowding and Sir Henry Tizard, a 'Night Interception Committee' was formed on 14 March 1940 to co-ordinate all efforts being made to solve the problems of defence against night attack by linking up research and development to the stage of practical trials; the expectation was that the day defences would prove so strong that the Germans would be forced into night bombing. Members were drawn from the scientific fraternity, and initially included Tizard, Sir George Lee (Director of Communications Development at the Air Ministry) and Watson-Watt; on the Service side were officers of high rank – Joubert de la Ferté, Brand, Orlebar, Hart, Dowding and Sholto Douglas, who took the Chair at the early meetings, and Army representatives. The membership was to change in the weeks ahead. Items under regular review were of a technical nature relating to development of radar equipments and techniques, aircraft detection using an infra-red apparatus, the use of aircraft-towed flares to provide illumination of the enemy and advancements in AA gunnery and searchlight efficiency. The sowing of aerial minefields became a common feature for discussion. Radar, especially AI, claimed much attention. Dowding was anxious to get it into service. After early disappointment and despondency, at a Meeting on 1 August he thought it had improved to such a degree with the arrival of the Mk IV sets that he offered the research organisations practically all the Blenheims in his Command for test purposes 'if that would be of help'.[43] On 12 September the Committee recommended eye tests for night fighter pilots and that the radar operators should be men of the highest possible standard. From Meetings in October, various components which were soon to become parts of the successful GCI Station system, were considered and recommendations made.

By now, the dynamic Wing Commander (later Air Vice-Marshal) Peter Chamberlain was attending; he was commanding the Fighter Interception Unit (FIU), the vehicle devised for conducting numerous trials and experiments in night interception. The special unit had been formed at Tangmere by the Committee at its first session in March 1940.

At the outset, he was summoned by Dowding to Bentley Priory, and for nearly two hours was given a comprehensive picture of the problems of night interception, and was much impressed by the C-in-C's knowledge of the subject; 'the most erudite Commanding Officer he had served under'. He was informed that the objectives of the Unit were to advance Air Interception Radar equipment AI, development of a technique using the Radar Stations, and trials of IFF equipment. When leaving the office, there was no doubt in his mind about what was required of him and his colleagues. He later wrote,

'Virtually my instructions were; no facilities will be denied, no excuses will be taken, go and find the answers – and get a move on.'

These words became the maxim by which the FIU lived and governed its affairs.

Within a week the new unit was into its stride and preparing for an influx of scientists. A camaraderie quickly developed between scientists and Service personnel. Peter Chamberlain was amused by the term 'Boffin', a name occasionally conferred upon his civilian

60

colleagues, and it was, to Peter's mind, worthy of personal interpretation. He reasoned that they were a genetic mix of the Puffin, a bird with a mournful cry, and a Baffin, a very obsolete Fleet Air Arm aircraft. The 'Boffin' he described as being a bird of astonishingly queer appearance, bursting with weird and sometimes inopportune ideas, but possessing staggering inventiveness, analytical power and persistence. With the pedigree now firmly established the name came into general use; there was not a scientist to be found anywhere, they were all 'Boffins'. The 'Boffins' were soon to endure the same conditions and deprivations as their Service colleagues, working and flying all hours of the day and night, often in bad weather and at no small risk to themselves. They came from the RAF, Telecommunications Research Establishments and from the civilian companies who were destined to undertake the manufacture of the sets. To form the FIU, the RAF provided ninety-two Officers and Airmen; they included pilots, aircrafthands, gunners, riggers, fitters and clerks. This highly motivated company of scientists and Service people laboured tirelessly to solve the many problems hampering the development and successful use of airborne radar in nightfighters and, in so doing, making it more practical for normal Service use. The number of hours devoted to this were staggering, enough for A.P. Rowe, at one of the weekly get-togethers of radar intelligentsia at Worth Matravers (known as the Sunday Soviets), to accuse Chamberlain of nearly working one of his men, namely Robert Hanbury Brown, into an early grave. This was received with a degree of amusement by the accused who knew that similar pressures were being experienced by many others at Tangmere; on one occasion he had himself worked almost continuously for three nights and two days.

Every week he wrote a detailed report which was sent to the C-in-C at the Priory. From these, Dowding kept up to date on all developments and they became the basis of lengthy discussions over the telephone in which he asked searching questions, frequently enquiring 'Have you tried this?' or suggesting another line of approach to solve a particular problem. He visited the Unit on at least one occasion, flying to see first-hand how things were progressing. Several times each week Dowding telephoned Peter Chamberlain during the day or night seeking information on current difficulties. How the telephone calls at night originated is perhaps worthy of explanation. The overall picture of air activity could be easily seen at the Priory by simply walking into the Filter Room and looking at the aircraft movements displayed on the plotting table; by using this facility, nightfighter operations could be comfortably observed. A good example of this is related in E.G. Bowen's book *Radar Days* where he describes how one night a Blenheim flown by Flight Lieutenant 'Jumbo' Ashfield, with Brian 'Chalky' White operating the radar set, was in hot pursuit of a contact which had almost reached German territory. It was at this moment that Dowding looked in on the Filter Room. The reply to his casual enquiry asking which squadron the fighter came from came as a shock when told that it was one of the FIU's Blenheims. He ordered the aircraft to return immediately, fearing that if it became incapacitated in any way and fell on German soil, the very secret AI radar set would be of great value to the *Luftwaffe*. (Later the most advanced radar equipment yet produced fell into German hands via Bomber Command. Their scientists were delighted to receive it and adapt it to their own requirements.)[44]

'Jumbo' Ashfield's efforts were not entirely without success. On the night of 22/23 July, 1940, from radar information supplied by Poling to the Tangmere Operations Room, Peter Chamberlain was able to direct Ashfield into the proximity of a hostile aircraft. An AI radar contact was picked up by Sergeant R.H. Leyland and Pilot Officer G.E. Morris, the observer, saw an aircraft crossing the path of the Blenheim. Ashfield turned after it and, aided by the light of the moon, identified it as a Dornier 17 and shot it down into the sea.

No facilities were denied, and when a request for a certain item was made by the Wing Commander during one of their daily discussions, the C-in-C would often say, 'Why didn't you ask me for it before?', to which Chamberlain honestly replied, 'Sir, until last night I didn't know that I wanted it'. He made an appeal for the ultimate in equipment after a particularly frustrating night flying a Blenheim; several attempts to catch his prey had failed due to the Blenheim's inadequate speed. Leaving the aircraft and walking back in the early morning to the Tangmere Mess to have breakfast, a phrase from the Bible came to mind. By the greatest good fortune he came upon the Padre who gave an on-the-spot verification of the quotation. When he got back to his office, he made a signal to Bentley Priory and asked that it should be brought to the C-in-C's attention. It simply said, 'Luke 5, verse 5'. (Master we have toiled all the night and have caught nothing. Nevertheless we will let down the net and try again.) Raymund Hart took the signal, together with the Bible, and placed it in front of Dowding. 'Take it away, I know what he is after', said Dowding. Four days later (12 August), Bill Pegg, Chief Test Pilot of the Bristol Aircraft Company, delivered a Beaufighter to FIU.[45] Fast and heavily armed, this was the new aircraft which carried high hopes for the future of nightfighting. On 16 August all the Unit's aircraft were damaged or destroyed in a raid on Tangmere, including the Beaufighter. The Unit moved to Shoreham.

While the Battle of Britain was in progress in the Summer of 1940, the FIU continued relentlessly on their scientific development flights and eventual Service trials; something which, it might well be argued, should have taken place much earlier in the introduction of AI radar, but it must be said that up to that time no formula for bringing sophisticated electronic devices into RAF service existed because there had been nothing of a similar nature; perhaps it is also worth recording that there were some influential people who suggested that the AI sets were of little value anyway. With the application of careful scientific study and total commitment by those concerned, most problems were methodically overcome, but it took time.

It was not fully realised then how great were the difficulties inherent in effecting an interception at night. The knowledge gained by the FIU people after their many hours of analysis and test flying of the equipment was freely passed to the squadrons; even then it took a great deal of experience and personal aptitude for crews to achieve success. The problem was how to position the fighter in darkness, getting it moving in the same direction as the bomber and at the same height; this was achieved by total reliance on good instrument flying. It required steadily creeping to within the operating sphere of the AI radar, which was roughly two to three miles, then, having made contact, the pilot being able to follow accurately the directions given by the radar operator, who would be interpreting the indications showing on his cathode ray screens. It also required a constant adjustment of the aircraft's speed to match finally that of the prey, by which time it was hoped that a 'visual' would be made. As can be seen, successful night interception depended upon a high degree of skill. When in its infancy, only a few expert crews achieved a measure of success.

The leading scientific figures in the field of radar research and development were never given adequate public recognition for their work. Recorded history has been deservedly generous in its praise of the coastal radar chain and Sir Robert Watson-Watt, but the importance of the other comparatively sophisticated equipments and their creators has seldom been stressed.

While work in the Tangmere Sector continued, experiments using radar information for ground control of night interception were going on elsewhere. A.F. Wilkins from Telecommunications Research Establishment was persisting with using the CH station at Pevensey in September and October 1940 endeavouring, with a small degree of success, to bring about interceptions over the sea, and I.H. Cole of the Stanmore Research Section was also conducting similar experiments. In the Kenley Sector overland plotting using a chain of small gunlaying sets coupled to searchlights was being used for tracking aircraft. On many nights, Dowding could be seen quietly studying the results in the Sector Operations Room.*

The arrival of the Ground Control Interception (GCI) stations, mentioned earlier, the first of which began trials in late October/early November 1940 at Durrington, near Littlehampton, was a giant stride along the road to combating the night raider and basically followed the idea first mooted by Hanbury Brown nearly a year earlier. They gave an all-round radio picture of the sky, and the controller, by watching the movements of the aircraft in the shape of small luminous blips on his radar screen, could guide his fighter pilot by R/T to a favourable position astern of his prey and into the narrow field being scanned by the fighter's AI radar set. The nights of groping in the dark were becoming fewer. Interceptions could now be effected at night, and in times of bad visibility during the day; they detected aircraft flying over land, which eventually made inland raid reporting possible. An inland network of GCI stations later formed the basis of a new system which supplemented the Observer Corps.

Jim Crofts, MBE, AE, who after the war became a Flight Commander and Fighter Controller with No. 3618 (County of Sussex) Fighter Control Unit of the Royal Auxiliary Air Force, served in the Sector Operations Room at RAF Kenley during the Battle of Britain; in 1941 he was working with one of the early GCI stations:

* See *RAF Kenley* by Peter Flint, published by Terence Dalton.

'It became blatantly obvious that in order to effect a successful interception at night, a means had to be devised whereby the Controller could see his fighter and target at one and the same time. Late in 1940, a cathode ray tube known as a P.P.I. (Plan Position Indicator) was developed. This tube produced a radial time base rather like the face of a clock with the time base in the middle and sweeping round a centre pivot. An aerial known as a 10-foot split was in use which produced a beam of energy approximately 10–14 degrees wide and was capable of being rotated through 360 degrees. Its movement was synchronised with the time base of the P.P.I. Tube so that if it was looking due south, the time base was aligned in the same direction. One small snag with this system was that on the cathode ray tube the echoes returning from aircraft representing 10 degrees of beam width, were shown as arcs of light rather like little sausages. One other snag in those early days was that a system had not yet been devised whereby the same aerial could be used for transmitting and receiving. In view of this, two independent aerials were used, and this presented problems on occasion. The aerials were manually driven by operators turning what looked like bicycle pedals mounted on a three-foot high column. The operator turning the Transmitting aerial was in touch by landline with the plotter on the P.P.I. tube in the mobile Operations Room vehicle, and in addition the P.P.I. plotter had a bell-push. When the Controller was carrying out an interception in a particular area of the tube, the P.P.I. Operator would merely push the bell when he wished the aerial to be turned in the reverse direction. This procedure was known as "inching". The snag was, however, that the operator in the Receiving aerial cabin had to keep his aerial aligned with the Transmitting one. To achieve this, he had turning gear similar to the Transmitting aerial but in addition, he had on his column a galvanometer (a sensitive instrument for measuring small electric currents).

This showed a central position when he was turning on the same bearing as the Transmitting aerial. If the operator managed to get ahead of the bearing, the needle would drift to the *plus* area showing the number of degrees off bearing. If he got behind, the needle would drift to the *minus* area. It will be seen that the operator in the Receiving Aerial cabin had the hardest job as he not only had to turn the aerial but keep his needle in the zero position. Oft times, these two operators became confused and the result was that the signals on the P.P.I. tube would disappear as the Transmitter aerial would be looking in one direction whilst the Receiver was looking on a completely different bearing. A few words were exchanged between the P.P.I. operator and both operators in the aerial cabins and the picture was eventually restored.

'The first G.C.I. Station of which the equipment is described above was known as a Mobile G.C.I. (Type 7). It was entirely mobile and travelled the road in the form of a number of special vehicles. There was a standby power system, Transmitter Vehicle and the Operations Room Vehicle with the Transmitting and Receiving Aerials mounted on their cabins. One of the first stations of this type was sited on the marshes just west of the village of Wartling, East Sussex.* The station became known as RAF Wartling and by coincidence was across the road from the C.H. Station of Pevensey. To man it, a crew of six airmen was posted from the Operations Room at RAF Kenley in April 1941. I was selected as one of the operators and when we arrived on the marshes having been conveyed to the area by a 3-ton RAF lorry, things looked pretty primitive. On entering the field, there was an old bell tent which we discovered was the Guard Room and was manned by a member of the RAF Special Police. However, we were pleased to learn that we would be billetted in civilian billets. We had one Controller who had arrived a few days before the operators. This was Squadron Leader Charles Elderton and he was billetted in a house at Westham adjacent to the village of Pevensey. He had been a Sector Controller. It was explained to us that our job would be principally to operate against the night raids which were being directed at London, so our duties usually covered the period from dusk to dawn and it was not long before we recorded our first success. It is interesting to note that the nightfighter squadron we controlled came from West Malling (No. 29 Squadron I believe) and for a brief spell one of their pilots was Squadron Leader Guy Gibson who was at that time flying nightfighters, having transferred from Bomber Command. The Wartling score sheet, which is now preserved in Bexhill Town Hall, shows that he was responsible for shooting down at least two aircraft whilst under Wartling's control.

I served at Wartling until May 1942 when I was posted to RAF

---

* Apparatus for the first six stations was constructed by hand and with remarkable speed. By the end of January they were providing cover over South and Southeast England.

Station, Blackgang on the Isle of Wight (just above St Catherine's Point) as a deputy GCI Controller'.

All of these events were many months in the future; during which time the whole of Europe was being further plunged into turmoil.

The Observer Corps had its Headquarters at Bentley Priory. It was the centre of a vast organisation which at its peak had 1,400 Posts providing surveillance throughout the country, and feeding forty Centres who disseminated information into the air defence system. Their Commandant, Air Commodore A.D. Warrington-Morris, like many of his colleagues, disliked having the Observer Corps separated from the control of the Home Office, which earlier had been the controlling body to whom they owed their allegiance as Special Police Constables. There was no possible way that this vital component of the air defence organisation could be permitted to receive instructions or be subject to any regulations other than those enforceable by RAF laws. Dowding made this point very clear in the Spring of 1937 when he advised against having members of the Corps as part of the plotting staff in his Operations Room. Liaison Officers were not included in this restriction.

During the Spring of 1940, while the debate about staffing Operations Rooms was in progress, a decision was made which enabled eighteen Observer Corps members from the Group Centres at Colchester, Watford, Norwich and Winchester, to receive direct entry into the RAF, and serve in the Filter Room. This was short term; as more members of the WAAF became available to take over their duties, ex-Corps members moved on, at least two becoming aircrew. Leslie Butt, who was an undertaker by profession, became an AI Radar operator in a Beaufighter before becoming a pilot. (He was later to lose his life in a collision with another aircraft when an instructor.) Another member, Douglas Finch-Beavis, also joined aircrew and served as an air gunner in Palestine and India. Douglas's only real complaint while at the Priory was a certain Sergeant Dawson's insistence that the airmen should have their hair cut with alarming regularity. This enthusiasm was so marked that there was some suspicion that he might be creating a full day's work for the barber. What never failed to make him smile, however, was the barber's final remark, 'Do you require any rubber goods?'

Roland Hammersley, the young barber, cycled each week from 'Alf Hunt's' hairdressers in the St Albans Road at Watford to spend a day administering the official 'short back and sides', at sixpence a time. The room reserved for him beneath the house witnessed a steady flow of unenthusiastic clients; no head ever left with anything remotely resembling a 'style'. The weekly clipping was a source of amusement to some members of the WAAF who, when passing through, often stopped to peer through the open door and were unable to resist making appropriate comments. On the subject of his sale of 'goods', he later wrote with tongue in cheek, 'I was very young and innocent in those days and had little idea of what use the product would be put to', adding, 'Time and the RAF changed many things.'[46] He also joined the RAF and became a member of aircrew, and by 1944 was flying on operations with No. 57 Squadron at East Kirby, winning a DFM in the process.

In the late 1930s the level of Regular staff in the Filter and Operations Rooms throughout Fighter Command had arrived at a point where it could barely cover the essential functions of the organisation and certainly not if ever called upon to work a three-watch around-the-clock system. Earlier, the suggestion had been made that perhaps Officers' Batmen and Mess Servants, Orderlies, Musicians, Groundsmen and men of that category could perform the less skilled tasks on a part-time basis, but it was the Regulars, the Aircrafthands, who were given the jobs, and their numbers were increased to a level able to undertake half of the proposed wartime establishment. Members of the Royal Air Force Volunteer Reserve, who had been training evenings and weekends, became the source from which the immediate expansion became possible at the outbreak of war.

On 19 September 1939, thirty-three members of the WAAF were sent to the Priory for Filter Room duties and were welcomed by the Director of the WAAF, Air Commandant Trefusis Forbes. Initially they took over the daytime watches, their presence attracting much interest from the resident male Officers. The girls noted how the temporary wood scaffolding supporting the balcony overlooking the table was almost groaning under the weight of bodies anxious to study their progress; the true interest was very evident. In charge of this first batch of women were Joyce Pearman-Smith and Sadie Younger, both of whom had been sent to Bawdsey for a short intensive course in the intricacies of the radar system and its procedures.

Soon after their arrival, Sadie Younger noticed Dowding standing behind her and gazing intently at the Filter Room plotting table. He casually asked her to show him certain procedures giving the impression of being anxious to learn: the 'teacher' was happy to comply. After he had left, a Scientific Observer asked Sadie what Dowding was concerned about and she told him that the C-in-C had asked a few questions to help him get a clearer idea of the working of the table. To her surprise, this had the same effect as telling him a joke; through the broadest of grins he told her, 'Dowding knows more about radar than anyone – he's been testing you.' Sadie's friends enjoyed her embarrassment; it amused them for quite a while. Dowding also remembered the episode; very soon, on his recommendation, she was commissioned. Joyce Pearman-Smith and Sadie were on a number of occasions selected to act as guinea pigs when studies were being made on procedures; at one time they had psychologists from Cambridge University watching their every move. (One of their recommendations after the studies, and which was later adopted, was that members of the Stock Exchange should be introduced as Filterers.) Sadie Younger later became a Filter Controller and was mentioned in Dispatches for her work. (After the war, Raymund Hart recognised her when attending a celebration dinner. He was heard to remark, 'Ah! here comes the first WAAF in Radar.')[47]*

The employment of members of the WAAF for duty in the Operations Centres was accepted but with some misgivings, one being that it was thought that they would not be able to sustain the necessary long periods of intense concentration; the most debated aspect was how they would react if ever subjected to bombardment from the air. Security was also thought to be a likely problem if ever they left the Service to return to civilian life for whatever reason. They had been trained in the working of the highly secret radar operations and were at that time able to change jobs and leave the Service. The feeling was that mixed watches of male and female personnel would give the women confidence if ever under attack. It was in staffing the Filter Room that this policy was most questioned, and as late as February 1940, although women had been employed there since September, supposedly on an experimental basis, the debate continued and broadened. In a communication to Group Captain Storrar (Vice-Chairman Establishment Committee), J. N. T Stephenson, a Wing Commander in the Operations Section, wrote;

* Many years later when writing to Sadie Younger about the WAAF, Dowding said, 'I was positively amazed at the way in which the so-called weaker sex stuck the gruelling effects of their war service. I am sure that not only I but the whole nation must feel a debt of gratitude which will remain for all time'.[48]

'Owing to the limitations of space in the Filter Room, which are imposed by the maximum practical size of the map, the Filterers are working not only close to their WAAF Plotters but have constantly to lean over them and push past them. It so happens that many of these young women are extremely attractive and with equal and similar attraction on the other side of the table, they cannot fail to make some claim, even if only subconsciously, on the attention of the men Filterers working with them.'

To improve the standard of Filtering, the idea that Filterers should be drawn from men of a more scientific background was considered, but Storrar commented, 'This gain may be to some extent offset by the unnecessary distraction of the beauty chorus'.[49] Another Officer commented:

'I must say that when I visited the present Filter Room I found the WAAFs more attractive than the plotting table and feel that, unless we limited the field to eunuchs, we should be unlikely to find Filterers who could give to their work the individual attention that is so vitally necessary.'[50]

Shortly, this problem was to solve itself; it had always been agreed that the women were very proficient and the turn of events left very little time for change. When the greatest demands were being made on the Filter Room, the minds of the staff had little time for extraneous thought.

On 9 March 1940 concern for the safety of the nerve centre of Fighter Command's defence network lessened when the underground Operations Block was brought into use. The mechanics of the organisation were the product of years of experiment and improvisation carried out in the incongruous setting of the old house. A duplicate of the final set up was installed within the concrete and steel structure many feet beneath the ground. One hundred and sixty-seven telephone lines serving the Filter and Operations Rooms were switched over in two and a half minutes. The lines to the Teleprinters, four serving the Intelligence Section and two carrying Home Office traffic were switched over immediately; sixteen others for the Administration were soon to follow. Some indication of the total reliance of the air defences on the GPO engineers can be seen by the number of other lines which were brought into use; two days later two hundred and fifty extensions, seventy exchange lines and private wires were switched to the PBX (telephone exchange) in the underground building. Carrying the great wealth of wiring, three separate cables in steel pipes,

70

laid six feet beneath the surface, ran outwards in different directions for two hundred yards, thereafter at a depth of three feet, before terminating in concrete-protected interconnection panels. This arrangement allowed for re-routing of all lines should one feed cable become damaged by bombing. (The demands for military communications were so great that a new telegraph system was introduced in the Spring of 1939. Known as the Defence Teleprinter Network, it carried a prodigious quantity of information between the Commands of the RAF.)

The underground block, soon known as 'The Hole', housed the Filter and Command Operations Rooms with departments for Intelligence, Home Office, Code and Cypher Section and Type 'X' Coding apparatus. Offices were provided for C-in-C, SASO and Air Staff; there were also rest rooms with kitchens and toilets for officers, airmen and women, these were later additions provided at Dowding's insistence, and a cleaners' room.

Four days later the underground operations block at Newcastle, Headquarters of No. 13 Group, was brought into use, but Headquarters No. 12 Group had to wait until 31 May before it could move from Hucknall into its new underground centre at Watnall, Nottinghamshire. No. 11 Group Headquarters at Uxbridge had been in use since ten days before the outbreak of war.

The amount of work being done by the GPO engineers was remarkable. They were providing landlines and equipment for the entire air defence, e.g. new radar stations, gunsites, Observer Corps, etc.; they were also installing telecommunications for all the other armed forces and civilian defence organisations. At the same time they were working to improve their own civilian telephone system.

Chapter 5

The Fall of France

On 10 May, Neville Chamberlain resigned and was succeeded as Prime Minister by Winston Churchill who immediately set about forming a coalition Government. On that same day, German forces moved against Holland, Belgium and Luxembourg. A brilliantly executed plan made it possible for them to make rapid advances across the European mainland, including France, which was thought to be the stone on which the sword of German aggression would be blunted. There were many contributory factors promoting the successful German advance, not least of these being the use of fast moving armoured units closely supported in the field by a dominant air force, a new concept in warfare. The air tactics had been developed by them during the Spanish Civil War. Dowding had studied them very carefully.

At the time of the German breakthrough, the British fighter forces on the Continent were operating in two separate capacities, four squadrons were serving as the Air Component supporting the British Expeditionary Force (BEF) and two others were providing cover for the light bomber units of the Advanced Air Striking Force (AASF). As part of the general plan, four further squadrons based at forward aerodromes near the South East coast of England could be used, if required, to cover the left flank of an Allied advance and provide cover for naval forces should they wish to carry out operations against North Channel ports. At the start of the German advance, reinforcements were sent immediately; four of the Home Defence squadrons were dispatched and divided equally between the two forces.[51]

By 13 May, the battlefield situation had already become alarming; requests for air assistance had come from Queen Wilhelmina of the Netherlands and her Prime Minister, the Belgian King and the British Ambassador in Brussels, Sir Roger Keys. The French Premier, M. Paul Reynaud, telephoned asking for more assistance. The Chiefs of Staff Committee of the War Cabinet met in the morning to discuss events. The prevailing opinion on sending more fighters was that it was difficult to see what further assistance could be given without weakening the home defences. It was noted that the French had large numbers available but it was not known to what extent they were being employed. The Prime Minister commented that the home defence resources should not be reduced below a minimum safety figure although there was a great deal to be said for making further efforts to give additional support. At the full War Cabinet meeting later in the day, how to give further assistance was debated and centred on whether the bomber force could be employed in attacking targets in the Ruhr district of Germany and whether retaliatory air raids would be directed against Britain. It then discussed the question of the strength of the home fighter force. The Secretary of State for Air, Sir Archibald Sinclair, expressed concern about sending any more fighters out of the country, saying that the Air Staff had estimated that sixty squadrons were required for home defence whereas there were only thirty-nine available. This requirement for sixty squadrons was confirmed by Chief of the Air Staff, Sir Cyril Newall, who added that it was doubtful if this figure would be sufficient if operations were carried out from Holland. The Prime Minister's view was that air attack against the homeland was inevitable; he followed by saying,

'Whatever course the war in France took, we could not afford to use up our fighters day by day until the defences of this country were seriously impaired. It was true our fighters would find it difficult to deal with German attacks by night, but on the other hand they would be unable to bomb our vital points with any degree of accuracy.'

Sir Cyril Newall, replying to a question whether we could send more fighters, asked that, before a decision was taken to reduce the number of fighter squadrons in this country by sending further squadrons to France, the Commander-in-Chief Fighter Command should be given the opportunity of expressing his views. 'His present view was that if it were decided now to reduce the fighter defences of this country he would ask to be formally over-ruled by the War Cabinet.'[52]

Newall's request was granted two days later when on 15 May Dowding was party to the deliberations of the War Cabinet. At 10 a.m. a meeting of the Chiefs of Staff Committee was held in the Cabinet War Room with Newall in the Chair. Those present were Sir Dudley Pound, Chief of Naval Staff; General Sir Edmund Ironside, Chief of the Imperial General Staff; and General Ismay, representing Officers of the War Cabinet General Staff; the Secretariat on this occasion was Colonel L.C. Hollis and Lieutenant-Colonel E.J.C. Jacob. At 10.30 a.m. the meeting was adjourned and discussion resumed immediately under the Chairmanship of Prime Minister Churchill who had just arrived. Churchill gave a resumée of the general situation on land and said that he had been telephoned that morning at 8.30 by French Premier Reynaud whose confidence appeared to be considerably shaken and had said that the battle was lost and the road to Paris open. (The previous evening Reynaud had telephoned to ask for ten more squadrons, a request he had now repeated; that evening he made yet another call for reinforcements.)[53]

At this point Dowding and Sir Richard Peirse, Vice-Chief of the Air Staff, entered the meeting and the discussion turned to whether more fighters should be committed to France. Dowding's view had been made known at the 13 May meeting and he now spelled out a warning to the new Prime Minister, Churchill, and Chiefs of Staff Committee, informing them how he saw the possible outcome of events now being enacted out, and the likely effect of further reducing his fighter force.

The Minutes of the Meeting record him saying that

'we were faced with a tremendously important decision in view of the situation developing in France. How the matter would end he was not in a position to judge, but if things went badly we would then have to face an attack directed against this country, possibly from France in addition to Holland and Germany. Provided no more fighters were removed from the Air Defence of Great Britain, he was confident that the Royal Navy and the Royal Air Force would be able to keep the Germans out of this country. If more fighters were taken from him, however, they would not achieve decisive results in France and he would be left too weak to carry on over here. He was absolutely opposed to parting with a single additional Hurricane. If we were not further weakened, he would be prepared for any German attack here in retaliation for action by our bombers.'[54]

These words were very important. There was now on record a clear and concise statement about the state of the home defences and the possible consequences if bad judgements were made. The Prime Minister and Chiefs of Staff would necessarily have to weigh future action against this warning; interestingly, Dowding was not asked to repeat it at a full War Cabinet Meeting later that day. Peirse said that the demand for ten more fighter squadrons made by the French Premier the previous day was made without any reference at all to the British Air Officer Commanding-in-Chief in France, Air Marshal Barratt, but Barratt had now reported that he was short of fighters. Churchill thought that the time had now come to reconsider the use of heavy bombers against German industry; until this time, concern over retaliation against British cities had prevented this action.

At the meeting of the full War Cabinet later, two major topics were introduced for discussion by Churchill; whether the appeal by Reynaud for more fighters should be granted and whether military targets in the Ruhr and elsewhere in Germany should be attacked. Churchill thought there would be little difficulty in deciding against the dispatch of further squadrons, no demand had been made by the French military authority; he was, however, reminded that the Commander-in-Chief of the British Air Forces had sent a telegram that morning stressing the need for additional fighter support; Newall commented that they could only be found by withdrawing them from the active defences of the country and he would not at this moment advise the dispatch of any additional aircraft. Dowding welcomed the proposal to attack targets in the Ruhr, saying they should not be deterred by the fear of attacks by Germany since these were bound to come sooner or later. Churchill agreed.[55] It was agreed not to send more fighters for the present.

Dowding arrived back at his office at the Priory in a more settled frame of mind. Replying to a letter sent by Keith Park, Air Officer Commanding (AOC) No. 11 Group,* in which Park had criticised the arrangements for the recent dispatch of Hurricanes to France, he added:

> 'We had a notable victory on the 'Home Front' this morning and the orders to send more Hurricanes were cancelled. Appeals for help will doubtless be renewed, however, with increasing insistence and I do not know how this morning's work will stand the test of time; but I will never relax my efforts to prevent the dissipation of the Home fighter forces.'[56]

The Chiefs of Staff Committee was a sub-committee of the War Cabinet and its members were the Senior Staff Officer from each of the three Fighting Services, plus the Prime Minister. Generally speaking, they met alone, usually starting at between 10 and 10.30 a.m., with one of their number taking the Chair, and later continued in the presence of the Prime Minister, who became Chairman as of right. At this time,

---

* On 8 March, Park, then SASO at Fighter Command, was taken ill with appendicitis. On returning to duty, he was posted as AOC No. 11 Group, and was replaced at Fighter Command Headquarters by Air Commodore A.D. Cunningham, CBE. When Park first became ill, Group Captain Orlebar stood in.

General Ismay was the Prime Minister's representative and it was through him that Churchill passed matters to them for discussion. The Committee collectively advised the Cabinet on defence problems as a whole and was the recognised channel through which the armed forces kept in very close contact with the Government of the day. Their sphere of influence ranged through offering advice on long-term planning during times of peace to becoming a battle headquarters during war.

The morning after Dowding had spoken to the War Cabinet, and they decided that no further fighters could be spared from the home force, the Chiefs of Staff met at 10.15 a.m. in the Cabinet War Room to discuss information received during the previous twenty-four hours; Sir Cyril Newall was in the Chair. While the meeting was in progress, a message was received from France saying that the Germans had broken through near Sedan and French forces were being overwhelmed. Newall told of how he had spoken earlier on the telephone to Air Marshal Barratt in France and the picture Barratt had painted was one of French loss of morale and imminent catastrophe, but Barratt had thought he would be able to 'stop the rot if he could be sent four additional fighter squadrons at once'. Newall went on to say how during the night further calls for assistance had come from the French. General Gamelin was requesting ten squadrons at once; 'If they did not come, the battle would be lost'. He recalled how on the previous day the War Cabinet had decided against sending more aircraft but, 'in the light of this new and critical development, he thought that he would have to recommend sending additional fighters to France'. Part of his reasoning was that he had information that a high percentage of German bombing strength was being used in the Continental battle, making it unlikely that it could be diverted away to attack Britain in any strength and also 'every bomber shot down over France was one less to attack this country'. He said that it was worse than useless to send only a small number of fighters and had reluctantly come to the conclusion that eight Flights, the equivalent of four squadrons, and a repair unit should be sent at once. It was agreed that this course of action should be recommended to the War Cabinet, but the Committee felt that further air assistance to the French Army was valueless if they were not going to fight. The Meeting then adjourned and continued at No. 10 Downing Street with Winston Churchill in the Chair. He was advised by Sir Cyril Newall of all that had gone before and agreed, but suggested that two further squadrons, those guarding the Fleet at Scapa Flow, should also be sent. Newall repeated the Committee's conclusion; 'four squadrons was the length to which we could go in sending further fighters to France at the present time.'

When the recommendation was put before the full War Cabinet later, it was not accepted. While stating the very grave risk involved in dispatching them particularly when retaliatory attacks on the country were expected after the bombing of the Ruhr the previous night, Churchill asked for the two squadrons protecting the Naval base at Scapa Flow to be sent, making a total of six squadrons; the first necessity, he thought, 'was to support French morale and give them a chance to recover'. Newall disagreed, suggesting if those at Scapa were available they should be employed in home defence. Secretary of State for Air, Sir Archibald Sinclair, also expressed disquiet and recalled Dowding's words of the previous day; he reported, 'He had not changed his views even when told of the situation in France'. Sinclair supported the view not to send more than four squadrons. Earlier in the day an arrangement was made for Air Marshal Joubert de la Ferté to go to France to discuss the situation with Air Marshal Barratt and in particular to find out what use the French were making of their own fighters. Sinclair thought a decision on whether to dispatch the other squadrons should be delayed pending Joubert's report. He also emphasised that 'the War Cabinet should realise that they were acting contrary to the advice of the AOC-in-C Fighter Command who was responsible for the defence of the country'. Sinclair's opinion was accepted; even so two additonal squadrons were to be prepared for dispatch at very short notice. It is surprising that at the time there was so little information available on what the French Air Force was actually doing. By recommending the dispatch of four squadrons, Newall had inadvertently released a strong emotional trait within the Prime Minister which would now be difficult to contain.

While the Cabinet was reaching its conclusion, Dowding sat at his desk in the calm of the lofty room which was his office at Bentley Priory, unaware of the latest threat to Fighter Command. Whatever his superiors decided, he was duty bound to implement; he had no authority to override their decisions. The only avenue open to him was one of forceful persuasion. With the catastrophe on the Continent in mind, and the prospect of a strain being put on Fighter Command the like of which he had foreseen several months earlier, and the reduction of his fighter strength which could possibly now become a wasted asset being too weak to offer sustained resistance, he wrote to Under Secretary of State Harold Balfour, at the Air Ministry. He told him how he assumed that if defeat were suffered on the Continent, no one would deny that England should fight on and for this purpose a minimum fighter strength would be necessary. Dowding asked that the Air Council should inform him of what that strength should be. He reminded them that they had estimated fifty-two squadrons would be required to defend the Country; his strength was now reduced to the equivalent of thirty-six squadrons. (News of the latest reduction of four squadrons was yet to arrive.) He requested that once the Air Council and the Cabinet had decided the limit on which they 'were prepared to stake the existence of the Country' it should be made clear to Commanders on the Continent that not a single aeroplane from Fighter Command above that figure would be sent out. He concluded,

'I believe that, if an adequate fighter force is kept in this country, if the Fleet remains in being, and if Home Forces are suitably organised to resist invasion, we should be able to carry on the war single-handed for some time, if not indefinitely. But, if the Home Defence Force is drained away in desperate attempts to remedy the situation in France, defeat in France will involve the final, complete and irremediable defeat of this country.'[57]

Later that day the Prime Minister and his delegation flew to France and met French leaders; they were much concerned by what they saw and heard. After their discussion that evening, Churchill asked General Ismay to telephone London and ask that the Cabinet should meet to consider sending six more fighter squadrons. (This would bring the total agreed number for 16 May up to ten squadrons, the figure asked for by Gamelin.)

The War Cabinet was well aware of the parlous state of the Home Fighter strength; with the equivalent of four more squadrons sent abroad only thirty-two squadrons of single-seater fighters would remain in the United Kingdom. From the reserves of the Home Defences thirty-two Hurricanes were taken and to get new aircraft serviceable, accessories were being stripped from damaged aircraft. However, Churchill's request for a further six squadrons was granted. (Had they been sent in entirety, just twenty-six squadrons would have remained to defend the country. Exactly half the estimated number required.) Sir Cyril Newall informed the Cabinet there were only six complete Hurricane Squadrons remaining in the country. He questioned the availability of airfields in Northern France; at most only three squadrons could be accommodated. As a compromise, he suggested all six should be based in Kent and an arrangement made whereby three could fly over and work from French airfields during the morning and they would be replaced by three others leaving Kent to relieve them at noon; these would return in the evening. The proposal was agreed.*[58]

Sir Cyril Newall, who had been subjected to immense pressure during the previous few days, was very much aware of Dowding's totally uncompromising view and now in possession of his letter of 16 May, which spelled out the reality of the situation now facing the country. He also knew that, in spite of the Prime Minister's expressed concern about home fighter strength, it did not deter him from asking the War Cabinet to agree to dispatch more to France. Deeply concerned and agreeing with the views in Dowding's letter, he used it as the basis for a note which he wrote on 18 May and circulated to his fellow Chiefs of Staff asking for their support when the subject was debated by the War Cabinet. To each note a copy of Dowding's letter was appended.[60]

The Chiefs of Staff discussed Newall's note, also an appreciation by the Joint Planning Committee on strategy. In the afternoon they met again and directed the secretary to convert Newall's memo into a Chiefs of Staff Report and submit it, over their signatures, to the War Cabinet. There could be no more weighty advice than that coming from the senior officers of the three Services.

On that same day, the Prime Minister wrote to General Ismay asking for information about the actual strength of the fighter squadrons in Great Britain. He also advised him, 'No more squadrons of fighters will leave the country whatever the need in France'. There would be a need for them for a covering operation from English bases if it became necessary to withdraw the British Army from the Continent. He also asked that the utmost Anti-Aircraft strength should be concentrated on protecting aircraft factories, commenting, 'These are more important than anything else at the moment'.[61] (On 20 May, Fighter Command Order of Battle shows that there were thirty squadrons of Spitfires and Hurricanes available on which so much depended; there were six of Blenheims and one Defiant, four others deemed

---

* John Colville, Churchill's Private Secretary, recorded in his diary on 9 July 1941 how that night Churchill and Sinclair, speaking of the French, had agreed they had acted shamefully by demanding more fighter squadrons after they knew the battle had been lost.[59]

to be for Trade defence were evenly divided between Fighter and Coastal Command.) Perhaps a clearer indication of the gravity of the situation in the home defence units can be seen by the number of aircraft available for operation; 247 Spitfires and 99 Hurricanes. Dowding made a point of keeping Spitfires out of the Continental battle because the supply position was so poor; they could not have maintained their existence in the face of such heavy losses. By now, the rapid German advances on the Continent made airfields over there untenable, and all British aircraft supporting the British Expeditionary Force were being withdrawn home to operate from airfields in South East England; their return bolstered the much depleted home force but their efficiency was greatly impaired. Only three Hurricane squadrons remained on French soil; these were with the Advanced Air Striking Force.

The Air Council replied to Dowding's 16 May letter seven days later. In it he was requested to develop the necessary plans for a covering operation if it became necessary to evacuate the British Expeditionary Force; also 'that the air defences of this country should be deployed in such a manner as to afford the maximum protection to the aircraft industry'. The emphasis was now on the preservation of the home base; they also agreed to the further development and deployment of the fighter defences in the West of the Country and between the Firth of Forth and Orkney.[62]

Dowding, when replying to the letter, remarked that the withdrawal of seven squadrons had 'converted a desperate into a serious situation'. He dealt with losses of aircraft and the benefits gained by fighting over Britain as opposed to France, i.e. battle damaged aircraft could be repaired when descending on British soil, shot down pilots could often be returned to their bases and would soon be in the air again. (When France surrendered, all German prisoner of war pilots held by the French were released to fight the British again in spite of a British plea that this should not be done.) He also reminded the Air Council of the many extra commitments he was now asked to fulfil and asked that these should be kept to a minimum; the general deployment of the Fighter Command had 'been arranged largely with the view of protecting the aircraft industry but the task will be rendered easier when the concentrated operations from the South East of England come to an end'. He asked whether it would not be a wise policy to bring the remaining three Hurricane squadrons home and also whether the efforts of Bomber Command could be directed against targets which would slow up the impetus of air attack.

'Damage done to crossroads or railway sidings is very quickly repaired, but damage done to enemy aerodromes and aircraft on the ground will have an immediate effect, while the destruction of industrial plant and oil stocks will have an effect which, though slower, may prove decisive.'[63]

On 26 May the Chiefs of Staff Committee summoned Dowding to an afternoon meeting to explain the AA gun and searchlight disposition he had made to provide special protection for the aircraft factories. When this was concluded, it was decided that the whole of the production of heavy and light AA guns and searchlights should go to the air defences. It was also agreed that two mobile AA units (twenty-four heavy and twelve Bofors) should be located in London and the Midlands, as arranged by Dowding. An AA Regiment earmarked for France should be retained in Britain. There was to be maximum production of balloons to strengthen the incomplete searchlight belt in the West and provide increased dazzle effect in the vicinity of vital points of industry.[64]

About the time the meeting was in progress, the machinery for the evacuation of the British Expeditionary Force by sea from Dunkirk was set in motion. That night Dowding was ordered to protect the beaches using standing patrols in strength from dawn until dusk. *Reichsmarschall* Goering had indicated to German leaders that the *Luftwaffe* could destroy the bottled up army of the British Expeditionary Force but, as the German aircraft made their approach to the embarkation beaches, the Fighter Command Hurricanes and Spitfires engaged them.

The direction of air operations fell within the province of No. 11 Group and it was from Keith Park's airfields that fighter protection over the Channel and behind the Dunkirk coast was directed. To achieve this, there was much movement of squadrons in and out of No. 11 Group aerodromes; the evacuation required almost the entire resources of Fighter Command. Patrols of three or more squadrons were sent after some had complained about the policy of employing weak patrols to provide continuous cover. Park informed them that this was an Air Ministry order, but his headquarters was now insisting they were undertaken in three-squadron strength.[65] Inevitably, the use of forces in such large numbers could not be sustained and there were periods when no cover could be provided; it was then the German aircraft did most damage. By liaising with the Admiralty, operations were arranged to try to coincide with specific shipping movements.

While the air battle over Dunkirk continued, the battles for France raged on and aircraft of the Advanced Air Striking Force continued their support of British ground forces in Northern areas. At a War Cabinet meeting on 3 June, recommendations made in a report by the Chiefs of Staff were discussed. This had been formulated as a basis on which a reply could be made to the French who were asking for assistance and was in essence a review of the current strength of British land and air forces, and what could be provided. For the air, it recommended there should be a smaller force than that at the beginning of the Continental battle. Sir Cyril Newall pointed out that the Advanced Air Striking Force was a part of the home Metropolitan Air Force and had been sent abroad for operational convenience, not to defend France or the French Army; it should now be incorporated in the Air Component. He emphasised that our fighter defences were organised to meet an attack by bombers operating from Germany and were inadequate to meet short-range attacks accompanied by fighters. (Events were soon to prove that it was the single-seater fighter which was to have greatest influence.) Newall emphasised the high losses which had been incurred by the RAF. Dowding had been invited to attend, and he now produced a graph illustrating the high wastage of Hurricanes in France during the period 8 to 18 May; 250 had been lost and he suggested that, if the wastage had continued on that scale throughout May, with the low output from the aircraft factories, the ratio being twenty-five lost per day against four being produced, there would not have been any Hurricanes left by the end of the month.

Replying to a later question, he said that on the previous day there were 244 Hurricanes and 280 Spitfires serviceable,* but this did not represent a true picture as a number of pilots had not yet done their first solo on eight-gun fighters; it would take six weeks before they were sufficiently proficient to take part in active operations. He reported on the great demands made on his Command during the fighting over Dunkirk; that very day the last three squadrons of Fighter Command were being withdrawn from Scotland to take part, and on the previous evening, to make up a strong patrol, eight squadrons were needed to provide the necessary strength. At the moment, he reported, the bottleneck was trained fighter pilots and, if the enemy developed a heavy air attack on the country,

* The aircraft, although amounting to the equivalent of thirty-nine squadrons, were spread throughout all home defence squadrons.

he could not 'guarantee air superiority for more than 48 hours'. The Prime Minister reminded him of the heavy strain being felt by the German Air Force. The Minutes of the meeting show that Dowding spoke at some length, and stressed the need for careful husbanding of resources. He spoke of the numerical superiority of the German Air Force, advising that

'we should use our resources economically. Our fighter operations must be regulated by the rate of output in such a manner as to ensure that we were not squandering the capital of our fighter aircraft. This meant that we must not send to France more fighter squadrons than we could see our way to maintain'.

He dwelt on the importance of maintaining the high quality and fighting spirit of the fighter pilots, by saying that

'our pilots must not be sent out except after adequate training, and in strong numbers, under conditions which would make them feel that their chances of survival were good'.

He reminded the Cabinet of the formidable task ahead to repair the damage suffered by the squadrons over France; this had to be done with the prospect of an immediate air attack against this country.[66] The meeting then moved on to discuss the future use of the long-range bomber which, at this time, was the only weapon available which could adversely affect German industry's war capacity. It was formally agreed that the six bomber and three Hurricane squadrons in France should be brought up to full strength and the home-based bomber force would give priority to supporting the land battle. Serious losses made it impossible to send further fighter squadrons to France but the door would not be entirely closed to reconsideration in the future. Churchill clearly did not like the fighter decision and reintroduced the subject at a War Cabinet Meeting the following day. He now wanted a further review. The discussion centred on the statistics of aircraft production and losses. The Minister of Aircraft Production, Beaverbrook, had provided Churchill with figures stating there were about forty-five squadrons for use in home defence; this, according to Churchill, was more than those available before the battle commenced. At one stage the Prime Minister suggested that 'we could never keep all that we wanted for our own defence while the French were fighting for their lives': the realisation that his own people were also fighting for their lives had perhaps not occurred at this stage. Beaverbrook gave figures for all aircraft production and emphasised twenty fighters were being produced each day. Sir Archibald Sinclair challenged Beaverbrook's figure of twenty fighters, pointing out that ancillary equipment to make them operational was not available. He described the parlous state of affairs existing in Fighter Command, telling how after the battle in France much reorganising and training was needed; although statistics looked good, in reality things were not so. He stressed the high loss of pilots and their leaders. He also reminded the meeting how the home fighter force had now been numerically decided at fifty-seven squadrons. Lord Halifax, Secretary of State for Foreign Affairs, suggested that it should be emphasised to the French that the 'whole success of the Allies depended on keeping up the production of our aircraft factories. If these were lost, the French as well as ourselves could not avoid defeat'. Sinclair suggested there was some indication that the French Air Force was 'not pulling its weight'. A report had been received that, despite adequate warnings by the British about a forthcoming raid on Paris, when it started only three out of forty French aircraft at Villacomblay had taken off to intercept. (The Deputy Chief of Air Staff had seen this when he landed there.)[67] No decision was made at the meeting to send fighter reinforcements.

On 4 June, operations over the Dunkirk area ceased; over 338,000 British and Allied troops had been evacuated from the beaches by using an amazing variety of craft; it was a triumph for both professional and amateur seamen. In the air, the British and German Air Forces had for the first time met on something like equal terms, with Spitfires being used in strength; losses on both sides had been heavy.

On 8 June the Prime Minister gave his view of the fighter situation to the War Cabinet.

'We could regard the the present battle as decisive for France and ourselves, and throw in the whole of our fighter resources in an attempt to save the situation, and bring about victory. If we failed, we should then have to surrender. Alternatively, we should recognise that whereas the present land battle was of great importance, it would not be decisive one way or the other for Great Britain. If it were lost, and France was forced to submit, we could continue the struggle with good hopes of ultimate victory, provided we ensured that our fighter defences in this country were not impaired; but if we cast away our defence the war would be lost, even if the front in France were stabilised, since Germany would be free to turn her air force against this country, and would have us at her mercy . . . He felt it would be fatal to yield to the French demands and jeopardise our own safety'[68]

It was agreed to keep the now five fighter squadrons in France up

Air Vice-Marshal Sir John Salmond and Group Captain Hugh Dowding during a visit to Kenley by Crown Prince Hirohito of Japan. 1921.

King George VI and Sir Hugh Dowding. *("Chic" Willett)*

King George VI and the Queen during their informal visit to Bentley Priory on 6 September 1940, escorted by the A.O.C.-in-C. Fighter Command, Air Chief Marshal Sir Hugh Dowding. *(Ministry of Defence)*

Dowding's desk and chair in the Dowding Room at Bentley Priory. *(Author)*

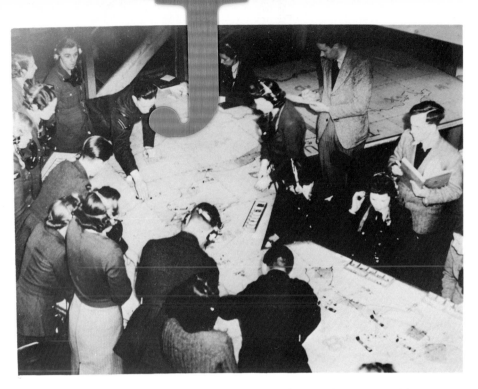

Filter Room in the house (circa late 1939 – early 1940). Note the trays containing plotters' counters. Scientific Observers (*top right*) are taking notes. *(Crown Copyright)*

Air Raid Warning Section on the balcony of the Operations Room in the house. Group Captain Smallwood is working on the table. *(Crown Copyright)*

The Filter Room in the house. Note the plaques on the map carrying raid information. Top right can be seen a time indicator numbered 1–5, each section of a half minute duration. Number 3 being lit up, plotters would be laying counters to coincide with that. *(Crown Copyright)*

Filter Room in the house. No. 3 is lit up on time indicator. *(Crown Copyright)*

5   Practice roadway with practice or local cover ascent place?

Cultivated areas (strong points)   approx. 19,400 sq. m.
Extent in total   approx. 202,000 sq. m.
Track connection not available   *(Christopher Elliot)*

350-foot Chain Home Radar masts supporting the transmitting aerials. *(R.A.F. Museum)*

Below: Chain Home Radar masts. The transmitter masts *(left)* were of steel and were 350 feet high. Those used for receiving *(right)* were constructed of wood to eliminate stray reflections which might affect direction finding and height reading. They were 240 feet, which was the highest it was practical to build. *(R.A.F. Museum)*

to strength; other, home-based, squadrons, up to a total of six, should operate under AOC-in-C Fighter Command when he could make them available.

The only major blunder the Germans had made occurred at the highest level, when it was decided to halt ground operations against the BEF at the Dunkirk perimeter in favour of destroying it from the air and, in so doing, allowing it to escape. Final collapse of the French came on 22 June with them signing an armistice, by which time the remainder of the BEF and the air support had been evacuated.

In his book, *Their Finest Hour*, Winston Churchill makes the assertion that Dowding told him the British Isles could be defended by twenty-five fighter squadrons; not surprisingly, this was vigorously denied by Dowding. The impression gained from the book is that this figure was conveyed to him at a War Cabinet meeting and on this understanding rested his decision to ask for a further six squadrons for France, leaving only twenty-five squadrons for Home defence. Dowding, until that time, had attended one Chiefs of Staff meeting followed on the same day by a full Cabinet meeting. No mention of an exact number of units was made at either meeting; two days earlier both the Secretary of State and Chief of the Air Staff informed the Prime Minister of the Air Staff's most recent estimate that sixty squadrons would be required for home defence. In reality, only twenty-six squadrons were available after Churchill's request from France. In his telegram to London, Churchill had commented, 'It would not be good historically if their requests were denied and their ruin resulted.'

Queries have since arisen about the number of French fighters employed in the battle for France when throughout that period their political and military leaders at every opportunity made strong pleas for more British fighters, invariably saying that they were being overwhelmed by numerically superior forces. Soon after the end of the war, the new French Government set up a Parliamentary Investigating Committee to analyse the failure of French arms. From this, it emerged that large quantities of their fighters had not been used at all and many had remained in storage. General Vuillemin, Chief of the Air Force, testified that, in spite of considerable losses, he had more front line aircraft available at the armistice than when the battle commenced. Statistics are often misleading and do not give a complete picture, but it is clear that the full potential of the French combat force was never fully used; events had moved so quickly that reserves were nullified. There is also evidence of aircraft being sabotaged.[69] The German Air Force had nothing like the estimated number of aircraft in operational service. It is generally agreed, however, that their aircraft were superior to those of the French.

Throughout this period, Dowding's predictions of the loss of the home force to France came true; it will be remembered that these warnings were made soon after the outbreak of war, long before large-scale operations commenced. In discussions at the highest level, he was fearless in expressing his view; in forthright terms he frequently warned of the likely consequences if the home defence squadrons were sent abroad. His words carried influence and formed the basis on which others constructed their argument for the retention of the home units. He remained steadfast, never faltering in his resolve to preserve the machinery of the air defence.

In his decision making he was not subjected to the pressures of international consideration like Churchill, nor like Newall, who was continually burdened with the onerous task of advising the War Cabinet, where military policy was sometimes shaped by broader political aspects. Dowding's responsibility was confined to the preservation of the homeland and its people from attack from the air, perhaps a narrower view which allowed for more objective thought.

Chapter 6

Breathing Space

While the German military forces rested and re-equipped after their victorious push through Europe, preparations were being made for the subjugation of the British people. During this period of relative military inactivity, which was also the occasion for the German High Command to make surreptitious whisperings about peace, the British were frantically working to regenerate their forces for the impending assault.

Those who had been fighting in the air over the battlefields of Europe had gained valuable experience of modern high speed aerial warfare. It was gained at a heavy cost of machines and men, equally there were many German aircraft and crews who would never fly against Britain in the coming conflict. The squadrons of Fighter Command were being hastily brought up to numerical strength, which is certainly not to say fighting efficiency.

In September 1938, the Air Staff had assessed the likely scale of German attacks on the country by estimating the range of each type of German bomber and drawing on a map an arc at that distance from a point in Germany. Estimates of bomb load and numbers of aircraft were introduced into the calculations and the result was an appraisal of the weight of bombing within a given area.

The air defence was planned to offer the earliest possible response to enemy long-range aircraft approaching from across the North Sea from bases in Germany. It followed then that the eastern and southeastern parts of the country were going to be the most heavily defended; this arrangement conveniently afforded a high degree of protection to London, always thought to be the most likely early target for concentrated attack from the air. The early warning CH Radar stations were sited in greater concentration in these areas. Recent German conquests changed the nature of things. Other parts of the country were now vulnerable, in particular the south and west. Before fighting ceased in France, Wing Commander

Theodore McEvoy* at the Air Ministry wrote the following to Air Commodore Donald Stevenson, Director of Home Operations, on 30 May.

'The German occupation of Northern France makes it necessary for us to consider how the air defences of this country should be reorientated to meet the new routes of approach to our vital points which will soon be possible. Examination of the map shows that German long-range bombers could fly up the Irish Sea to attack such objectives as Bristol, Liverpool and Belfast with little or no warning of their approach.'[70]

He went on to suggest measures for containing the impact of this latest development. He was also anxious to increase the fighter defences in the far northeast of Britain. Other than the airfield at Filton, being used for the protection of Bristol, initially fighter defences extended only as far as Tangmere. In January 1940, Dowding pressed for expansion into the south and western areas, but as yet the programme was still incomplete; this situation was to continue into the Battle of Britain period.

In June, Stevenson was asked by the recently appointed Vice-Chief of the Air Staff, Air Marshal Richard Peirse, to review the air defence requirements in the light of the latest state of affairs. He reasoned that the range and striking power of the Heinkel and Junkers 88 when used from the north and west coasts of occupied France would effectively deny the passage of convoys into the Irish Sea and Bristol Channel from the Southwest (the Western Approaches); the Admiralty had agreed that from 5 July, they would be re-routed to approach in a southeasterly direction down through North Channel into the Clyde, the Mersey and Bristol Channel. Only small coasters would trade along the southwestern coast, and provision for their security had now been made. His greatest concern was for shipping in the Irish Sea and he proposed creating several sector stations to provide air cover, but more than anything else, he was hoping that fighter stations would become available in Southern Ireland. (This was not possible 'until either we are invited to do so, or Eire is invaded'.) With regard to improved fighter strength, a future requirement of sixty squadrons to be available by September 1940 and rising to eighty by the Spring of 1941 had been approved in principle by the Chief of the Air Staff at a time when the threat arose solely from bombers based in Germany. Now the entire force of German front

* Later, Air Chief Marshal Sir Theodore McEvoy KCB, CBE.

line aircraft, estimated as being 5,400 aircraft, could be used.* To oppose such a force, by using the usual method of calculation, it was estimated that a requirement of one hundred and twenty fighter squadrons, each of sixteen aircraft, would be required. Stevenson reckoned that this figure would create an unequal balance with the proposed bomber force and adversely affect the nation's ability to strike at vulnerable German areas. He suggested a further ten fighter squadrons, five of which were to be of long range, for shipping protection, making a total of seventy, and when circumstances permitted, ten more. (At this time, Fighter Command Order of Battle stood at fifty-two squadrons, of these forty-two were single-seater aircraft. The figures are misleading; the actual 'strength' of Fighter Command was governed by the efficiency of the squadrons, most of whom were refitting and training.) He thought, not unreasonably, that to counteract British bombing, Germany's first line fighter strength would be widely dispersed at home to protect their exposed points; this in fact was not so, German defence at this time was reliant almost entirely on AA guns (Flak)†. The tactical use of the German fighter particularly the single-seater Messerschmitt Bf 109, was to have a considerable part to play in the planned offensive in the days ahead.

At the outbreak of war, it was not unreasonable to expect that if German forces were able to advance overland, it would be some time before they arrived at striking distance of the British Isles, a period during which home defence could be improved. But events had occurred at such incredible speed that in only twenty-six days of fighting, Germany had control of the Channel coast.

The layout of Fighter Command was changing. During the early part of the war, only three Groups were fully organised: No. 11 Group caring for South East England with Headquarters at Uxbridge; No. 12 Group with responsibility for the Midlands with Headquarters at Hucknall, Nottingham (soon to move to Watnall); and No. 13 Group, administered from Newcastle, which covered the area to the north. On 8 July, a new No. 10 Group was thought to be sufficiently well established to take over the administration of the south west area; it had Headquarters at Rudloe Manor, Box, near Colerne, and was divided into four sectors. All Groups were geographically divided into these small areas or Sectors; for example, No. 11 Group

---

* Quartermaster-General's Department of the German Air Ministry records for 8 June 1940 show figures of the entire strength as being 4,663 aircraft.
† *Flugzeugabwehrkanonen*

89

accommodated seven with headquarters at Tangmere, Kenley, Biggin Hill, Hornchurch, North Weald, Northolt and Debden. The Sector arrangement in the others was similar; in both Nos. 12 and 13 Groups there were six divisions. Each Sector had a premier fighter station with a fighter control organisation from which its squadrons, and those based at satellite aerodromes in the Sector, could be directed from the ground.

While every effort was being made to strengthen the defences, serious problems with equipment were emerging. A new Very High Frequency (VHF) radio system had proved very successful in trials at Duxford on 30 October 1939 and it was being introduced throughout the Command. Operations over Dunkirk had, however, highlighted the inadequacy of supplies; only eight squadrons so far had been switched over. Others, while waiting for sets remained on the old High Frequency (HF) network; the two systems were incompatible. Squadrons using VHF could not communicate with ground control working on the old system, nor could they communicate with HF aircraft in the air. Operations were now also being carried out using half squadrons to form composite units. Flexibility of the movement of squadrons in the Command was greatly reduced. Seeing the confusion, and seeking to conserve the new equipment, Dowding had been advised that no further supplies would be available until late Summer; he decided that the VHF system was to be indefinitely suspended in favour of overall reversion to the old HF system. Expressing his disappointment in a letter to the Air Ministry, he wrote, 'It is deplored that such an action should have to be taken as it has proved to be the most successful form of fighter communication and will result in a reduction of the efficiency of the Command.'[71] Gradual introduction of the new equipment which had more frequency channels, including one which a pilot could use for 'Homing' when lost, provided much improved range, direction finding qualities and clarity of speech. Installation began in December 1939 with the intention that by 1 September 1940 it would have entirely replaced the inferior HF network throughout Fighter Command. As an insurance against the situation now arising, the fittings in all aircraft were made so that both types of radio set could be accommodated; changeover from one to the other was reckoned to be one hour. Sets installed in day fighters were now stripped out, but VHF ground installations feeding Sector Stations remained functional. Sholto Douglas, DCAS had accepted a justifiable risk, which he termed 'a bit of a gamble',[72] when pushing to get the new system into service. Cutting corners, no normal service trials were carried out, and unfortunately modifications to sets and aircraft created delays. It became vital when the Blenheim nightfighters had AI radar installed that VHF radio was put in at the same time, and these aircraft gained full advantage of the new system. For the dayfighters the loss of the superior communication at this time did indeed cause a serious reduction in the efficiency of the Command. However, construction of the ground stations and communications transmitting and receiving blocks, and other parts of the organisation, continued while the system remained on ice.

The shortcomings of the early warning CH Radar stations were also causing anxiety. One problem was their inability to indicate accurately the number of aircraft in a group; another, and more serious, was their inconsistency when reading aircraft height.

It was an accepted fact that the terrain surrounding each site would have some influence on the performance of a station's equipment and these anomalies needed to be recognised and compensated for. But there were other influences causing variations in the comparative performance of each station and the scientists were carrying out a comprehensive analysis of each one to find out why. Their conclusions were far reaching. They noted operators were as yet unfamiliar with the apparatus at stations, also only occasionally were test flights being made for calibration purposes. No one knew at this stage how consistent the performance of a station would be; readings of height and direction finding were showing such great discrepancies that they always carried an inherent sense of doubt. The scientists found mechanics were given no opportunities for regular maintenance because the stations were ordered to remain in constant operation and as a consequence the apparatus ran until it broke down, then great pressure was applied by Fighter Command Headquarters to get it repaired. Test gear and the instructions on its use were scarce. Technical orders to staff varied considerably from station to station and depended largely on the discretion of the Commanding Officers. These generally were men with a very good background of normal radio skills and it was found extremely difficult to restrain them from putting into practice their personal ideas for improving the equipment's performance; it was found that no two stations were alike.

H. Larnder, the scientific head of the Stanmore Research Section, was becoming despondent. After studying a report on the recent performance of equipment at the stations, he wrote to The Superintendent of the Air Ministry Research Establishment, Dundee on 12 March 1940 as follows:

'The ability of the Chain, as a whole, to give accurate D/F (Direction Finding) reading or height measurements has not improved since the commencement of the present war. This seems a very sad state of affairs to us, and one almost wonders if it is worthwhile carrying out calibration tests for a system which appears to show no improvement in its ability to maintain constancy of calibration.'[73]*

Several days later, Dowding felt compelled to write to the Air Ministry on the subject of the inaccuracies of height reading. He reminded them that it was vital to show the precise position of raids on a map but, to effect an interception, the third dimension, that of height, was also necessary. Recalling the peacetime Air Exercises, he wrote of how the bombers usually came in at 7,000 or 8,000 feet (Bomber Command were generally unable to fly higher because the crews were not provided with oxygen or means of keeping warm), and it was rare for a raid to be staged as high as 12,000 feet. During the exercise, all interceptions had been carried out over land and with the benefit of Observer Corps height readings, now they were over the sea and Radar was the sole source of information; also fighters had to be prepared to intercept at more than double the height. He pointed out the Radar's limitations, saying,

'It is generally known that raids under 2,000 feet or over 25,000 feet are likely to be missed altogether by the Chain Stations, but there is a comfortable feeling that between these limits the Chain Stations can give height with approximate accuracy. This is far from being the case . . . 15,000 feet is about the best height, but even at this optimum altitude there are important areas where blanks occur.'[74]

The Radar was being pressed into use when not fully developed. It became a race against time; to delay and wait for improved apparatus inevitably meant it would not arrive on time.

A re-arrangement of Groups, and the possible creation of new ones, brought about by the recent changes in the position of German forces, and the tactics to be adopted in the event of invasion were discussed at a conference at Bentley Priory on 3 July, attended by Group Commanders, Officers of Headquarters Fighter Command and representatives of the Air Ministry.[75] Proposals for Group changes were the subject of a letter to the Command from the Air Ministry and comments were made on them. The conference then discussed the form an invasion was likely to

* The calibration was necessary for accurate height measurement.

take, and views on the tactics to be employed to defeat it, were sought. Dowding outlined what he thought could be the two main alternatives; a narrow battering ram attack on a particular locality or an assault on a broad front with the Germans not knowing where a breakthrough would occur; when one came they would then take every opportunity to pour through and exploit it, the latter had been their tactics in France. Small attacks could be undertaken from occupied territory against points in the British Isles. The opening attack, he thought, might come from the air, using parachutists and gliders (at Fighter Command they had been much impressed by this German method of attack). Alternatively, fast motor boats could be used to try to establish a foothold, then the slower, helpless tank-transporting barges could be safely brought ashore. He thought that the invasion would ultimately settle on one point, and in that area a glorified circus would develop where under a protective 'umbrella' of fighters a constant stream of troop carriers and bombers would operate. Air Vice-Marshal Leigh-Mallory, commanding No. 12 Group, thought that, before attempting a landing, the enemy would concentrate on air attacks against airfields for a week or so and the enemy bombers would be afforded a strong fighter escort. Dowding hoped that this would be the case, from the British point of view the enemy could do nothing better than spend a week this way; it would leave them exhausted and would crack their air force morale before they started the serious business. He said he would like to see them spend a month that way, since it would end in no invasion at all, but he feared that if the enemy did try anything of that sort, it would only be for about twenty-four hours.

If invasion came, initially only the normal number of aircraft sitting waiting at 'Readiness' could be used; it was impractical for whole squadrons to be kept at this advanced state of preparation while the invasion remained just a threat; until cast-iron evidence was produced or tracks could be seen coming in across the sea, only those in the Sectors at 'Readiness' at that moment could be employed, thereafter everyone would have 'to work day and night, figuratively speaking'. He went on to say that Group Commanders should keep a pretty good control of the situation and try to ensure generally that they get a force of three squadrons available. Everybody should know where the big attack is taking place and a proportion should be detailed to meet the fighters, and the rest, the bombers. It should not be left to chance; precise orders should be given by the Group Commanders. For instance, one squadron to tackle the fighters, two others arriving simultaneously to take on the bombers. Three squadrons should continually be thrown in at 2-hourly,

1½-hourly or hourly intervals, in this manner throughout the 18 hours of daylight. He was anxious that the fighter force should not be obsessed with the fighter escort above, and in so doing leave those beneath to go unmolested; a balance needed to be struck.

The C-in-C then moved on to talk about the pilots, emphasising that he wished it to be an accepted principle that during heavy and continuous fighting every squadron should be released for eight hours out of twenty-four and, no matter what happened, they should not be disturbed during that eight hours, otherwise everyone would crack up simultaneously after a while. After the first burst of activity, when everyone would be expected to work themselves to the bone, this 8 hours off principle would apply.

Air Vice-Marshal Saul asked whether in the event of a parachute attack the airfields should be defended or put out of action. Dowding replied that they were to be defended at all costs and for as long as possible. In the event of beach landings near forward airfields, the aircraft were to be taken away and Station personnel should join with the soldiers in defending the airfield; demolition should not take place except as a last resort.

The conference touched on several other items. Dowding thought the six cannon-firing fighters now in service should be retained for anti-tank purposes; he did, however, refer to recent practice firing carried out at Northolt where a Lysander fitted with cannon, after firing a considerable number of rounds at a ground target 20 ft × 10 ft had not scored a single hit. He ruled that more practise for pilots against ground targets should be undertaken. Night fighting was discussed and the stocks of ammunition; it was generally agreed that the Air Ministry's estimate bore no real relation to the stocks likely to be required to repel an invasion.

Earlier, mention was made about the role of the Navy, and Dowding was sure they would do everything in their power, and commented that 'we would be left to deal with whatever the Fleet were unable to deal with'. He added that he had not yet been asked to provide standing fighter patrols over the warships; 'it would appear that they would have to look after themselves on this occasion'.

It is clear that the leaders of Fighter Command had no positive intelligence on which they could make an assessment of the likely form an invasion would take, or where it would likely come from; they could only wait and see. Dowding commented that he did not wish to say what was likely to take place, but that he could say what was possible and reasonably probable.

Dutch, Belgian and French ports were continually watched for signs of a build-up of shipping able to provide transport for an invasion force; it was not confined to these alone as it was acknowledged that an expedition could be mounted from other directions; Norway could not be ruled out.

Replying to a letter of 4 July from Lord Beaverbrook, Minister of Aircraft Production, in which he asked whether he was satisfied to release Spitfires for Photographic Reconnaissance, Dowding replied,

'Of course I grudge every Spitfire which is taken from Fighter Command until the supply situation is improved, but I must take a broad view of the question. The Spitfire can do photographic work with few casualties, which could only be done by other types at a cost of heavy losses. Provided, therefore, that establishments are kept down to the minimum for genuine requirements, I do not wish to oppose the use of Spitfires in this role.'

Chapter 7

The Battle of Britain Period –
Stressed to the Limit

'Since England, in spite of her hopeless military situation, shows no sign of being ready to come to an understanding, I have decided to prepare a landing operation against England, and, if necessary, to carry it out.'

So runs the often quoted phrase of Adolf Hitler's Directive No. 16 of 16 July 1940. Five days earlier at a German Air Force Chiefs Of Staff meeting, their leader, Hermann Goering, told them,

'When the time comes, the enemy aircraft industry and air force must be destroyed at the earliest possible moment by the first blows of the attack. The defence of Southern England will last four days and the Royal Air Force four weeks. We can guarantee invasion for the *Führer* within a month.'

His intention was that, once the defences were suppressed south of a line between London and Gloucester, the daylight air offensive could be pushed steadily northwards until total air supremacy was obtained over the country. The other aim of the offensive was to cut off supplies to Britain by attacking shipping and the ports which handled the cargoes. An additional advantage of the destruction of the aircraft industry was that it would effectively inhibit the flow of aircraft to Bomber Command and, in so doing, preserve output of Germany's manufacturing industry. Goering complained of air raid warnings 'causing a loss of output whose consequences are far graver than those caused by the actual bomb damage. In addition, the frequent air raid warnings are leading to nervousness and strain among the population of Western Germany'.[76] At this stage of the war, bombing was one of the few avenues left to the British which was likely to affect German productivity and morale to any degree.

At the end of June and the early part of July, raids against the British Isles were on a small scale and in the main confined to targets closely conforming to German strategy, i.e. small night raids against the aircraft industry and anti-shipping mining operations. By the middle of the month, operations were directed towards the destruction of shipping and ports as the campaign intensified. Intelligence from interception of radio signals showed that German Air Force units were preparing for an offensive against Britain from their bases in the Low Countries and Northwest France, confirming evidence being gathered by photographic reconnaissance flights; it also suggested that most of the units would have completed their preparations by the middle of July.[77]

The forces ranged against Fighter Command were considerable. Of the main long-range bomber force, the Heinkel He 111 and the Dornier Do 17 twin-engined bombers were most numerous with the latter also being used in the reconnaissance role. The Junkers Ju 88 twin-engined bomber, occasionally used as a dive bomber, was the high performance bomber of the period, but was less plentiful. The company's other product, the Ju 87 *Stuka* dive bomber had achieved respectability for the accuracy of its bombing; it was, however, slow and vulnerable; an easy prey for fighters. The Messerschmitt Company produced the two front line fighters then in service. Their Bf. 110 twin-engined aircraft could operate at a good range and was heavily armed but lacked the agility of its Bf. 109* single-seater contemporary. This aircraft was the equal of any aircraft flying at that time. It was well armed and had high performance, but like its British counterparts, lacked range. In the middle of July the *Luftwaffe*, on paper, had 1,200 long-range bombers, 280 dive bombers, 760 single-engined and 220 twin-engined fighters; 140 reconnaissance aircraft were available. These made up *Luftflotten* (Air Fleets) 2 and 3 facing Britain across the Channel. *Luftflotte* 5, based in Norway, had one hundred and thirty long-range bombers, thirty twin-engined fighters and thirty reconnaissance aircraft; it was beyond the range of the single-engined fighter.[78]

Opposing them, Fighter Command, on 8 July, could put up forty-two squadrons of Spitfires and Hurricanes, eight Blenheim twin-engined fighters and two single-engined Defiant Squadrons; a number of other units were being formed or reformed.[79]

The Blenheim fighter had by now been almost entirely committed to the role of nightfighter. The Defiant, with its unconventional turret with

---

* Bf. The 109 and 110 were commonly known as Me 109 and Me 110, but were actually designated Bf, as they were originally manufactured to a Messerschmitt design by the *Bayerischeflugzeugwerk*.

four .303 machine-guns, achieved notable success during the Dunkirk evacuation when extraordinary claims for the destruction of thirty or so aircraft were made by No. 264 Squadron on 29 May, much to the pleasure of Dowding who sent Squadron Leader Hunter a congratulatory message. On 3 July, Hunter had flown his Defiant in assessment trials against a captured Bf 109 and reported that it should be able to 'deal with the Me. 109 very satisfactorily at all times'.[80]* The Defiant, however, was not favoured by Dowding. As early as June 1938 in a letter to Air Vice-Marshal Sholto Douglas at the Air Ministry, when complaining about the lack of consultation over the acquisition of aircraft for Fighter Command, he wrote,

'The first essential of a fighter is performance, and the second is hitting power. In both these respects, the Defiant is inferior to contemporary fighters . . . When we get the Defiant in a year's time, or whenever it may be, it will already be semi-obsolete.'

He was also critical of the early decision to purchase the 20mm cannon saying,

'I have seen no sort of proof that this gun will give decisive results. We ought to have carried out the most careful experiments to prove the value of the gun before we adopted it in anything but experimental types, and we have acted in woolly imitation of woolly Continental air forces.'[81]

It would appear that the French had accepted it because it could effectively fire through the airscrew boss of their Hispano Suiza engines, which dampened the recoil; when fitted to a wing it was much less efficient.

Dowding had in 1936 foreseen that there would come a time when enemy aircraft would have their vital areas protected by armour, and Browning .303 calibre machine-guns become insufficient. At a meeting on 26 August 1940, he recommended a change over from the current eight machine-gun installation to one of four cannons. It was decided to commence with the Hurricanes, which if it proved suitable, would

---

* On their arrival at Hornchurch on 21 August 1940, Keith Park gave specific instructions to his Group Controllers that No. 264 Squadron Defiants were 'not to be detailed to intercept fighter Formations'; whenever practical they were to be sent against bombers. Within a few days the squadron had been practically destroyed, mostly in combats with Messerschmitt Bf. 109s, and was withdrawn. Squadron Leader Hunter was killed.

go into production followed by Spitfires when the Mk III version came out. The meeting was told of malfunctions of the existing two Hispano cannon equipping No. 19 Squadron; a set-up using two cannon and four Browning machine-guns was replacing them.[82] Dowding had stopped the trials of the two-cannon installation at the request of the Squadron Leader; the squadron reverted to the eight Browning type for a short period. The Minister of Aircraft Production was not satisfied with results from the American .5 machine-gun at this time.

The eight machine-guns of Hurricanes and Spitfires then in service could each produce a rate of fire of 1,200 rounds of .303 calibre ammunition per minute. With each gun having storage for only 300 rounds, a burst

Battle of Britain – Main Area of Conflict
Each group was divided into sectors which had a premier fighter station receiving information from the Fighter Command Filter Room, Observer Corps centres, Group Headquarters and gun and searchlight locations. These sources enabled a reasonable picture of the air situation to be shown on operations rooms tables for controllers to act on.

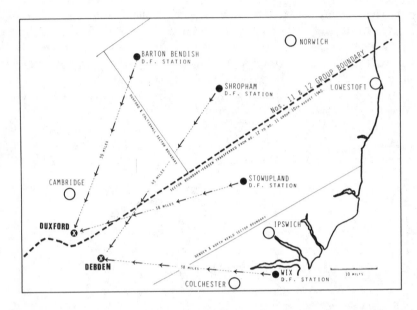

Limitations of High Frequency Radio in the Battle of Britain
A 35–45 mile radio range greatly restricted the area in which fighters could be effectively controlled. Two Direction Finding stations sited roughly equidistant from the one at the Sector Station and each other gave a small increase in range. Best results were obtained from aircraft operating within the triangular space of the three. Voice production quality, centred on the Sector Station's equipment, was not good. The whole system was badly affected by atmospheric conditions. Understandably, Dowding wished to use the new V.H.F. throughout the Command as soon as possible. The increase in range was threefold.

of fire of only 15 seconds duration was the limit of the aircraft's capacity. The eight wing-mounted machine-guns were adjusted so that their fire converged at a point 250 yards ahead. This distance was agreed after careful study of attacks made by aircraft using cine-camera guns and a study of Combat Reports. (Dowding had been urging the Air Ministry to provide cine-camera guns and, as late as May 1940, there were only six available for each squadron.) Some confusion has since arisen about what the C-in-C decided as being the correct distance for harmonization of the guns, that is to say the point ahead of the aircraft where the fire from the eight machine guns converged. In a letter of 14 January 1940 to the Air Ministry[83] he wrote,

'*The Opening Firing Range* for eight-gun fighters should be, for the present, 400 yards, and fighters should close in to the attack so that the bulk of the firing takes place at *shorter range*.'

This opinion was formed because it was noticed that attacks were being made at too short range and too high closing speeds. Dowding quoted the case where one pilot made five separate attacks before he had expended his ammunition. By 5 May, after having studied a large number of cine-gun films, he had accepted that most pilots, when opening fire from a stern chase, did so at much too great a range; a fault he would correct. In a letter he informed the Air Ministry that 250 yards could be termed the 'decisive range'. When going closer there was a tendency for the pilot to focus his eyes on the aircraft and look away from the gunsight. It also created problems of parallax, where because of the nearness of the target, the view through the gunsight differed from that of the line of fire of the guns. He concluded his letter, 'In my opinion, therefore, efficiency falls off progressively as the range deviates from 250 yards in either sense'. He added that this opinion was shared by the Staff of the Air Fighting Development Unit (based at Northolt), and went on,

'Group Captain Vincent has in fact informed me that, in his opinion, we have gone to too short a range in concentrating fire at 250 yards. The results which we have obtained with this harmonization, however, have been quite satisfactory and I am convinced that when a higher standard of training has been reached with the aid of cine-camera guns, in judging range, "holding on" and regulating overtaking speed, the results will be extremely impressive.'

In December 1939 No. 111 Squadron harmonized their guns to give a pattern 12 feet vertically by 8 feet horizontally at a range of 250 yards; this was changed to 350 yards the following January. Range was finally settled on the original distance at a meeting of Fighter Command's Gun Sub Committee on 20 February 1940.

The recommended approach when attacking an enemy aircraft was to creep up on it from astern, and then with both aircraft moving in the same direction it gave sufficient time for the pursuing pilot to register the gunsight on the target and open fire. A recent innovation practised by German fighter pilots, and incidentally Gladiator pilots of No. 263 Squadron when in Norway, was the attack into the side of the aircraft. This required precise judgement on the part of the pilot, who needed to make an allowance for the target's movement across his path by aiming at a spot slightly ahead of it. This was deflection shooting, and Dowding felt that his pilots would soon be compelled to use this type of interception when the *Luftwaffe* increased protective armour plate to vital parts of their machines. The 'head on' method of attack was suggested by the Air Fighting Development Unit at Northolt.

Earlier, at a conference held at the Priory with his Group Commanders, Dowding addressed the subject of aircraft in trouble while flying over the sea and not being able to regain the safety of land. He told them Hurricanes and Spitfires would immediately sink thirty to forty feet if alighting on water, and instructed that pilots should bale out if there was sufficient height.

From the middle of July, German air activity escalated in the run up to the launching of 'Eagle Day' (13 August), when large-scale operations were to begin to prepare the way for an invasion of Britain. On 21 July at a *Luftwaffe* conference, Goering gave instructions to his commanders for prosecution of the air war against England. Attacks on shipping in the Channel and off the East Coast were to be carried out by all three Air Fleets engaged in the campaign and, where possible, damage to the Royal Navy should be inflicted. Strong action against British fighters should be undertaken and seeking out targets in the aircraft industry was essential. While this was in progress, other units were to prepare for the air campaign in the coming weeks. Early success was necessary against targets in the areas allotted to *Luftflotten* 2 and 3 (south and southeast England) making it easier to send in low level attacks on particular targets. The combined strength of *Luftflotte* 2 and *Fliegerkorps* VIII and including fighters from *Luftflotte* 3 were to be used against enemy fighters based around London. By this time, forays against aircraft factories would be of secondary importance. Basically the tactics were to concentrate on weakening British fighter strength to pave the way for the use of heavy bombers. Mass attacks using bombers with fighter escort could then be made while smaller raids could operate to draw off British aircraft; attacks by bombers and *Stuka* dive bombers on ground installations could also be achieved more easily at this stage. Goering in his instructions was emphatic that early destruction of the enemy fighter force was of paramount importance. At this time, effort was being directed on to shipping and much use was made of the *Stuka*, the aircraft which had earlier proved to be very successful in support of ground operations.

Prime Minister Churchill paid a surprise visit to Bentley Priory on 4 August and Dowding showed him a map he had produced for a recent meeting he had attended at the Admiralty, and remarked on the thinness of his forces when it became possible to occupy the new Sector Stations being prepared for the defence of the now threatened Western flank of the country. Churchill said to him, 'If you want a hundred Fighter Squadrons you shall have them'. In reply Dowding said it was

'quite obvious that we could not win the war if we pushed everything into defence; we must have regard to building up the bomber force in order to hit Germany hard and, therefore, no more fighter squadrons should be formed than those which were absolutely essential for our security'.

Churchill asked him to put a figure on it, and he said he would be happy with eighty squadrons of sixteen aircraft.[84]

German operations increased with large formations of bombers supported by strong fighter cover attacking shipping and ports on the southeast and south coast between North Foreland and Portland, including the Naval base at Portsmouth. Incursions against fighter airfields on the coast were extended to include operations against Bomber and Coastal Command airfields; light attacks were made against inland targets. The Junkers 87 *Stuka* dive bomber continued to be extensively used, and shot down by the defending fighters.

At 11 Group Headquarters, at Uxbridge, Keith Park and his Controllers were now frequently engrossed in the dilemma of deciding which raid was being put in as a diversionary measure to attract their fighters, while the main attack was in preparation against a port or airfield elsewhere. This usually arrived thirty to forty minutes later when the fighters were low on fuel. Because of this, it became necessary to keep nearly all squadrons at a state of 'readiness' (able to get airborne within five minutes) when they were at the forward airfields such as Lympne, Hawkinge, Manston and Rochford. A very high standard of preparedness was required for fighter units to engage the enemy before they reached their coastal objectives. This put a greater strain on ground staff; there was always the danger when refuelling and re-arming their aircraft that a German fighter sweep would come in low over the sea and strafe the airfield. It became essential to exercise extra vigilance and employ a fighter patrol overhead for protection.

The fighters of No. 11 Group, when attacking large formations, were usually employed on the basis of half the force intercepting the bombers and the remainder taking on the fighter escort. Defending fighter pilots were learning through experience; they found attacks from astern were effective on fighters, but were less so against the bombers which were

103

now thought to have their vulnerable parts protected by armour. It was advised that deflection shooting should be practised; also that they be engaged from above and below. It was found that the German fighter escort operated at 5,000 to 10,000 feet above the bombers, a tactic which later caused Park to comment, 'These tactics were not very effective in protecting the bombers'.

He was much concerned, however, that their combats were over the sea; his pilots were drowning after baling out of stricken aircraft. He instructed Controllers to dispatch fighters to engage the enemy over land or within gliding distance of the coast and to avoid sending them over the sea to chase reconnaissance aircraft or small groups of enemy fighters. Provision of Air-Sea Rescue craft and preservation of men who were unfortunate enough to come down in the water had been badly neglected. This can only be described as astonishing when one considers that at this time the Radar network was geared almost entirely to surveillance of the air space above the sea, and it was earlier assumed that most air fighting would take place there and over the coast.

In January 1939, Air Chief Marshal Ludlow-Hewitt, AOC-in-C at Bomber Command, had complained to the Air Ministry about the inadequacy of air/sea rescue for his bomber crews when they were engaged in training flights and joint exercises with Fighter Command which took them beyond the coast. He had written saying that if something was not done soon 'exercises over the sea would have to be limited'.[85]

A meeting had been held under the chairmanship of Sholto Douglas who had confined the debate to 'peacetime requirements'. An interim scheme operated by Coastal Command using nine high-speed launches had been adopted; the intention had been that there should eventually be nineteen such vessels. In May 1940 seven such launches were available for the entire British Isles.

On 9 July 1940, Donald Stevenson wrote to Sholto Douglas at the Air Ministry, 'I think the time has now come to review our safety arrangements for crews shot down – particularly fighter pilots – in the Channel. Under the present arrangements two high-speed boats are kept, I understand, one at Felixstowe and one at Ramsgate.' He gave examples of pilots recently lost. He suggested using the fast motor-boat type, civilian owned, small craft which had been used on the beaches at Dunkirk – thirty-three would be required. An approach was made to the Admiralty who told the Air Ministry, boats for a proposed scheme were 'not even in existence'.[86] An interim arrangement was made with the Admiralty for some measure of pilot rescue and on 6 September control of RAF launches was taken over by the RN. Lysander aircraft were used by the RAF for searching. Air/sea rescue operations reverted to Coastal Command in August 1941.

On 14 July, British pilots had been instructed to shoot down German rescue aircraft. German aircrew were already being comparatively better served by a well organised system using search and rescue Heinkel 59 float planes. By July, they had twelve such aircraft operational, all of which were clearly marked with red crosses and unarmed. The British order that they should be shot down came about because it was thought they might be collecting intelligence on shipping and land near the coast. All this was, of course, an irrelevance if you happened to be an airman on the point of drowning; they were also saving RAF people.

On 31 July, *Grossadmiral* Raeder, C-in-C of the German Navy, had warned that the necessary preparations for an invasion of the British Isles (Operation SEALION) could not be completed before 15 September. *Feldmarschall* Keitel, issuing a directive the following day after a meeting of the OKW (Supreme Command of the German Armed Forces) stated that fourteen days after the launching of the air offensive against Britain, scheduled to begin on approximately 5 August, the *Führer* would decide whether the invasion would take place that year: his decision depending largely on the outcome of the air offensive. By that date, however, the air offensive was already deeply beset by problems. At a conference held on 15 August, Goering directed that fighter escorts for Junkers Ju. 87 *Stuka* formations should be increased 'as the enemy is concentrating his fighters against our *Stuka* operations'. Three fighter *Gruppen* (ninety aircraft) were to defend one *Gruppe* of *Stukas* (approximately thirty aircraft). He was already concerned with preserving his force of the Messerschmitt Bf. 110 twin-engined fighters; they were to be used only when the range of other fighters was inadequate or to help them break off combat. He decreed that attacks on large naval vessels were to be attempted only when circumstances were especially propitious. Orders were given that operations were to be directed exclusively against the enemy air force, including the targets of the enemy aircraft industry, and all other targets should be ignored. 'We must concentrate our efforts on the destruction of the enemy air forces.' Making a serious error of judgement, he went on, 'It is doubtful whether there is any point in continuing the attacks on Radar sites, in view of the fact that not one of those attacked has so far been put out of action.'[87] This was a poor understanding of the situation and it was to have a notable effect on the future course of events. Already Keith Park at No. 11 Group was suffering from the inability to discern a main attack from a diversionary one because, he claimed, of the 'very unreliable information received from RDF, after they had been heavily bombed'.[88]

The early warning Radar chain was, in the main, so arranged that each station's area of detection was overseen by its adjoining stations, and so to cripple the system satisfactorily it was necessary to reduce the efficiency of two or three together. Much depended on how close the stations were to each other, e.g. in the south and southwest they were more widely spaced, making the cover less concentrated. There were mobile reserve units on call to plug gaps where enemy action had put Radar stations out of order or if cover suddenly became necessary in a hitherto unprotected area, but they were less effective than the original. The Interservices RDF Committee decided at their meeting on 25 April 1940 to have a pool of MB2 equipments on call for such emergencies. They were fitted into suitable vehicles and provided with their own power generators.[89] Goering's decision to stop attacks on the stations was fortuitous for the British. It is often said they were difficult targets, the masts supporting the aerials providing protection against low level raids, but the buildings, their land-line telephone communications and power supply were vulnerable. A good example of what could be achieved occurred at Ventnor, on the Isle of Wight.

At midday on 12 August a large enemy formation flying down the English Channel had been reported by the Radar Stations to the Bentley Priory Filter Room. At Ventnor, WAAF member Audrey Brown watched the raid divide into two, one formation heading for Portsmouth, the other turning towards Ventnor. She later recalled,

'We knew we were to be attacked before it happened. Very soon we were bombed and almost straightaway everything went dark and the radar went off the air. We lay down on the floor; there was nothing more we could do.'[90]

The damage was serious, fires were unchecked due to damaged water mains. Delayed action bombs forced emergency services to retire. By the greatest good fortune, there was only one person injured. Earlier in the day, other Stations had been bombed but damage was less severe and they were on the air again within hours. Dowding sent a signal expressing his 'satisfaction and pride in the behaviour of the WAAF in the face of enemy attack'. It did show that given heavier concentrated attacks, it would have been possible to punch a hole in the radar cover for a period long enough to give the *Luftwaffe* a big advantage.

Air Commodore Gregory, AOC No. 60 Group inspected the damaged stations and reported to Dowding at Bentley Priory, who told Gregory he was not prepared to increase radar stations' gun defences because this could only be done at the expense of the protection for aircraft factories.[91]

Four days after the 12 August raid while repairs were in progress, five Junkers Ju. 87 *Stukas* dive-bombed Ventnor. Apparatus was now installed in makeshift accommodation, which was little more than a hut protected by sandbags. The girls sought protection under a table which, as each bomb exploded, vibrated its way across the floor from above them. Good fortune had remained with Ventnor; once more there were no fatalities. The Station was now inoperable; after the two raids only the diesel generator house and the Receiving Block were left standing. It took until 23 August before they could get a Mobile Reserve Station functioning at Bembridge on the Isle of Wight. Members of the WAAF were sent on nine days 'survivors' leave while Ventnor was being tidied up.

If the *Luftwaffe* had set out to give Fighter Command the opportunity to prove the effectiveness of its defence organisation, it could not have improved on the strategy it adopted on 15 August when directing raids against northeast England. Soon after midday, sixty-five Heinkel 111s, escorted by Messerschmitt Bf. 110 twin-engined heavy fighters, were sent from Norway to attack targets in the Newcastle area, which fell within the boundaries of No. 13 Group. At much the same time, an unescorted raid by fifty Junkers Ju. 88s was sent from Denmark against targets North of Hull in No. 12 Group; this was in line with Goering's orders on 21 July, that aircraft of *Luftflotte* 5 were to 'tie down hostile fighter strength on the east coast of the Midlands', preventing it being transferred down south to assist with the heavy engagements being fought there. Both the northeast raids were repelled with the German units incurring heavy losses. They had provided the defenders with the very conditions on which their organisation had been originally planned. The CH Radar located them while they were well out over the North Sea, giving adequate warning of their approach. Air Vice-Marshal Saul's No. 13 Group was able to put up five full squadrons to cover the Newcastle area; Air Vice-Marshal Leigh-Mallory's No. 12 Group met their raid with one and a half squadrons. The long over-sea flight ruled out using the short-range Messerschmitt Bf. 109 fighters to provide an escort; the bombers and their largely ineffective Bf. 110 protectors paid a heavy price. The 15 August raids in the North confirmed what already had been proved beyond doubt, that during the hours of daylight the agile single-seat fighter was dominant in every way. The Messerschmitt Bf. 110

twin-engined fighter was shown to be in itself impotent and all unescorted bombers were effectively 'sitting ducks'. Such raids during daylight were not attempted again.

On 15 August, there was a marked escalation in the ferocity of the air war in the south; aerodromes of No. 11 Group were now attacked in strength. This Group covered a smaller geographical area than the other three, but it was here that activity was now concentrated and fighter defence was strongest. It was closest to the German forces.

On 19 August, Goering directed that the main task of *Luftflotten* 2 and 3 was to inflict the utmost damage to British fighter forces combined with attacks on the ground organisation of the British bomber force. He gave orders that only part of his fighter strength was to be employed in direct escort of bomber units, insisting,

'The aim must be to employ the strongest possible fighter forces on freelance operations in which they can indirectly protect the bombers and at the same time come to grips under favourable conditions with the enemy fighters.'

Goering wanted them, whenever possible, to make attacks against ground targets and also form special formations to protect bombers and fighters when they returned over the Channel. Units were instructed to make provision for defence of their own ground organisations.* Goering was imposing a heavy burden on his fighter units; whether they could cope was questionable. He was already showing some concern about his aircraft losses, insisting that 'as long as the enemy fighter defences retain their present strength, attacks on aircraft factories must be carried out under cover of weather conditions permitting surprise raids by solitary aircraft'. The cloudy conditions expected during the next few days should be exploited. He sought the destruction of the 'relatively small number of aircraft engine and aluminium plants', stressing their importance and directing that attacks should also be made at night. He concluded,

'The vital task is to turn all means at our disposal to the defeat of the enemy air force. Our first aim is the destruction of the enemy's fighters; if they no longer take to the air we shall attack them on the ground or force them into battle by directing bomber attacks against targets within range of our fighters.'[92]

* The Germans were surprised that no retaliatory attacks were made on their airfields at this time.

Increased effort was required against the ground organisation of the enemy bomber units.

That very day, Keith Park issued instructions to his No. 11 Group Controllers saying,

'Against mass attacks coming inland, despatch a minimum number of squadrons to engage enemy fighters. Our main object is to engage enemy bombers, particularly those approaching under the lowest cloud layer.[93] If all our squadrons are off the ground engaging enemy mass attacks, ask No. 12 Group or Command Controller to provide squadrons to patrol aerodromes Debden, North Weald, Hornchurch.'

The air battle was now becoming concentrated more over the land where the chances of survival for pilots of stricken aircraft were better, even so he warned against sending aircraft out over the sea.

The latest change of German emphasis became apparent to Fighter Command; inland aerodromes and aircraft factories were seen as the priority targets. It was also observed that diversionary attacks were on a wider front using small bomber formations. A greater number of very high-flying fighters were being employed to protect their heavy attacks; on several occasions recently large formations of bombers with substantial close escort had managed to carry their way through to their objectives by sheer weight of numbers.

Selection of the inland targets was seen to be more widely spread with deeper penetration. Park's tactics were to meet those of greatest strength using squadrons in pairs, while relying on support from neighbouring No. 12 Group, and now also No. 10 Group, to provide patrols to cover his No. 11 Group aerodromes near London, which were now being sought out for heavy attacks; this also made it possible for their returning squadrons to refuel and re-arm in comparative safety. There were occasions when it became practical for No. 11 Group to detail a pair of Spitfire Squadrons to engage the fighter escort while a pair of Hurricane Squadrons dealt with the bombers.[94] When combating the large closely-escorted bomber attacks, Park emphasised that the sole object of attacking fighters was to uncover the bombers, allowing more to be shot down 'in order to protect our aerodromes and aircraft factories against heavy damage'. There had been several occasions when the defenders had been unable to break through the escort and all units resorted to individual fighter engagements. To overcome this, he advised that head-on attacks could be used effectively; the bombers were vulnerable in front and, being in close formation, evasive action was difficult. Fighter leader Gerry Edge, a pioneer of this form of attack had shown how a handful of determined fighters could break up large formations. In No. 12 Group, on the other hand, No. 19 Squadron, when experimenting with the method later, was unable to reach a decision about its effectiveness. They recorded that the 'closing speed was rather frightening' and it left 'little time for sighting'. In his instruction to Sector Commanders, Park spelled out what their policy should be and the order in which it should be accomplished. Bombers were to be destroyed:

'(1) before they reach their target; (2) when in the act of bombing their target; (3) during the return flight when they will have been separated from their escort and have expended their ammunition'.[95]

Park was now effectively supplementing his own No. 11 Group strength by drawing in and relying on reinforcing squadrons from neighbouring Groups and the co-operation of their respective Commanders. During mass attacks they would defend the areas to the rear of the Group. This procedure had first been envisaged as early as 1936 and more recently brought into being by Dowding. But it was not being carried out correctly. By 27 August, Park was instructing his Group Controllers to request assistance from No. 12 Group only through the Controller at Command Headquarters at Bentley Priory and not, as previously, by asking the relevant Group Headquarters directly. When offers of assistance had been made by No. 12 Group, their squadrons had not patrolled the places that were requested and, in consequence, on two occasions the aerodromes they were supposed to protect were heavily bombed. He contrasted this with the actions and co-operation given by No. 10 Group.[96] When asking for reinforcements, No. 11 Group Controllers were advised by Park that from the time of their request to the squadron reaching its patrol area they should allow up to 20 minutes for a No. 10 Group unit to arrive at its Brooklands/Northolt line; a second unit would require an extra 10 minutes. A No. 12 Group squadron operating North of the Thames on lines North Weald/Debden and North Weald/Hornchurch would need 25 minutes. (They were not normally expected to patrol south of the Thames.) Anticipating their arrival after these times, a staff officer at No. 11 Group Operations Room placed a plaque on the plotting table in the relevant patrol line position and Observer Corps and Gun Operations Rooms were to be informed accordingly. This was to prevent the squadrons being mistaken for hostiles.[97]

The heavy fighting in the southeast was putting a great strain on pilots and ground staff. All German incursions had to be met, including reconnaissance flights by single aircraft and this could only be achieved by pilots flying several sorties each day.

Fighter Command losses were such that the situation was becoming critical and Dowding was much concerned. So much so that he summoned senior members of his staff, including Keith Park, AOC No. 11 Group, to a conference on 7 September. Sholto Douglas, Deputy Chief of the Air Staff at the Air Ministry, was also present. Dowding told them he had convened the conference to outline the fighter defence situation and decide the steps to be taken to 'go down hill' in the most economical fashion (if it should be necessary to do so), leaving the pathway back uphill again as easy as possible when the present situation improved. He was assuming that the situation would arise when efforts to keep fully equipped and trained squadrons in the battle became ineffective. He explained how when a squadron became tired it was the policy to replace it with one from a less active Group. This course he would continue to follow but it would not be operable if the present scale of attack continued; pilot strength would have to be made up with non-operational men who would be made operational as soon as possible. He later reminded the conference that it took time for a newly trained pilot to become operational. Sholto Douglas questioned whether it was not being a little too pessimistic to speak of 'going down hill'. Dowding strongly disagreed, saying that at that very moment No. 11 Group were calling for reinforcements for five squadrons which had lately come into the line.

Shortage of pilots was a major item for discussion, with Sholto Douglas submitting 'that there should be no question of a shortage'. Sir Douglas Evill, the SASO at Fighter Command, had earlier worked out the comparative figures of pilots arriving from the Operational Training Units (OTUs) against combat losses. On balance over a period of four weeks, at the current casualty rate, there would be a deficit of sixty-eight pilots. Park told of how that very day nine of his squadrons had started with less than fifteen pilots; before lunchtime on the previous day squadrons had to be joined up and sent up as composite units. In 11 Group casualties were rising to somewhere in the region of one hundred a week, there was a grave shortage of pilots. Dowding expressed his concern about the weakening of morale when squadrons operated with insufficient numbers.

The minutes of the conference record him saying to Sholto Douglas, 'I want you to take away from this meeting the feeling that the situation is extremely grave.' Park later went on to tell of the heavy burden being carried by his men; some were flying four full squadron patrols each day, often engaging in three heavy combats against superior forces; he told of their lack of rest and how meals were being affected by the bombing of their aerodromes.

Park recalled how, before the heavy fighting, there had been a scheme where new pilots fresh from the OTUs were given instruction in their Sector's Training Flight, but because of prevailing circumstances, neither experienced pilots who did the training nor the aircraft could any longer be spared. He suggested that all new OTU pilots should be given this training in squadrons in the quieter area of the north and their experienced men could be used for duty in the front line squadrons of No. 11 Group. In the earlier discussion on losses, Dowding reported how some less battle-hardened units had sustained heavy casualties after only two or three days fighting when sent down to the southeast and needed replacing. He was looking for a solution to the problem of maintaining them in the front line for a minimum period of at least a fortnight. He had proposed taking Nos. 266 and 616 Squadrons and stripping them of their operational pilots, who could be posted into squadrons being moved into the front line, and replacing them with men fresh from training units. This way, those units would remain in being and could be used for less hazardous work. In the light of what Park was now suggesting, Dowding agreed that non-operational pilots should be replaced in the front line squadrons and none should be sent with the replacing units. He expected five or six squadrons based in quieter areas could be treated in this manner. He hoped to always maintain some fresh units to change round with those most fatigued in No. 11 Group.

Prior to the conference, on 4 September, Dowding had spoken to Donald Stevenson expressing his great anxiety regarding the immediate ability of Aircraft Storage Units to supply replacements for lost aircraft. On that day none of the fourteen Hurricanes and thirteen Spitfires asked for arrived at the squadrons.[98] Dowding accepted these figures might not have been accurate. The following day they were unable to send six aircraft. At this time Evill was looking into discrepancies occurring between figures supplied to the Air Ministry by three separate departments within Fighter Command; he found only one of them was giving accurate day-to-day returns for battle-ready aircraft and pilots. Others were being calculated on statistical returns with no consideration for operational fitness of personnel and aircraft serviceability. The returns were also being prepared at different times of the day. It was suggested that in future all figures should carry some explanation of their origin.

The position of aircraft wastage and supply was questioned at the conference by Sholto Douglas and it was pointed out that the figures he was quoting were several days old and since then a squadron's strength was now being based on eighteen aircraft and not on an earlier figure of twenty-two. Dowding suggested that it might become imperative to remove Spitfires and Hurricanes from those unlikely to become involved in the fighting and replace them with American Buffaloes and Curtiss aircraft. Sholto Douglas was unconvinced of the desperate shortage of fighters.

Discussion was concluded with Dowding strongly emphasising that what had been debated should be kept a close secret.

It was absolutely essential that the enemy should be made to believe that our strength was in no way diminished. No. 11 Group must have the best of everything, and go on fighting until, if necessary, everything had been used up, and then we would go on fighting with anything which could be fought in the air.[99]

Ideas on pilot replacements put forward by Park and Dowding were incorporated in a new policy where a category system was adopted. 'A' squadrons were those in the forefront of the battle, 'B' were maintained at full operational strength and could be put into the battle as replacements and 'C' would have a nucleus of five or six experienced men who would train pilots coming from OTUs in quieter areas; it was thought that these would be able to deal effectively with any incursions by unescorted bombers in their own area if the occasion arose. In normal times, a policy such as this would have been totally unacceptable to Fighter Command.

At a No. 11 Group Meeting of Sector Commanders a week before the Conference, when discussing the escalating losses, it had been generally agreed that this was due to the employment of 'new Squadrons with little experience of engagements with enemy fighters, and an increasing proportion of new and inexperienced pilots in existing Squadrons'. There had been general agreement that a request should be made to Command asking that whenever Squadrons were reduced to fifteen, operationally trained pilots should be posted in from other Groups.[100] This had now prompted some action.

Other Commands in the RAF had already been scoured for prospective fighter pilots and the Fleet Air Arm had also made a substantial contribution. There were a few French and Belgians; Czech and Polish squadrons were already formed and in action.

After the conference, Evill studied No. 11 Group returns of pilot and aircraft strengths for 15 September and he wrote from Bentley Priory to Keith Park pointing out that as a rough average pilots were 17 per squadron, whereas serviceable aircraft were 12, and operational strength 10. This suggested that the number of aircraft was now limiting the strength of formations and Evill questioned whether they should 'turn the searchlight on to the Aircraft Maintenance or Supply Organisation'. . . . Park replied, 'Until a few days ago, shortage of operational pilots limited the strength of our fighter formations. Except in the instance of our nightfighter squadrons, shortage of aircraft now limits the strength of formations'. He did point out, however, that the day Evill chose for his study had been an exceptionally heavy day's fighting; it was not the 'average state of affairs'.[101] It was hoped recent moves would improve the situation.

Vickers aircraft factory at Brooklands had been attacked and suffered severely on 4 September; a further raid was sent against Shorts factory at Rochester. The destruction of Fighter Command's southeastern aerodromes continued to be the *Luftwaffe*'s principal occupation, but this shift in German target selection and its threat to the supply of aircraft was quickly discerned at Bentley Priory. Dowding, needing little reminding of the September 1939 Directif giving defence priority to aircraft factories, instructed Keith Park to provide 'maximum fighter cover' during the next week to Hawkers, who were manufacturing Hurricanes at Kingston-upon-Thames, and their other factories at Brooklands and Langley.

The Vickers factories at Southampton, making Spitfires, were also singled out for extra protection. Park accordingly had instructed his fighter Controllers to arrange for two No. 10 Group Squadrons to patrol lines (a) Brooklands – Croydon, and (b) Brooklands – Windsor, when heavy attacks were being made south of the Thames. This was more or less in keeping with the tactics already being employed. He put his squadrons in forward positions between the coast and Sector aerodromes and relied on the support from Nos. 10 and 12 Groups to protect their bases around London and the aircraft factories to the west.

The analysis of reports showed that some bomber formations were proceeding uninterrupted to their objectives, as in a raid on Brooklands, and this was successful because defending fighters were operating at too great a height and had been concentrating on the enemy fighter screen; this was usually at above 20,000 feet. The No. 11 Group Commander reasoned that his Group Controller was ordering a patrol at 16,000 feet, the Sector Controller added one or two thousand more and the squadron put on a further two thousand in the hope that no enemy fighters would

114

be above. In consequence, while they were up there, bomber formations were slipping in below. At this time, bombing was rarely conducted from above 16,000 feet by day and the aircraft were being given a clear run. In conclusion, Park estimated that during the previous week the majority of interceptions had occurred after the bombs were dropped, the very antithesis of his policy.[102]

While the conference at Bentley Priory on 7 September was in progress, in the sky over London events were occurring which are now often referred to as the turning point in the Battle of Britain, and it is now recognised as the time the *Luftwaffe* made the strategical error which ended any possibility of victory, and as can be seen from the conference, a time when success was within their grasp. Thinking that the remnants of the British fighter force would be lured into the air to defend London, and seeking reprisals for a recent raid on Berlin by Bomber Command, Hitler withdrew his prohibition of the bombing of cities; London was to become the prime target. Effort was diverted from the destruction of Fighter Command's airfields and the aircraft industry when they were in a state of crisis. Park later wrote, 'This change of bombing plan saved 11 Group Sector Stations from becoming inoperative and enabled them to carry on operations, though at a much lower standard of efficiency.'[103] He reported that daylight attacks had created extensive damage to five of his forward aerodromes (Manston and Lympne were unable to operate fighters for many days), and six of his seven Sector Stations. Biggin Hill was so badly damaged that for over a week only one squadron could be accommodated there; its two other squadrons were sent to adjacent Sectors.

The change of strategy employed new tactics by the *Luftwaffe*. Bombing large cities with their large sprawling mass of buildings was not difficult. The requirement for great bombing accuracy was no longer necessary when the objective was to terrorise the civilian population. It was hoped a breakdown of civilian morale and subsequent political peace settlement would be forthcoming.

With the sky filled with aircraft, the radar organisation was reaching saturation point when every incursion, be it one or two aircraft or a mass formation, was being plotted. On 9 September, No. 60 Group, responsible for the radar chain, sent instructions to the Stations telling them to concentrate more on plotting the mass formations so that a clearer and more accurate picture of the main thrust of enemy activity could be seen. Earlier, to supplement the raid information supplied by Radar and the Observer Corps, and bring about an increase in the number of interceptions, fighter formation leaders in No. 11 Group were instructed, when sighting the enemy, to report over their R/T the numbers of bombers and fighters present, their height, position and the direction in which they were proceeding. Park now decided also to employ single VHF radio-equipped Spitfires who, while flying at great height, shadowed raids and reported on them to his Sector Controller; the details were then passed to the Group Operations Room. This supplementary method of reporting raids could be used only when aircraft could be spared from combat duty. The success of the reconnaissance flights eventually led to the formation of No. 421 Flight at Gravesend, who specialised in this type of work.

Other important intelligence sources were also supplying information to Fighter Command. The day before the 'going down hill' conference at Bentley Priory, Donald Stevenson, Director of Home Operations, wrote to the Vice-Chief of the Air Staff advising him that he had told Dowding that he could 'thin out' his eight-gun fighter strength protecting the north and, in so doing, transfer eight squadrons to give extra strength against heavy attacks coming in over Kent.[104] He wrote how Dowding 'was in great opposition to the idea' saying 'that squadrons in the north were his only reserve'. (This coincided with the introduction of the C-in-C's new policy of non-replacement of squadrons in the south, and using experienced pilots from elsewhere to keep them up to strength.) Stevenson's plan most likely centred on information received from an Intelligence source which showed that the German Air Force had withdrawn its long-range bomber units from Norway and based them in France; he reasoned that the threat to the north had diminished. Whether the south's ground organisation, i.e. airfields and control system, could cope with this is debatable. Information such as this was obtained and corroborated by several intelligence sources, in the main, from monitoring German radio transmissions. To do this, the British 'Y' Service gathered and deciphered information from enemy low-grade radio signalling. From these and high and medium frequency signals decoded at the main RAF interception station at Cheadle, a flow of intelligence was established. This was supplemented by decrypts made at Bletchley Park (The Government Code and Cypher School) of signals traffic emanating from German Enigma coding machines, although this process was still in its infancy and had little tactical value. Another source of information was the R/T voice transmissions of *Luftwaffe* aircrew which was assimilated at Kingsdown in Kent. There was soon enough available material on which to form a clear picture of the German Order of Battle, i.e. the units, aircraft types and where they were based, etc. The Kingsdown organisation relied on the skill of German-speaking WRNS and WAAF

116

members serving in Home Defence Units (HDUs), a small number of wireless listening stations sited on the east and south-east coasts. There they carefully recorded aircraft call signs, the frequencies being used and, most importantly, the ever increasing utterances of German pilots. Their reports were telephoned by direct land line to Kingsdown, local Sector fighter stations, and Group Headquarters, also the Admiralty and to the Command Operations Room at Bentley Priory. During the latter stages of the Battle of Britain, it is said they could, on occasions, determine where raids were building up outside radar detection, give their height and, knowing their unit call signs, work out whether they were bombers or fighters.

Operations reports and analysis of data from Radar and Observer Corps records was evaluated and, if of operational value, immediately passed to those most able to use it. The Intelligence Section, now housed in one of the many huts in the grounds of the Priory, produced a daily summary of events compiled from reports sent in from various quarters of the Command. This covered a wide spectrum of German equipment and activity, including descriptions of raids (both day and night), studies of crashed aircraft, i.e. their armour, weapons and ancillary equipment; also any alterations to markings and camouflage. Any odd behaviour of crews, e.g. throwing out wires in the face of a pursuing fighter, or new formations being flown, was carefully noted. Movement of bombers and fighters to different bases were written in when they were known to have changed. The summary occasionally went to the lengths of mentioning the contents of German propaganda broadcasts. On the home front, from the daily Squadron returns the true strength of Fighter Command in pilots and aircraft was published. Activity of Bomber and Coastal Commands was also put on record. In all, a comprehensive statement of affairs was produced by the Intelligence Section at Bentley Priory for those who needed to know.

What it was like to experience the early days of the war at Bentley Priory when people were rushed in to get the air defence organisation on a firmer footing and how the activity down 'the hole' was directed can best be described by those who were there. (The procedures were to undergo many changes in the years to come.)

Joan Clarke (née Crawford) enlisted at Speke Airport, Liverpool in September 1939 and, after several weeks of waiting, together with seven other Liverpudlians, she was posted to Leighton Buzzard to receive just two weeks training in Filter Room plotting. As an Aircraftwoman 2nd Class (ACW2) Joan was posted to Bentley Priory in December and recalls the following:

'I'll never forget my first sight of Bentley Priory; passing through huge ornate gates supported on each side by beautiful pillars, then driving on down the long curving drive to finally catch sight of the old house, We were all lined up outside what looked like the stables, and were greeted by a WAAF Officer, the formidable Section Officer McLeod. The Liverpool contingent, plus a few others, was assigned to "C" Watch and we were driven to our billet. (There were four Watches.) This was "The Warren", a lovely country house not far away in Bushey Heath, opposite St Peter's Church. The house gave every appearance that it had only recently been requisitioned because when we were shown to our bedroom on the ground floor, we noticed the chandeliers were still hanging there. Across the road from "The Warren" were several terraced cottages and one had been converted into a shop dealing with electrical goods and such like. We had no wireless in our bedroom; portables in those days were unheard of, so we persuaded the old gentleman in the shop to rent us one. It was a huge, ugly contraption with an "accumulator" (a sort of battery) to supply the power; it wouldn't work without one. We somehow staggered back to "The Warren" with it, stood it on the mantlepiece and attached the "accumulator", Hey Presto! it worked. There was one snag, however, "accumulators" had to be recharged, so we took it in turns to take ours back to the old boy and he substituted it with a fresh one. This and the cost of the rental was a shilling (5p) a week. There were twelve of us in the room, so I used to collect a penny from everyone, and we were able to keep up with the news.

'We had no proper uniforms. Raincoats, black berets, blue shirts and black ties were issued; the shirts we wore were our own. When eventually uniforms were issued, acting on a tip from my brother, I made sure my one was very, very big. I then found a little tailor in Watford to alter it; the fit was so good that other girls who had had theirs tailor-made at Moss Bros couldn't believe it had originally been an old standard issue uniform. Everyone bought their caps from Moss Bros.

'We were given our Watch duties which were spread over twenty-four hours, and were four hours at a time. We went on at midnight 00.01 hours, then had eight hours off, and returned at 12 noon until 4 o'clock in the afternoon. This was followed by a further eight hours off, then we started the routine again at midnight. The following week it changed to 4 a.m. to 8 a.m. and 4 p.m. to 8 p.m., and so on. It seemed to be all bed and work and, when you were going on at 4 a.m., it meant you had to get up at 3 a.m. to be in time for "Phoomph", our name for the coach. Thankfully our duty times included one week of eight hour shifts, which ran from midnight to 8 a.m., a great relief because you could if you wished occasionally sleep all day outside in the sun, go to a dance in the evening, maybe at Watford Town Hall, then catch the last bus back to Bushey and go straight on duty.

'Life in the early days was easy as there was little to do; it was a time of waiting. I have never written so many letters or read so many books. I read *Gone with the Wind* in about a week. People around the Filter Room table would be knitting or doing crosswords, etc. Occasionally someone would happen to cast an eye up at the balcony and notice dear old "Stuffy" Dowding was peering down at us. We would give each other a nudge and immediately the knitting, writing and books would disappear. I'm sure he must have inwardly chuckled seeing our reaction; no one knew how long he had been standing there. It was a very relaxed atmosphere; you spoke to the people at the radar station you were covering every fifteen minutes to check that the telephone line was in working order; it should have been every five minutes. Their shift times were different from ours so that continuity could be maintained. We got to know them very well and would discuss everything under the sun – hobbies, pastimes, state of the weather, anything that came to mind. Quite suddenly things would change. The voice at the other end would say, "Hang on, we've got something showing on the screen. Something is coming up. Standby. The plot reads V Victor 8565". This I repeated as a check then placed a counter on that position on the table. I asked, "Have you got a height and number of aircraft?" The Filter Officer on the balcony wanted to know and it went on the raid plaque. More plots came through; the track continued.

'By the time the war hotted up, we were well set in a routine. All our Watch lived at "The Warren", and "Phoomph" regularly took us to the Priory; later, when the summer weather was nice, during the day, we walked. Camouflage netting covered the Operations block area even though it was underground. Showing of identity passes became almost unnecessary when our faces became familiar. Dim blue lights lit up the many steps of the passageway down to the Operations Centre. All was quiet inside as we walked along the corridor; doors along there never seemed to open. By contrast, when entering the Filter Room, you were struck by the noise and twenty-eight members of our Watch moving in to take over didn't help. People on the balcony would be talking with the Filterers beneath them at the table, perhaps querying or altering details of a track, etc.; it all added to the general hubbub. Other voices; WAAFs speaking to their radar stations and "Tellers" reading off the plots showing on the table to Operations Rooms throughout the country.

'When taking over there was a well practised procedure. Plotters selected from the rack a telephone headset and mouthpiece which was hung around the neck. WAAF Sergeant Harland had the list of Radar Stations from which she selected the one you were to man; after a while this became almost a formality. I usually had Ventnor on the Isle of Wight, and would just say "Ventnor" and she would confirm. (My first station was Kirkwall up in the Orkneys.) I would walk to the table, sit down beside the girl working on Ventnor, plug my headset into a duplicate socket, listen in to check that the line was in order, then if all was well she unplugged her headset and departed. This procedure ensured that there was no break in continuity; no plots were lost. If we were not busy, I would make a friendly remark, like, "Is there much on?" and she would have a quick word and then go. In front of me, illuminated from above by strong lights, was a very large table map of the British Isles showing the location of all coastal radar stations and at each position was a telephone socket, like the one I had just plugged into, which had a direct line to that station. The map was formed in the shape of a giant letter "J" because it followed the shape of Britain's coastline stretching from Scotland, right down the Eastern side and turning round the South. There was not much land shown, our stations at the coast showed only activity over the sea and into the countries beyond; when aircraft passed inland behind them, we finished plotting. (From Observer Corps plots the track was then continued overland on Operations Rooms tables.) Stations were generally quite close to each other and so, to make space for us to work, plotters were arranged on both sides of the map, some working towards themselves, others away; roughly about twelve or fifteen on one side and eight on the other. A grid was marked over the whole map, the bigger squares being something like three feet (picture, if you can, large graph paper) and these were further divided into ten lines horizontally and vertically and numbered one to ten; further divisions of the grid were not marked and had to be calculated by eye. Each large square had a letter of the alphabet marked in the centre to distinguish it from the next, and each side of the square represented 100 kilometres. A plot would come through from Ventnor and I would place a counter at that point on the map. The counters, which we unofficially called

"Tiddlywinks", were about the size of a one new penny coin and were the colour associated with your particular station; Ventnor was orange and Poling, next to me, I think was blue. These we placed by hand, unlike the Operations Rooms who placed plots with long rods. Fanning out seawards at range gradations of 10 miles, using the station as a centre point, arcs were drawn and individually numbered 10–20–30, etc. as the distance from the station increased, up to 180 miles.

'The system worked efficiently but, it totally relying on the human factor, only a small plotting error could result in our pilots being given wrong information and missing an interception. Roughly speaking, it worked like this. At each station on the coast the readings from their radar screen were converted into map reference "plots" and shown on a small table map which geographically covered the area watched by the station. The grid of this map was exactly the same scale as ours and plots of approaching aircraft were "told" or read from it to me in the Filter Room. I placed counters on the given points. WAAFs with stations on each side of mine would be plotting at the same rate with their stations locating the same raid, but obviously they would be recording things from a different position along the coast and the ranges would be different; if we were getting it right, most of the counters would fall near to each other and a clear track could be seen emerging. Beside us stood an Officer Filterer watching the table very carefully and, as soon as the counters began to take the form of a track, he put down a plastic arrow at its head to show the direction in which it was moving and where he calculated, from the trail of coloured counters, the aircraft would be. (Later he placed an arrow after the first plot so that time was not lost waiting for a track to form.) If one station's plots were inconsistent, he would tell the plotter to ask the station to check their sendings. The track continued; after several more counters another arrow was placed, and so on. Counters were removed after 2½ minutes.

'The Filterer's job was a very difficult one. The radar plots we received from the stations as a single grid reference were made up of readings of "range", that is to say the distance the aircraft were from the station, and "bearing" which was, roughly speaking, the angle made between the aircraft, the station and True North; all of this being calculated from the display on the station's cathode ray tube. This gave the position on the map. Their recording of range was accurate, those of bearing were less so and it was on the former, the range readings, that work was concentrated. The Filterer watched each plot's relative position to the Range Arcs on the table map and compared one station's output with that of its neighbours. For example, if my station was assessing aircraft to be on the line of the arc at 80 miles and the one next to me at, say, 60 miles, where our arcs crossed on the map at these ranges is where the aircraft would be.* Usually he would similarly be using the plots of another neighbouring station which was also helping to form the track. It was not quite as simple as this, however, because he had to calculate by eye the unmarked distances between the ten mile spacings of the arcs and by using a rule of thumb method make a decision where to place his arrow. He also calculated a mean reading of the height and number of aircraft from information received from these stations. Sometimes our area had several tracks being worked on simultaneously

'As a track began to develop, a Raid Orderly nearby made up a "raid plaque" by fitting magnetic numbers and figures on to a small tray. This was placed at, and moved with, the head of the track. It showed the given track number, the estimated number of aircraft and their height, also whether the raid was hostile, friendly or "X" unidentified. Later Radar operators could see on their screen whether the aircraft carried IFF (Identification Friend or Foe), a device fitted to our aircraft which altered the shape of the blip, but until then movements liaison officers, watching the table from the balcony, and who had advance knowledge of the expected location of their respective Bomber and Coastal Command aircraft, identified their aircraft by shining a light producing a bomb or anchor silhouette on to the table below.

'On the balcony watching the table sat the Filter Officer who controlled the working of the table and was responsible for the efficiency of the reporting of the entire radar chain. Three "tellers" with headsets were also up there. Over direct telephone lines they read off the position of the arrow points, and other information showing on the plaques to waiting Operations Rooms in their area. The arrow points were now the "true" plots. WAAF Recorders wrote down all those broadcast from the Filter Room to their Operations Room listeners so that they could be scrutinised later.

---

* The official title given to this procedure was 'Range Cutting'. The principle was not new; it existed in the First World War when used to pinpoint the position of enemy artillery fire.

A small PBX exchange took care of the numerous telephones up there, and the Filter Officer could speak on the phone to every radar station or anyone he wished to discuss or query anything with.

'Measurement of speed was calculated by a WAAF who stood beside you using a stop watch. She could see the number of miles being covered by the aircraft and, by measuring the amount of time taken, could work it out; this was of some help to the Operations Room. Scientific Observers often came in to make checks on how things were going. When the bombing really got going in August, the number of raids increased daily and by September they were coming over in droves; it was quite terrifying; we knew how few we had. As the Battle of Britain developed, the increased tempo in the Filter Room could be measured by the increase in noise. I was receiving plots normally at 20 second intervals but often as fast as speech would allow; the voice speaking to me from the radar station never seemed to stop for breath.

'They bombed the radar stations. I remember on one occasion* my WAAF teller at Ventnor saying to me, "We are being bombed, Joan, and are now under the table", but they still remained in contact. I could hear all this going on, suddenly the line went dead. Then they hit other stations as well, Dover, Rye and Pevensey; I remember them going off the air and it seemed unreal; after all the activity there was nothing, just an empty space on the table. Nothing else affected our plotting except perhaps during a quieter period when our station would go off the air for a half hour's maintenance. Once or twice all the lighting went out, probably from bombs falling close by, and we continued our work by torch light; the torches were provided for such emergencies.

'It was a very hot Summer, so back at "The Warren" we moved our beds out on to the terrace; the rose gardens stretched a long way and beyond that, in the distance, was Hartsbourne Manor, so we were not overlooked. It was wonderful sleeping under the stars but it didn't last long. In September the Port of London docks were bombed and from the terrace you could see the sky over London lit up bright red by the fires. We were made to bring our beds indoors because it was no longer safe.'

* 12 August 1940.

The girls at the plotting table were each in turn allowed a ten-minute rest period and two girls moved around the table systematically plugging into each position in turn. When they had completed their circuit, being reliefs, it fell to them to disinfect with Dettol the headsets that had been used by the earlier Watch; they also swept the floor.

On the balcony overlooking the plotting table sat the Tellers. Their job was to read off grid references and information on raids approaching in the sea area beneath where they sat. This roughly coincided with the Group area they were serving, plus a generous extension on both sides. Through direct telephone lines Plotters in Operations Rooms at Sector, Group and the Command room next door received their commentaries simultaneously and thereby all information showing on all the tables was the same in content and placed at the same time. In this manner radar was able to alert defences in all threatened areas throughout the British Isles.

'Telling' was another demanding job, and it required good eyesight. From the display on the table a Teller was required to read the track details on the plaques and quickly interpret the points of the filterer's arrows into grid references for her listeners; these were now the 'true' plots. It also required good powers of concentration which in busy periods needed to be sustained under pressure for long periods. She followed the progress of tracks in her area and moving from one to another, 'told' the latest arrow plots as they were positioned. When a new track appeared, she warned, 'Stand by for new raid', then, after a short pause, would begin to read the relevant details. During periods of high activity, with several tracks being worked on, she could be heard passing an endless flow of readings. Plots on the table remained there for just two and a half minutes before being collected up; long trails of stale plots were of no value in the fast moving air war; they were, however, recorded for later analysis.

On the Filter Room wall was a standard one hour Operations Room colour change clock with its face divided into five-minute segments by the addition of colours. (Not to be confused with the five-number two-and-a-half-minute indicator used for Filter Room plotting.) It commenced on the hour with a five-minute red section; next came yellow, then blue, and this sequence was repeated throughout the sixty minutes. As the minute hand swept over each colour, Plotters in Fighter Command Operations Rooms, all of whom had identical wall clocks, matched the colour of the plots they were placing to that of the section currently being swept by the hand. This particular clock in the Filter Room was not used in plotting but was basically for maintaining synchronisation of all such clocks within the system. As the hand began its travel across the red segments, the Filter Room tellers alerted Operations Rooms, thus all clocks were kept in step. The clock was also used in keeping logs and other records.

Margaret Taylor (née Doll), a WAAF Flight Officer, was at that time a Clerk/Special Duties Sergeant and a plotter in the Command Operations Room. She was a recipient of the Filter Room Tellers' information. She recalls:

'The first thing you did when arriving on duty was to have a good look at the table to see what was going on. Each Plotter collected her headset, put it on and plugged it into her position at the table. On the hour and every quarter hour the Filter Room Teller next door would call, "Colour change red", and then go through all the Stations on her lines; for example, if it were No. 11 Group area, it would be Uxbridge (Group), and the Sector Stations at Tangmere, Kenley, Biggin Hill, Northolt, Hornchurch, North Weald, Debden; this procedure was to check their phones were serviceable; the Plotters there each answered to their Station's name. (When extremely busy, this was dispensed with and checks made only when a small lull in activity occurred.)

'Each of our Plotters had a rod with a battery operated magnetic tip and also at the table edge a small tray filled with red, yellow and blue metal arrows which were approximately 3/4" long. There were also numbers and letters for track details: red letter H for "Hostile", black X for "Unidentified", F for "Fighter" and C for "Coastal" (aircraft of Coastal Command). These pieces fitted on to small plaques (not magnetic) to make up the track number, height and number of aircraft. The plaques were positioned at the head of tracks and moved using a small stick.

'At 1207 hours, say, a track might appear near the French coast and the Teller in the Filter Room would commence giving information for the first plot, starting with the track designation (e.g. "Unidentified", and its allotted number), the direction of flight and the grid letter and four figure grid position. This was followed by the number of aircraft and their height. She would say, for example, Raid X49 – North West – A 3752 – ten aircraft at 10,000 feet. The Plotter then looked at the colour clock on the wall and seeing the hand was in the yellow section, picked up a yellow arrow, laid it on the table in front of her pointing North West and picked it up on the end of the rod by activating the magnet, then placed it with its point on the given map position, and released it. With practise, you could develop a very quick rhythm, make up a plaque and be ready waiting for the next plot. A large group of aircraft that could not be counted individually would be estimated at, say, 30+, or whatever. If activity were very hectic then two Plotters could plug into the same line and share the work; at such times as many as ten Plotters could be seen at the table, including those receiving Observer Corps information. Only hostile or "doubtful" overland Observer Corps plots were passed to us from Group. Chatting to the Teller was not encouraged, but we might on occasions ask whether there was "any height available yet" or if the aircraft was using IFF. We would be getting plot positions of the tracks of all aircraft and you could on occasions see raids coming in and our fighters going out to meet them; in every instance the plot colour was matched to that being specified on the face of the clock. Old plots of a particular colour were taken off when the hand of the clock moved into the same colour section of the next quarter; this meant that none of the information displayed on our table was more than ten minutes old. Our two Tracers in the gallery near the Controller, used two map boards over which sheets of tracing paper were laid and they drew all the tracks plotted on the Operations Room table. They too changed their colours to coincide with the clock by using coloured pencils; the times were recorded also. As I remember, the tracing was changed to a fresh one every hour during busy periods. These tracings were a permanent record that could be referred to later.'

Observer Corps plots were sent to the Operations Room via Group Headquarters. These were plotted by girls working alongside Margaret Taylor.

A number of other indicator markers, e.g. position of convoys, were placed on the table. In the Operations Room, a close liaison was maintained with the Royal Navy. Lieutenant-Commander W.D. Swinerd, VRD (Retired) was a Lieutenant in the Royal Naval Volunteer Reserve when sent to Bentley Priory in April 1940 to serve as a Naval Liaison Officer (NLO), and remained there until 1944, when he was appointed to HMS *Leigh* (the Admiralty designation for the Naval Control of Shipping base at Southend) to work on the routeing of convoys out of the Thames Estuary. Of his time at Bentley Priory, he writes:

'The Naval Liaison establishment in the "Hole" was originally made up of a Captain, four Commanders, one Lieutenant-Commander and four Lieutenants. About October 1940, we were so busy our numbers were increased by the addition of more Lieutenants and some WRNS Ratings. The reason for the Royal Navy being represented at Fighter Command Headquarters was to advise on shipping movements around the coasts of Britain so that fighter cover could be provided speedily in case of calls for help. Also we were ideally situated to inform the Admiralty about any activity in the air likely to threaten that shipping. There was one other naval Captain at Bentley Priory who was not on the Naval Liaison strength but on the staff of the Commander-in-Chief Headquarters Fighter Command as naval adviser.

'On the balcony in the Operations Room looking down at the table and watching every movement and change of situation as it developed, there would be a Commander and a Lieutenant on watch. Close to them was a plotting table on which the Lieutenant would be preparing the charts on which the positions of convoys were plotted. (Later we were provided with an office off the Operations Room.) Information was supplied by various sources; the Admiralty sent theirs by Code and Cypher or over the telephone, and every hour or so we unfailingly telephoned places such as the Naval Operations Rooms in Chatham, The Nore, Tyne, Rosyth, Western approaches, Milford Haven, Pitreavie, Portsmouth, Liverpool and various other points up and down the coast to obtain their latest sailings, arrivals and estimates of convoys' positions. Naturally we were supplied with signals giving, in advance, the full details of all convoy sailings. Telephone communication was by secure lines and direct; you picked up the telephone, pressed the button down for Chatham, for example, and you went straight through. These sources we used as points of reference and from their reports we could work out the convoys' estimated future positions by "dead reckoning". Every hour the results of our calculations were plotted on our chart and then the positions were given to the Operations Officer in the Operations Room who passed them down to the girls at the table, who moved the convoy markers (shaped like a lifebelt with the convoy's code name displayed) to the latest indicated grid positions. Occasionally, due to bad weather or lack of accurate information, errors crept in and we had to move the plots forward or back; sometimes this could be as much as twenty miles or so, but we got it right eventually.

'Convoy positions were relayed by the Filter Room Teller to Groups Operations Tables for the information of RAF pilots, so that they could find the convoys quickly if they were being attacked. Also the pilots could avoid flying over the convoys if they were on other missions; this avoiding stratagem was most wise, as the Navy were in the habit of firing at any unidentified aircraft first and asking questions afterwards, especially if the aircraft came at them out of the sun, a favourite ploy used by hostile planes!

'The pilots used to complain about being shot at by the Navy so we used to take RAF Officers to join a Convoy now and then so that they could see the problems from the Navy's point of view and pass the information gleaned on to the squadrons' pilots, etc.

'We would frequently wander down into the Filter Room to see if they had got their table up to date, (we had a responsibility to them as well as to the Ops Room) as it was from there that convoy positions were told to all RAF Operations Rooms. When a convoy arrived at its destination, the marker would be removed from the table; on one occasion I was carrying out the usual check and there were two convoys showing on the table, one codenamed "Bacon", the other "Bosom", and the latter had just arrived in port. I can clearly remember the smiles when the Filter Officer leaned over the balcony and called down to a shapely, large-busted WAAF, "Remove Bosom" from the table, please'!

'The Filter Room was much smaller than the Operations Room and on a lower level. To get there from the Ops Room you would walk along a short gangway and go down a little, narrow staircase which took you on to the balcony of the Filter Room. On the opposite side of the room from us was the Air Raid Warnings Section, which was under Group Captain Smallwood; among his fellow officers was the Marquess of Carisbrooke, of immaculate uniform and bearing; there might also be the actor, Ronnie Squire, or perhaps June Clapperton, one of "Tom Arnold's Young Ladies", on duty. We had a lot of theatrical people and members of the Stock Exchange in the underground block. The Air Raid Warnings Section took up a lot of space; they had their own plotting table and a large illuminated display map of the British Isles. Sitting on the balcony and presiding over all the activity there and on the floor beneath would be the Operations Officer. The senior figure present in the Operations Block was the Duty Air Commodore, either Air Commodore J.M. Bonham-Carter, Air Commodore Sir John Webb-Bowen or Air Commodore H.B. Russell. They were not always there; if it was quiet whoever was on duty would retire for a while. The atmosphere in the Filter Room was always hot and seemed cramped compared to the loftier Operations Room, and there always seemed to be a lot of bodies down there and a continual buzz.

'It was customary to go on watch at least ten minutes early to allow time for a smooth change over. One would arrive in the Operations

Room, having come down the long flight of stone steps and along the corridor. After the freshness above ground the air appeared noticeably stuffy and oppressive, even though there was air conditioning. We worked in our shirt sleeves and the dryness of the air gave one quite a thirst; there was a rest room where one could take refreshment and, incidentally, spend a little time at backgammon, the favourite game at H/Q Fighter Command. However, on entering the Operations Room you would come to the balcony, have a quick study of the table below, have a word with your opposite number whom you would be relieving to find out what was going on, take over the plot and then he would be off. If there was little activity, the girls at the table would be sitting down and half asleep. Quite suddenly the Filter Room would come through on the telephone saying there was a raid; immediately everything would come to life – the girls would jump to their feet and begin placing and pushing around various indicators on the table, chaps on the balcony would look over to find out what it was all about and others would begin talking on the telephones. Suddenly it was all bustle. You might arrive on watch in the middle of one of these flaps and it was always difficult to pick up the threads of what was going on. If a raid was coming anywhere near one of our convoys it would be showing on the table and we would ring up to advise the Duty Commander at the Admiralty on our direct line; this information, of course, was initially supplied by the coastal radar stations and came via the Filter Room.

'With us on the balcony overseeing the table there were various sections which had their own allotted space. There was Army Intelligence with such well known personalities as Clifford Mollison, the actor, and Fred May, the caricaturist, who worked next to us of Naval Liaison. To keep our papers tidy we had a lectern fixed to the rail and looked over it to view the table; the Duty Commander usually sat there all the time writing up the Log Book, especially when there was activity going on. Then there was RAF Intelligence in touch with Cheadle ("Y" Service) and Kingsdown where German wireless traffic was intercepted and interpreted; the actor, Reg Tate and Lord Douglas Hamilton were in their section. Somewhere in the organisation was a Meteorological man and Observer Corps representative.

"Stuffy" Dowding, the Commander-in-Chief, usually came down two or three times a day and watched from the balcony. He was a grand character really, a shy and retiring man. Once or twice I went up from the Operations Room to take a message to him in his office in the main building and he was always courteous and quiet, more like a schoolmaster. His successor, Sholto Douglas, an extrovert, was always full of fun, and so was his wife. He used to come up quite often to use the swimming pool at No. 2 Mess, the house just across the field from the Priory, called "The Cedars", requisitioned from Mr Maclean of toothpaste fame!'

June Esau, née Clapperton, became a Section Officer and later a Filterer but during her early days in 1941 served in the Operations Room in the Air Raid Warning Section (ARW), which at that time was directly controlling a countrywide network, made up of 130 Warning Districts, through which the civilian population was warned of air raids. The degree of threat was conveyed in a colour coding.

'On the balcony the ARW table was a large map of the country lit from below. When an ARW "Yellow" was given to a particular district, a yellow light from beneath illuminated that part of the map. To the Police and Fire Services of that district our telephonists sent preliminary warning of the impending raid through operators at the civilian telephone exchanges. If the raiders continued on course this would become ARW "Red" (full alert and sirens sounding), but it occurred only after we established that none of our own aircraft was due back from a raid, or a returning reconnaissance flight was the object of our concern. From the balcony we watched the tracks relayed from the Filter Room forming on the Operations Room table, and acted upon them. The Filter Room housed the Movements Liaison Section (MLS) and their job was vital; they had all the information about our aircraft crossing the coast; their outward flight times and when they were expected to return (ETA)*, also numbers of aircraft involved. They were aware of what height the Squadrons or Sections would be when crossing the coast. Using this knowledge, they were able to work out where our aircraft would be at a given time and assess whether tracks on the table were of hostile aircraft or not.

'If the CH or CHL Radar Stations picked up a single aircraft coming in and we were not expecting anyone, it was possible that it could be one of ours in trouble and we would expect the pilot to switch on his IFF. This was a device in the aircraft which, when switched on, would flash through the blip it was making on the screen of the Radar Stations every 6 seconds. So you got the V-shaped blip of the aircraft and the extra flash down and up of the IFF blip making the V elongated for a

---

* Estimated time of arrival.

second. Sometimes the pilots were naughty and forgot to switch it on; this resulted in an "X" being put on the raid plaque which signified it as "doubtful" (Unidentified). The Observer Corps obtained visual identification and their information was wonderful for sorting out what the aircraft was and often prevented the ARW "Red" being given. The reason for not sounding the sirens at the drop of a hat was because the factories in the areas concerned would be shut down and only re-start once the "All Clear" was given; this was shown as ARW "White". If a large number of aircraft were approaching and we had fighters up, they helped by transmitting back a warning. A huge illuminated ARW map of the whole country was on the wall north of the plotting table which also showed the yellow and red warnings for everyone to see. "All Clears" were usually given after enemy aircraft had crossed the coast going home.'

Like most other sections, the ARW had undergone changes; at the end of July 1940, 'White' replaced a 'Green' phase in the sequence and a 'Purple' warning was introduced which was sent out only to dockyards, railway marshalling yards and factories so that their exposed lighting could be left on until the very last minute. The warning sequence became Yellow, Purple, Red and the 'All Clear', White.

Those in the Operations Room have not forgotten the unnerving experience during the night 'blitz' when looking up at the illuminated map on the wall, they could see the whole of the country showing red. All their families were under threat.

The work done by the ARW Section was of great importance and generally made it possible for the civilian population to go about their daily business, and factories to operate, without the constant fear of surprise attack from the air. It is impossible to estimate the number of lives which were saved by this organisation, its great value to the manufacturing industry and the country's economy.

From his seat on the balcony in the Operations Room the Duty Air Commodore kept watch on the table below. In front of him was a complete picture of all current activity over and around the British Isles. Through a number of liaison officers and other sources of information he was kept up to date on sea traffic, the passage of convoys, fishing fleets and naval movements. He knew of balloon barrages, searchlights, guns, flights of friendly aircraft, both bombers and civilian; for the latter advising on timings, routes and signals before giving permission for flights. He knew of events and incidents; the details of all raids were logged as were many other activities. Information on the strength and employments of the fighter squadrons was to hand. On the table an assortment of markers not directly related to fighter interceptions showed other activity. On the balcony the apparatus of the Air Raid Warning System, the use of which was his primary responsibility, demanded attention. The Command Operations Room projected a picture of the entire air defence situation but very rarely interfered in the control of operations.

The indomitable spirit of the WAAF cannot be overstated and it had an important influence throughout Fighter Command; earlier doubts were expressed about how the girls would behave if subjected to bombing and whether they would be able to withstand the rigorous way of life. At Bentley Priory the around-the-clock shift work system inevitably led to great tiredness which was further exacerbated if doing a demanding job in the stuffy, oppressive atmosphere of the underground Operations Block. In spite of this, they somehow managed to maintain a remarkable degree of social activity, much of which was of a sporting nature. They went swimming, played tennis and formed a hockey team to play local clubs. Two, noting the empty stables when they were billeted at 'The Warren', arranged to have their horses sent from home. Dancing was a much favoured pastime and each week, to music provided by a band made up of musicians from Bentley Priory, and for sixpence admission, many practised their nimble art. The events were well organised and disciplined with only the occasional minor departure from this practice, one exception being on the occasion when Sholto Douglas was guest of honour. One can only speculate on what the reaction of his wife would have been had she known that the attraction of her expensive mink coat had become too much for the members of the WAAF supervising the cloakroom and it was being handed round for each in turn to try on.

In the early days living accommodation for some was particularly spartan; large and often damp huts were in use. Other girls lived in hostels, usually large requisitioned houses; here again facilities were very basic. Each day a large RAF lorry could be seen leaving 'The Rookery' in Stanmore village where the food rations were stored, and slowly driving its regular route around the district dropping off supplies to the kitchens of the hostelries. The quality of the meals was generally thought to be of a good standard.

Fortunately only one hostel was damaged by bombing and this occurred on 15 November 1940 at 'Rosary Priory', a Catholic convent and boarding school in Elstree Road. There was no air raid warning and some of the girls were settling down to their evening meal in a hut in the grounds when a violent explosion rocked the building. Blast shattered the windows showering lethal splinters of glass in all directions. The chapel was badly damaged; the huts in the grounds got off comparatively lightly in losing their windows; remarkably no serious injuries had occurred. Having recovered from the shock of the explosion, the girls who had been eating supper were surprised to see much of their meals firmly stuck on the ceiling. One of them, Evelyn Bugg, who was eating liver and bacon at the time, was so affected by the trauma of it all that she has been unable to face eating it since.

The stringent conditions and discomfort shared by the girls in a strange way bound them together, creating a strong camaraderie. There was a great sense of purpose and fulfilment which stemmed from the realisation that they were personally making an important contribution to the defence of the country and the war effort as a whole. Nearly all signed on not knowing what to expect. The poster on the wall of the recruitment offices advised them, 'serve in the WAAF with the men who fly', but few ever got close to an aircraft. One of Bentley Priory's girls later commented lightheartedly, 'The only flying we ever saw was back to the billet at the end of a shift'. Later, when men were required elsewhere within the Air Force, the girls took over a high percentage of their work.

Operations Rooms on Sector Airfields in No. 11 Group were in buildings of poor quality and sited in vulnerable positions close to the flying area; this meant that their power supply and communications were equally so. Several had already been damaged, resulting in loss of ground control. The wisdom of Air Vice-Marshal Gossage, Park's predecessor at No. 11 Group, who had suggested that 'Standby' Operations Rooms should be made available two or three miles from the airfields, showed its worth. By 10 September, the damage to Sector airfields was so severe that Dowding gave instructions that control should be moved to these emergency standby centres if this had not already been done. Very soon most of the control of British fighters in No. 11 Group was carried out from the most unusual places, e.g. in the case of Kenley, a disused butcher's shop. Although this makeshift arrangement led to a certain loss of efficiency, it was far outweighed by the safety aspect. Meanwhile, immediate construction of more permanent Operations Rooms, each with a full communications system, was begun in locations far enough away for them to be free from attacks on aerodromes.[105]

Thirty-six Bofor anti-aircraft guns were taken from the air defences and passed to the Home Forces 'for the defence of the troops' on the stretch of coastline from North Foreland to Dungeness. Dowding protested at this interference with his responsibility for the disposition of air defence weapons, and carried out the Air Ministry's order under protest. It had previously been agreed by the Chiefs of Staff that only if invasion became imminent would weapons be transferred. Dowding commented, 'I have no information of such an event'. The instruction, he was told, had come from the Prime Minister at a War Cabinet Meeting; Dowding insisted that his protest be conveyed to the War Cabinet 'where the decision was made'.[106] (No reference to movement of guns appears in the War Cabinet meetings' minutes.)

Where, until recently, German strategy had been to use two or three hundred aircraft a day, spread over two or three separate raids, now three or four hundred were being sent in two or three waves, and in quick succession. The entire process would be over in about forty-five to sixty minutes. Keith Park in his instructions on 11 September emphasised that squadrons should be committed in pairs against heavy raids, and the raids should be met in maximum strength. Squadrons at 'Readiness' (ready to take off in 5 minutes) were to be dispatched against the first wave in pairs, the Spitfires taking on the fighter screen, and the Hurricanes intercepting the bombers and their close escort. Squadrons 'Available' on 15 minutes standby were to be sent in a similar fashion to engage the second wave and those 'Available' at 30 minutes would be dispatched singly to protect aircraft factories or Sector aerodromes, or to reinforce units already in the air; if there were a third wave, then they would be committed in pairs. Squadrons from Tangmere, when not protecting Portsmouth and Southampton area with No. 10 Group squadrons, were to patrol the Kenley Sector or to the rear of their own Sector to block German aircraft approaching from the south from either bombing London or creeping through to the aircraft factories at Kingston, Brooklands and Langley. The Group Controller would designate where pairs of squadrons would join up and when this was achieved, the Controller at Sector, who was in direct contact with the pilots, would advise his opposite numbers at Group who would then detail which raid they would be sent to intercept; the Sector Controller would take it from there.[107] Park gave instructions to his Controllers and they endeavoured to put them into practice but, as with all air fighting, how effectively they could be carried out depended on the conditions at the time; i.e. weather and the all important time factor.

The air fighting in No. 11 Group area was a continuous process of tactical changes and counter moves. Throughout the battle the protection of aircraft factories and airfields was in the forefront of Park's mind, his instructions to Controllers and Sector Commanders adequately confirm this; that is not to say that this was done to the exclusion of everything else; ports, harbours, docks and other sensitive areas were seen as likely targets. Later, cities, particularly London, required special attention. Interceptions engineered on Sector Operations Rooms tables were not always entirely successful, leaving pilots to rely on their own resources to engage enemy formations wherever they met them within their own Group area.

Battle casualties were high. From 8 August to 16 September they averaged 80 pilots per week; in the two most intensive weeks, 194 had become victims. When figures for non-combatant wastage were added, i.e. sickness, accidents, etc. it was estimated that a loss of at least 100 per week was a realistic average. Fighter Command was now facing a deficiency of 98 pilots; moreover, many of its most able and experienced men were gone.

Park carefully studied the reports flowing into No. 11 Group Headquarters at Uxbridge searching them for changes in enemy tactics and scrutinising them for any weakness in his own organisation. Where necessary he was critical of his Group and Sector Controllers; for example he was quick to spot that they had been detailing individual squadrons on to big raids and some pairs of squadrons were being patrolled too far forward and too low, with the result that they were attacked by the fighter screen. High German fighter formations of 100 to 150 aircraft were being allowed to draw up nearly all of the Group's resources, making it possible for a bomber raid sent in about forty-five minutes later to have the advantage of a number of British units being on the ground refuelling. His instructions to repel mass attacks, issued on 16 September, were for pairs of Spitfire Squadrons from Hornchurch and Biggin Hill, in clear weather, to engage the high fighter screen which was normally at 25,000 to 30,000 feet. In overcast conditions, squadrons should rendezvous below cloud or high over an airfield in a reasonably safe place where they could not be dived upon when climbing. Whenever raid information on strong incoming raids was unreliable, squadrons were to be held in wait patrolling in a given area at that height; if necessary, two squadrons very high and two between 15,000 and 20,000 feet. If the first wave of a raid was by high-flying fighters, several pairs of Spitfires were to engage them and Hurricane Squadrons sent to rendezvous in pairs near Sector Airfields. In the meantime, Northolt and Tangmere units were to be brought to 'readiness' in preparation for a possible third wave, which normally contained the bombers, and sent in as a Wing of three squadrons.[108] Tactical planning at No. 11 Group was a complex business and most of the resources were being used.

All was not well on the German side; their losses were high and they had no accurate assessment of the remaining strength of the British. It was now assumed erroneously that the defending force was numerically much depleted. (Claims for aircraft destroyed were found to be over optimistic by pilots on both sides.) German pilots were sceptical of the assessment made by their intelligence service; they were daily witnessing a different picture. Air supremacy, the vital prerequisite for a seaborne invasion, was not being achieved. On 15 September, the heaviest attacks yet had been directed against London. On this day the RAF met the attacks in strength, which included the full weight of five reinforcing squadrons of the Duxford Wing and five squadrons sent by Quintin Brand of No. 10 Group. German losses were high and it proved beyond doubt that any hope of gaining air superiority was still far off. With the onset of Autumn and deterioration of weather, time was of the essence if an invasion were to remain in prospect.

Goering criticised his fighter pilots for giving poor protection to the bomber force; bitter arguments occurred between the fighter and bomber forces; he began casting around for scapegoats, with his own credibility now at stake. A big disadvantage was the amount of time it took for the great aerial armadas to form up over their airfields in preparation for an attack; British radar was able to record this activity and give sufficient time for a response. The manoeuvring, particularly in cloudy conditions, also wasted the precious fuel of the Messerschmitt Bf.109 escort, shortening the time they were able to stay over England, which under the best of circumstances was minimal.

Hitler studied the situation closely and vacillated. On 17 September he decided to postpone Operation SEALION. The undermining of civilian morale by bombing cities was given preference, but an illusion that an invasion was imminent, he insisted, should be maintained. The strategy where attacks on cities had in effect led to the Polish and Dutch armies capitulating and the Danish Government doing likewise by the threat of it, had proved very successful earlier. Where before, night raids were more widespread, now London became the main objective. The policy had many advantages: because of its size, the capital was easily found in darkness; it was densely-populated and, by bombing at night, due to the inadequacy of the night defences, raids could be carried out with minimum losses. From now on, in what became known to the British as 'the Blitz', and to the Germans as 'Nerve Warfare', London was subjected to a nightly storm of explosive and incendiary bombs; the only comfort for the citizens was the sound of anti-aircraft gunfire, which fostered the belief that the enemy was being hit back, but in fact very few enemy aircraft were being destroyed. The courage of the civilian services, the ambulance crews, rescue workers, firemen and those responsible for maintaining the life of great cities would now match that of their Service colleagues.

Night bombing was not a one-sided affair. Since the middle of May, small forces of Bomber Command's long-range aircraft had been seeking out targets on the mainland of Europe, including Germany. As with Fighter Command, the *Luftwaffe* had not as yet found a successful interception technique for their nightfighters; they were relying on the use of Flak (guns) units. Blenheims were being continually used on daylight raids with the emphasis of Bomber Command as a whole increasingly directed against airfields in occupied Europe and on Channel ports. Together with Coastal Command, they were also attacking Channel shipping; these daylight operations required protection by fighter escorts, an additional strain on the already overstretched Fighter Command. In the current state of the battle, arrangements could not always be fulfilled when the squadrons were re-directed on to heavy raids. The Air Ministry was not slow in asking for a report when plans went awry.

On 25 September, using diversionary fighter-bomber attacks to deceive the defences, a large force of sixty He 111s and Bf. 110s bombed the Bristol aircraft factory at Filton, causing much damage and destroying a number of Beaufighters, the heavy fighter on which the RAF was pinning its hopes as a nightfighter and anti-shipping strike aircraft. The following day, the Supermarine Works at Southampton, producing Spitfires, was heavily bombed. Dowding quickly moved No. 504 Squadron from Hendon to Filton to protect the Bristol factory. A cypher message was sent to all Groups reminding them of priority to be given to the factories. Park, in a signal to his Sector Controllers and Squadron Commanders, emphasised the importance of breaking up bomber formations before they reached aircraft factories and Sector aerodromes. A further cypher message from Bentley Priory reiterating the earlier one said, 'This applies to all major aircraft factories'.[109] At Southampton, Lord Beaverbrook, Minister of Aircraft Production, looked at the damaged works and gave instructions that in future manufacturing should be dispersed. Components were soon being produced in all manner of requisitioned premises throughout the Southampton area, including motor garages and showrooms.

The latter part of September saw a steady decrease in the use of the German long-range bomber force: by day their losses had been heavy and it had now become prudent to concentrate on sending smaller forces, generally the fast Ju.88 bombers, accompanied by a strong fighter escort;

these were being interspersed with fast fighter incursions flying at great altitude. This greatly reduced the time available for the defences to prepare their response. Squadrons from forward airfields in Kent were being attacked while climbing and Park withdrew them to inland bases. Earlier, given ideal conditions, it had been possible on occasions to assemble No. 11 Group Squadrons in three-unit Wings; even then a small amount of cloud had delayed their forming up and retaining contact when on patrol. It was estimated that they took twice the time to arrive at a given point than paired squadrons.[110] The time factor and deteriorating cloud conditions were now making this increasingly difficult. As always, it was left to the Group Controller to assess whether time and weather allowed for such measured response; a bad decision could result in squadrons being caught by German fighters while still climbing to reach their designated height. Park advised that unless there were clear skies and ample radar warning, squadrons were to be dispatched in pairs during the winter months. Even so, he instructed his Sector Commanders to 'continue to study and develop fighting tactics in Wings of three squadrons, which will probably become more common in the Spring of 1941'.[111] With an eye to the future, he was hoping that then he would be able to take a more offensive role and attack the enemy before they reached the Kent coast.

Normally, when raids penetrated as far inland as London, there was sufficient time for paired squadrons to be positioned for interception. 'Tip and run' raids by bomb-carrying Bf. 110s were, by 4 October, coming in so fast across Kent that on occasions it became imperative that Controllers directed on to them any single units that happened to be in the air at the time to prevent them reaching aircraft factories, Sector airfields and other vital areas. No. 11 Group Controllers were being beset by problems created by unreliable height readings of incoming raids being supplied by the radar; and by delays in receiving these and Observer Corps reports; it was also noticed that squadrons were now taking longer to get off the ground. Their instructions were much the same; whenever time permitted, squadrons at readiness were to be sent off in company, to join up over Sector airfields; Spitfires to 25,000 feet, Hurricanes 5,000 feet beneath. When they reported their arrival in position, they were to be either directed to intercept an approaching raid showing as a good track on the Operations Room table, or were to be sent on a patrol line while awaiting instructions.

During early October, German strategy once more underwent funda-mental change. The long-range bomber force, save for a few fleeting attacks using cloud cover, was almost entirely removed during the hours of daylight. In its place, when weather permitted, mass high-flying fighter formations were sent over at various times of the day. Occasionally, and at lower altitude, attacks in the London area were made by formations of Bf. 109s and 110s which had been adapted to carry bombs; many of these were seen to jettison them when encountering defending fighters so as to assume the role of fighter. They were skilfully using high cloud cover to conceal their presence as autumn cloud and mists were having an important influence on operations. It was quickly recognised that German intentions were to destroy the British fighters using fighter patrols and sweeps at very high altitude, seeking to draw them up into combat on unfavourable terms. Raids were frequent and spread over a wide area. To assist Controllers, Park sent them information on times attainable by the combatants. Enemy fighter squadrons could be over London within twenty minutes of the first plot showing on the Operations Room table; on occasions it could be as little as seventeen minutes. For a Spitfire to reach 20,000 feet, on average it would take thirteen minutes; a Hurricane three minutes longer. To reach 30,000 feet a Spitfire took twenty-seven minutes.[112]

On 15 October, Park advised Sector Commanders of results calculated from a study of recent combat reports sent in from the squadrons, and after having had discussions with their Commanders. He had added to this his own experiences while observing the situation from his Hurricane while flying over Kent. He suggested that, against the current enemy tactics, using very high fighter patrols or raids in mist and cloud, Wings and paired Squadrons were seriously disadvantaged. (They took 15–18 per cent longer to reach the combat height than a single squadron.) Radar warnings gave insufficient time to get fighters high enough to intercept the first wave of enemy fighters and interception was made only if a second or third wave came in. Combat with the first wave was usually only achieved by a Spitfire squadron operating as a Standing Patrol; these were regularly used between 0800 and 1800 hours and by units flying at 15,000–18,000 feet, moving to full operational height when raids were detected. Enemy fighters coming in at between 25,000 and 30,000 feet found the 'Achilles Heel' of the radar system; it was here the CH Stations remained least efficient and was a factor in the introduction of wasteful standing patrols. The size of enemy fighter incursions was varying. Small numbers of up to seven aircraft were proving effective, and these formations were compact yet remaining flexible. If they had a height advantage, any numerical inferiority did not worry them. It was noticed that, when they dived to attack, the mistake of staying down at the lower level to become embroiled in a dogfight was not made; their tactics were to dive, attack and immediately zoom upwards. Park recommended that, when the situation was reversed, his fighters should copy this idea. He also gave instructions to alter the time-honoured practice of rigid Squadron 'Section line astern' formations, earlier adopted as a standard method of attack. He had witnessed events while over Kent and noted that pairs of squadrons were climbing in rigid order inviting attack from the German fighters above. The Sections should be trained to break away and, if necessary, work in pairs. When two or three squadrons were on patrol, they should be spaced 2,000 to 4,000 feet apart and not be in a rigid mass. If the top one was attacked from above, it should attempt to draw down the enemy across the bows of those flying beneath. Park finished his assessment in an encouraging frame of mind, pointing out the disadvantages endured by German fighter pilots when weighed against the British; how some had to carry bombs a hundred or so miles into enemy territory and how they did not have the advantage of being kept informed over the R/T of the approximate strength, height and position of their opponents. He wrote that Nos. 12, 13 and 14 Groups were building up and becoming more fit operationally and the hope now was that No. 11 Group would benefit by the squadrons being relieved after six to eight weeks in the Front Line.[113]

To cope with the high fighter raids, as soon as enemy formations were plotted over the French coast or Channel, two reconnaissance aircraft on regular patrol near the Kent coast were sent to find and report their position as they came in. Standing patrols over Maidstone by Spitfires at 15,000 feet were ordered to 30,000 feet to cover others climbing to reach them after joining up over their base. Other units at 'Readiness' took off to rendezvous over their airfields at 20,000–27,000 feet then be put on forward patrol or interceptions. Further Spitfire Squadrons could, if necessary, be sent off to patrol to the rear at 25,000–30,000 feet in wait. Hurricane units could be used to combat any third wave after being put on back patrol lines. The plan was to have one or two Spitfire Squadrons to engage the enemy fighters from above at about mid Kent to cover others climbing to operating height from airfields to the east and south of London. Here again the success of the tactics relied heavily on time and weather factors.

In a letter to Evill at Bentley Priory on 23 October, Park wrote.

'From five and a half months of strenuous fighting in all sort of conditions of weather, we have learned that there is no one type of formation that is best. Conditions of time, location, weather and States of Readiness, demand that squadrons shall be trained firstly to fight offensively and defensively alone, secondly, fight effectively in pairs and lastly, fight in Wings of three when conditions are favourable. The German fighters, and their bombers too, have employed an infinite variety of formations and set formations, showing a remarkable flexibility in ideas.'

He pointed out the danger of squadrons trained in the northern Groups having a set idea that it was only safe and effective to work in Wings of four or five squadrons and having seriously neglected their offensive and defensive tactics as a squadron.* This would be all right for those not having to fly daily within the range of enemy fighters which were now known to fly well into Kent at great height without being detected by radar or Observer Corps.[114]

The great height at which fighter-versus-fighter engagements were now fought highlighted the weaknesses within the defensive system. At that altitude, the gaps in the radar cover were large enough for some aircraft to remain undetected but it was only on rare occasions that large formations were missed entirely and later located well inland. If there was no reported radar track to pick up at the coast, the Observer Corps was disadvantaged by having lost its prior warning of an incoming raid. They also had their problems if weather conditions were cloudy, which made both sight and sound reading very difficult.

With raid information uncertain, greater reliance was placed on the information radioed back to Group Headquarters from the few high-flying reconnaissance Spitfires of No. 421 Flight who were sent to detect the types of aircraft and course of approaching raids. The Germans were now adopting a similar tactic by having their aircraft send back reports on cloud conditions, weather and movements of British fighters. (The British 'Y' Service had noted a much increased volume of radio messages in this field.) They also had radio listening posts and for some time had been monitoring British ground and aircraft

---

* This was a reference to No. 12 Group. Earlier he noted how replacement squadrons 'possibly imbued with Big Wing idea' had not done as well as those of No. 13 Group 'trained to fight singly'.[115]

transmissions. Recognising that use of this information was very likely, Dowding gave orders for the wording of Controllers' instructions to their pilots which had definite codenames, e.g. 'Pancake' being an instruction to land, should be periodically changed, thus eliminating the danger of a squadron being caught on the ground. The height at which a unit was ordered to fly was given as 'Angels' followed by the number in thousands of feet – 'Angels 15' being 15,000 feet. It became prudent to introduce a measure of subterfuge on occasions by the addition of a pre-arranged extra several thousand feet, for example 'Angels 15' would then become an instruction to fly at 20,000 feet.[116]

The air war in the south was becoming a fighter-versus-fighter affair with, on the German side, the Bf. 109 being the principal antagonist. Aircraft were now being pushed close to their maximum height capability. Part of a report on operations sent to the Priory by Keith Park, compared the performance of German and British fighter aircraft. He wrote of how up until the end of September in combats below 20,000 feet British fighters had little difficulty in dealing with their German adversaries; the Spitfire was slightly faster and the Hurricane slower, but both types were more manoeuvrable. The Hurricane equalled the Bf 109's speed at ground level but became progressively incapable as the height increased; it had little difficulty in catching a Bf. 110 up to 20,000 feet but above this the Bf. 110 was proving definitely superior. The Bf. 109 easily outclimbed it but up to 15,000 feet it was outclimbed by a Spitfire. Both types of German fighters were now found to have superior speed above 20,000 feet; this Park attributed to them having two-stage superchargers fitted to their engines. As a result, British pilots were now at a serious disadvantage in engagements at heights above 25,000 feet; some interceptions were above 30,000 feet. At these heights Park reckoned enemy fighters were vastly superior. He complained that the new Mk.II Spitfire, now coming into service, had a higher operational ceiling but no other improvements; it was found to have serious faults – tail heaviness, bad starting, also it was difficult to maintain. The latest Mk.II Hurricane had improved rate of climb and operational ceiling; its manoeuvrability was, however, not enhanced above 25,000 feet; the engine was designed for 30,000 feet but the aircraft itself was never designed to operate at this height. Future aircraft, Park recommended, should be more heavily armed to penetrate the armour plating now installed in German bombers, and cannons were a necessity; a mixed armament using four machine-guns and two cannons would be the ideal. A speed of over 400 mph was required and an operating ceiling of 40,000 feet should be aimed at. Comfort in the form of cockpit heating was essential for pilots; the small air leaks in cockpits, if playing on any part of a pilot's body, were producing an almost paralyzing effect.[117] British pilots were now relying heavily on guile to match their opponents. Air fighting was never a comfortable occupation at the best of times but to the now tired fighter pilots of both sides the high altitude fighting carried with it the additional burden of intense cold. Windscreens and cockpit hoods iced over, both inside and out, impairing their vision; they were enduring periods of intense discomfort when on patrol as the cold penetrated clothing and bit into their bodies; returning earthwards was a very welcome relief. With no cockpit heating, at times conditions were agonising.

High combat showed the lack of experience of some pilots when manoeuvring their aircraft above 25,000 feet, and a lack of physical fitness in others. It was noticeable in No. 11 Group that some Squadron Commanders (average age 29½ years) became prematurely exhausted and recommendations were made by Park that consideration should be given in future to ensuring that they be no older than 25 years. (The fallacy of this proposal becomes obvious when one appreciates that today's fast jet pilot is at the early stage of his career at this age.)

The Battle of Britain had almost run its course. Although there was a certain diversity of effort in that destruction of shipping ports and harbours would hopefully strangle supplies into the country, the main thrust of German intention had essentially been to bring British fighters into combat to destroy them and to demolish their ground support, to make way for a seaborne landing. The initiative was always with the German air forces; where to fight, tactics to be employed and choice of the most favourable weather conditions for such operations. When it became clear in the early days that Fighter Command was not committing massive numbers of fighters to shipping protection in the English Channel and coastal targets as they hoped, the *Luftwaffe* was compelled to extend its operations further inland, eventually to London, principally to get them to employ more. In doing this there was a price to be paid; selecting more distant targets reduced the effectiveness of the bombers' fighter escort; because of its poor fuel capacity the Bf.109 could remain in the combat area no more than ten minutes. Fear of running out of fuel and coming down in the Channel became a nightmare for German airmen.

The advantages for the British were manifest. Damaged aircraft and pilots shot down over land would very likely be repaired and returned to service. Most importantly, the British were supported by the raid reporting and fighter control system. Nowhere else was there in existence a fully integrated air defence system which incorporated fighters, AA guns, balloons, searchlights and a means whereby it could be efficiently directed against an enemy. German pilots were shocked when first encountering this; their organisation was greatly disadvantaged by having no similar close ground control; once their aircraft were in the air, they were, generally speaking, left to carry out a pre-ordained plan.

British fighter control, designed to help pilots find the enemy, retained a degree of flexibility. It was left to the fighter leader in the air, having first been vectored on to a raid, to decide how the final act of interception would be made. With the benefit of experience, some fighter leaders whenever possible put their formation into a tactically favourable position.[118] Then, using the Controller's raid information, i.e. number of aircraft, their height (all of which he read off from the raid plaque on the Sector Operations Room map), and the course he had advised them to fly, which gave an indication of where the enemy was estimated to be at that time, they made a quick mental calculation, taking into account the distance which would have been covered by the raiders, and flew their interception course. Other leaders went strictly 'by the book'. Having been an experienced fighter pilot in the First World War, Keith Park was well aware of the thought processes of those at the 'sharp end' of air fighting. Writing a paper on 'Fighter Attacks' in December 1938, when SASO at Bentley Priory, he wrote, 'Moreover it is essential that some latitude be left to the Leader in the air in order to effect surprise'.[119] At a conference he called to discuss tactics with his Sector Commanders and Squadron Leaders on 21 September 1940, he reaffirmed the principle of raid interception being effected in this manner. The record states,

> 'Squadron Commanders also agreed with the AOC's condemnation of R/T chatter and the numerous vectors indulged in by Sector Controllers, preferring to rely on their own searching to find the enemy, providing they were given some information as to his line of approach.'[20]

This did not give them licence to wander beyond the range of their ground control and Group boundaries. Park also stressed the need for Squadron Commanders to get in touch with each other before the day's operations to work out a general plan of campaign for attacking in pairs or three squadrons. It was decided that, if practical, the Commanders should meet or telephone each other after every engagement.

Selection of squadrons being sent to engage raids was now being practised on a more flexible basis. As before, the procedure was initiated by the Controller at Group Headquarters, who decided which unit at a Sector aerodrome should be sent to engage a specified raid, but if by looking at the up-to-the-minute situation developing on his own table map, a Sector Controller could see that, for whatever reason, the unit was unable to do so, he filled the gap using another of his own choosing. He was often in conversation with the Controllers of adjacent Sectors, deciding which of their patrolling squadrons was best placed to intercept, and the Group Controller was informed accordingly. On Group Operations maps, fighter positions over land were shown but the units not immediately identified; only at Sector Control, where they had the apparatus for tracking their own aircraft, could this be reliably established. The Observer Corps was of assistance but its greatest value to all Controllers was in tracking enemy formations.

Park's written tactical instructions were sent to Controllers with the intention of nullifying changes in German tactics, but implementing them was not always possible; often, especially in the early days, there was insufficient time for two squadrons to join up. How a fight actually developed was not always of the defender's choosing; equally the opposition sought combat when the time was right for them.

Raids had been varying in size from one or two aircraft to two or three successive waves made up of several hundred, and Fighter Command's forces were compelled to try to respond with whatever strength they had available. Radar was of considerable importance but it did not follow that the build-up over France showing on the tubes was about to be a single raid as some large formations later divided into smaller raids, or feint attacks when over the Channel. (The *Luftwaffe* allowed ten minutes for bombers to join up with the fighter escort.) The No. 11 Group Controllers waited for a more positive picture to emerge; in the meantime they prepared their forces. If the threat appeared to be a substantial one, some squadrons were sent off on standby patrol while others were brought to an advanced state of readiness on the ground.

The strength of No. 11 Group was not being conserved, as has sometimes been suggested; the delusion is likely to have been created by Park needing to spread his resources thinly to cover the airfields and vital points within the Group. This strategy also was to create a feeling among some German pilots that the RAF were reluctant to get into the air.

The onset of winter and deteriorating weather gave Goering the ideal excuse to call off major attacks during the daylight hours. This did not, it would seem, have an adverse effect on the German long-range bomber force which continued a ferocious nightly assault on London and provincial cities, but the heavy daylight raids were no more.

For the first time the aspirations of the German forces had not been fulfilled. In equipment, skill and courage the antagonists were well matched; leadership at the highest level was a different matter. The conflict, without doubt, had shown the dominance of single-seater fighters and it could well be argued that on the German side without the Bf.109 the battle would have been very short. It was soon established that all bombers needed to be protected from the British single-seater fighters; the Bf.110, long regarded by the *Luftwaffe* as the élite of its fighter force, had failed. The daylight battle, therefore, mostly became confined to within the short operational radius of the German single-seater. By careful study and with the benefit of experience, pilots on both sides established tactics which used the strengths of their aircraft to exploit the performance weaknesses of their opponent, e.g. the Hurricanes and Spitfires could out-turn the Bf.109. Statistically the Hurricane became the most successful British aircraft; most of the Fighter Command losses can be attributed to the Bf.109. Having incurred very heavy losses and a falling off of morale, the German fighter force began to fail and with it the ambitions of its leaders. The *Luftwaffe* had been narrowly defeated by a numerically inferior force which, allied to the other components of the air defence system, out-fought it.

Of the men at the 'sharp end' in the struggle, much has been said; they were at an age when physical and mental alertness is perhaps at its highest; a time when most able to withstand the strain and discomfort of prolonged periods of combat flying. Their youthful spirit and personal pride carried with it the desire to suppress any signs of fear in the closely-knit community of a squadron. Although many were desperately tired and stressed, they carried on; in their opponents' camp things were much the same. An important feature for Fighter Command was how well the part-timers of the fourteen Auxiliary Squadrons had become integrated into the battle line up; often bringing a refreshing approach to Service life. Dowding later wrote, 'No praise can be too high for the Auxiliaries, both as regards their keenness and efficiency in peace-time and their fighting record in war.'[121] A total commitment by ground staff had kept the squadrons in fighting shape; it was a matter of personal pride how quickly and efficiently a fighter returning from a sortie could be refuelled, re-armed and checked in preparation for the next call. All of this was done out on the airfield and much of it with the ever-present risk of being attacked. All staff working within the raid reporting and fighter control organisation were magnificent, often coping with the technical shortcomings of a still far from perfect system.

That an invasion was not attempted was not solely due to the efforts of Fighter Command. Coastal and Bomber Commands played a significant part, the latter destroying many barges and transports assembling in Channel ports. The constant menace from the Royal Navy dampened the ardour of many German leaders. Here was the biggest obstacle to any seaborne invasion force, and it was hoped by the Germans that their air power could overcome it once the RAF had been subdued.

Prime Minister Churchill exerted much influence on morale. On 4 July he circulated a specially prepared statement to people in important positions; it said,

'The Prime Minister expects all His Majesty's servants in high places to set an example of steadiness and resolution. They should check and refute expression of loose and ill digested opinion in their circle, or by their subordinates. They should not hesitate to report, or if necessary remove, any officers or officials who are found to be consciously exercising a disturbing or depressing influence, and whose talk is calculated to spread alarm and despondency.'[122]

Very few entertained the thought that they could possibly lose anyway.

Chapter 8

Big Wing – Night Defence

Ith the threat of invasion gone and the air over the British Isles secure, critical elements within the air force made their case. Discontent between No. 11 Group and No. 12 Group over the provision of reinforcements became a focal point of their attention.

On 29 September Keith Park wrote a highly critical letter to Fighter Command Headquarters on the conduct of No. 12 Group reinforcing squadrons, and in it made recommendations that in future procedures should be more strictly enforced when they were assisting his Group against mass raids. He had made his feelings known in an instruction to his Controllers a month earlier when emphasising the friendly co-operation afforded by No. 10 Group, commenting, 'They are always prepared to detail two to four squadrons. No. 12 Group, on the other hand, have not shown the same desire to co-operate by despatching their squadrons to the places requested.'[123] Because of this, two of the airfields they were asked to protect had been bombed. (See Appendix 1) His orders to No. 11 Group Controllers had been amended so that all future requests to No. 12 Group should be made through the Controller at the Command Operations Room, Bentley Priory. This procedure had not worked; in fact the situation had worsened. In the letter, Park again referred to the two earlier airfield bombings of late August and complained of No. 12 Group formations now roaming into Kent seemingly at will and creating confusion; the Observer Corps recorded them as unidentified and his Controllers were compelled to take steps to intercept them. Unnecessary air raid warnings were issued and gun operations rooms alerted. It was these latest developments, which were totally alien to the Fighter Command raid reporting and control system, which sparked off Park's anger. On the day prior to his letter, he recalled how the Command Controller at Bentley Priory had asked if he required assistance; it had been a relatively small attack and he said he could cope; shortly afterwards he was informed that there was a Wing of five squadrons in the Hornchurch area. During a recent attack he had enquired whether No. 12 Group were patrolling North Weald/Hornchurch and was told the

The house, in spite of its green camouflage, remains distinctive. 1944. *(Air Vice-Marshal "Sandy" Johnstone)*

The house, top left, with hutted offices in foreground. The airstrip can be seen top left. 1944. *(Air Vice-Marshal "Sandy" Johnstone)*

Air Vice-Marshal K. R. Park prepares to fly a Spitfire. During the Battle of Britain he often piloted a Hurricane to get a personal view of how the squadrons of No. 11 Group were performing. *(A.H.B. Crown Copyright)*

Lieutenant W. D. Swinerd R.N.V.R. when Naval Liaison Officer, 1940. *(W. D. Swinerd)*

Field Marshal Montgomery and Air Chief Marshal Sir Trafford Leigh-Mallory inspect R.A.F. Regiment 28 May 1943. Visit to tell officers about Africa. *(I.W.M.)*

Visit by Mrs Churchill to W.A.A.F. Dining Hall July 1943. Accompanied by Group Officer F. M. Lewis *(2nd Left)*, Squadron Officer N. M. Salmon *(right)*, Section Officer A. Causton *(left)*. *(I.W.M.)*

A.E.A.F. 1944

Operation personnel including:–
Group Captain "Sandy" Johnstone, Wing Commander Watson-Smythe, Colonel
Morrow U.S., Colonel Peterson U.S., Colonel McKinnon U.S., Wing Commander
McPherson, Colonel Bagby U.S., Squadron Leader Taylor (Historian), Group Captain
Sharp R.A.F., Pat Kingsley A.T.S., Margaret Walker, Wing Commander Paul. *(Air
Vice-Marshal "Sandy" Johnstone)*

Left: Air Marshal Sir Arthur Coningham, Commander 2nd Tactical Air Force. *Right*
Major-General L. H. Brereton, Commanding General 9th U.S.A.A.F. 9 February
1944. *(A.H.B. Crown Copyright)*

Left to right: Air Chief Marshal Sir Arthur Tedder, Deputy Supreme Allied Commander; Major-General Butler; General Dwight D. Eisenhower, Supreme Allied Commander; Air Chief Marshal Sir Trafford Leigh-Mallory, C.-in-C. Allied Expeditionary Air Force. Photographed on the steps at the East end of the Priory in 1944. *(Ministry of Defence)*

Prime Minister Churchill signing the visitors' book watched by King George VI and Sir Trafford Leigh-Mallory *(extreme right. Left)*, General Smuts. D-Day 6 June 1944. *(I.W.M.)*

Allied Air Chiefs at Bentley Priory on 10 February 1944.
Left to right: Air Marshal R. M. Hill, Major-General William O. Butler, Air Chief Marshal Sir Trafford Leigh-Mallory (C.-in-C. A.E.A.F.), Air Vice-Marshal H. Wigglesworth, Brigadier-General Aubrey C. Strickland, Major-General L. H. Brereton (seated in foreground) and, extreme right, Air Marshal Sir Arthur Coningham. Note arrows on map! *(A.H.B. Crown Copyright)*

Prime Minister Churchill and General Smuts visit Headquarters Fighter Command. D-Day 6 June 1944. *(I.W.M.)*

The Auster ("Puddlejumper") Communications aircraft turned over while landing at Bentley Priory. Its pilot, "Batchy" Atcherley, one of the R.A.F.'s most eccentric characters who was concerned with A.E.A.F. training, can be seen far left. He had put forward the idea of an airstrip but Leigh-Mallory rejected it. By chance, an American Colonel with whom Atcherley had struck up a conversation in a club in London, let it be known that he commanded an engineering outfit and his men were "rarin' to go". "Would you like a job?" Atcherley enquired. "Certainly would", replied the Colonel. The Americans arrived the following Sunday morning and by nightfall all the trees had been removed and the landing strip was in being. When learning of its existence, it is said Leigh-Mallory was not at all pleased. Most flying was done during the period leading up to D-Day. Ironically, Atcherley's was the only accident. *(R.A.F. Museum Photo dated 2.6.44)*

Air Marshal R. M. Hill, A.O.C.-in-C., A.D.G.B. *(A.H.B. Crown Copyright)*

Air Vice-Marshal Sir Walter Pretty *(Lady Betty Pretty)*

Air Chief Marshal Lord
Dowding of Bentley Priory,
G.C.B., G.C.V.O., C.M.G.
1960. *(Courier Newspapers)*

Inscription on Lord Dowding's
statue. *(Christopher Elliot)*

AIR CHIEF MARSHAL LORD DOWDING WAS
COMMANDER-IN-CHIEF OF FIGHTER COMMAND,
ROYAL AIR FORCE, FROM ITS FORMATION IN
1936 UNTIL NOVEMBER 1940. HE WAS THUS
RESPONSIBLE FOR THE PREPARATION FOR AND
THE CONDUCT OF THE BATTLE OF BRITAIN.

WITH REMARKABLE FORESIGHT, HE ENSURED
THE EQUIPMENT OF HIS COMMAND WITH
MONOPLANE FIGHTERS, THE HURRICANE AND
THE SPITFIRE. HE WAS AMONG THE FIRST
TO APPRECIATE THE VITAL IMPORTANCE OF
R.D.F. (RADAR) AND OF AN EFFECTIVE COMMAN
AND CONTROL SYSTEM FOR HIS SQUADRONS.
THEY WERE READY WHEN WAR CAME.

IN THE PRELIMINARY STAGES OF THAT WAR, HE
THOROUGHLY TRAINED HIS MINIMAL FORCES
AND CONSERVED THEM AGAINST STRONG
POLITICAL PRESSURES TO DISPERSE AND MISU:
THEM. HIS WISE AND PRUDENT JUDGEMENT
AND LEADERSHIP HELPED TO ENSURE VICTORY
AGAINST OVERWHELMING ODDS AND THUS
PREVENTED THE LOSS OF THE BATTLE OF
BRITAIN AND PROBABLY THE WHOLE WAR.

TO HIM, THE PEOPLE OF BRITAIN AND OF THE
FREE WORLD OWE LARGELY THE WAY OF LIFE
AND THE LIBERTIES THEY ENJOY TODAY.

squadrons were somewhere down near Canterbury. The basis of Park's complaint was that No. 12 Group fighters did not confine themselves to the requested area; he suggested that while waiting for their squadrons to form up in the air as a Wing, valuable time was being lost. In contrast, an arrangement existed with No. 10 Group whereby if the scale of attack on No. 11 Group was becoming too great they agreed to take on responsibility for protecting aircraft factories or Sector aerodromes in the West and Southwest of London, if they were threatened. Quintin Brand, AOC No. 10 Group, had agreed with him that it was more essential to get a small number of squadrons quickly to the point requested rather than delay their departure while joining up in Wings. Doing this would have caused their late arrival, after vital objectives were bombed; undoubtedly a bigger 'bag' of enemy aircraft would be secured, but it did not achieve the main aim which was 'to protect aircraft factories and other vital points from being bombed'.[124] The letter finished on a sarcastic note making comparisons between the different fighting conditions within the two Groups.

Dowding sent a copy of Park's letter to Leigh-Mallory at Watnall, No. 12 Group Headquarters, asking for comment. In his letter he recalled how Leigh-Mallory had spoken to him about the 'desire to meet the enemy always in the maximum strength' and agreed that this was, 'of course, a sound principle of war'. Leigh-Mallory answered saying that when Park's aerodromes were bombed these were the first occasions on which reinforcements were asked for. (See Appendix No. 1.) He agreed with proposals in Park's letter that his fighter formations would not be sent into No. 11 Group area unless requested and when they were, Park's Group would be kept informed of their approximate movements. Also that no change of patrol line would be made without first consulting the No. 11 Group Controller. He disagreed with two other proposals because of the lack of time afforded to squadrons to get into the position requested by No. 11 Group.

On the question of the time taken to get the Wing airborne, he asked that they first be ordered up when indications over the French coast showed a heavy build-up; this would give adequate time for it to be in an advantageous tactical position on patrol. The allegations of his patrols operating over East Kent he agreed were true; they had been there on the request of Fighter Command (presumably the Controller at Bentley Priory) and combats had spread far and wide. Other Wing deviations he dismissed as occurrences where the Wing, while patrolling Hornchurch, had seen large enemy formations to the south, and had moved to engage them. (Park had related how a formation leader from No. 12 Group told a member of his staff that they never patrolled North Weald/Hornchurch but went off down into the Dover area when asked to reinforce.) He argued that, given the earlier warning, his formation could be at 20,000 feet in the Hornchurch/Biggin Hill area before the enemy reached there; many raids that had penetrated to London in the last ten days would have been engaged before they got there. He concluded by saying that he felt most strongly that the main object must be to prevent the Germans getting to London.

'With Duxford placed as it is, a convenient distance to the North of London, out of the area over which the Germans are operating, I feel I have a more favourably situated base from which to operate for the protection of London.'[125]

From these exchanges, fundamental differences of approach can be seen. Keith Park's personal relations with Quintin Brand at No. 10 Group were such that a reasonable policy for reinforcing was agreed, but the same could not be said for Leigh-Mallory at No. 12 Group, with whom affairs were a lot less than cordial. Leigh-Mallory was also consumed by the idea of using large formations and was pushing to change the system.

Within their Group boundaries, Group Commanders were marshalling their forces and deciding tactics relative to the situation in their particular areas. This was their intended brief. The fighter control system was based on the principle of the resources allocated to each Group being sufficient to protect that area with some provision for limited reinforcing from neighbouring Groups if the need arose. To effect an interception, Operations Rooms knew where the enemy was from the processed radar and Observer Corps observations. As mentioned in Chapter 2, Sector Controllers knew where their airborne fighters were from the direction finding system. The range of an aircraft's High Frequency TR9D radio set, as already mentioned, was very poor (approximately 36 or 40 miles). To make interceptions over and beyond the coast, where it was originally planned they would occur, it was necessary to have forward relay stations to improve the speech transmission between aircraft and Sector Operations Rooms; there was also a tendency for the sets to 'drift off tune', one effect being that it impaired pilots' voice transmissions. Difficulty was experienced by Squadron Commanders communicating with each other in the air. The short range of the Direction Finding 'Pipsqueak' 'fixing' station system was equally inadequate, thus restricting the field in which a fighter could be effectively positioned. This disadvantage meant that, if it became necessary for units to move to reinforce an adjacent Group, unless the fighters stayed close to their particular Sector/Group boundary, they moved beyond radio range of their ground control. They were now in another Group/Sector organisation which could only direct fighters based within the confines of its own area, and which generally had only raid information showing on its operations rooms tables relative to that area. This meant that they could not receive effective ground support and unless they stayed in a pre-arranged patrol zone decided over the telephone between the two Groups, the controllers on the ground did not know where they were. If they wandered from that zone, they were classified as unidentified. A programme for the reintroduction of VHF radio was beginning to get underway and limited use of it, with its superior range, made it possible for some No. 12 Group fighter leaders to maintain speech contact with No. 12 Group while over No. 11 Group, but the conditions governing identification of their position and lack of raid information remained the same. Because of the difference of radio frequencies, No. 11 Group Controllers could not communicate with them. The technical restriction imposed by the High Frequency system greatly reduced flexibility within Fighter Command and was most likely a factor which influenced Park's policy of, in the main, confining the reinforcing units to patrol zones on the northeast and western fringes of his Group. There was in being a definite agreement with No. 12 Group that they were specifically to patrol Debden–North Weald or North Weald–Hornchurch lines when called upon. Using squadrons of one Group to reinforce another was not a simple affair.

A report by Leigh-Mallory, dated 17 September, on the recent exploits of the No. 12 Group Wing was passed to Group Captain H.G. Crowe, Deputy Director of Air Tactics at the Air Ministry, who commented favourably on the tactics employed. The file passed to Sholto Douglas who remarked,

'I have received a number of criticisms recently from several sources about the combined tactics employed by Fighter Command squadrons (particularly by those in No. 11 Group) to deal with the large enemy formations that come over by day. It is alleged that squadrons go up with no instructions as to how they are to work with them.'

He offered an example, how 'as a very obvious piece of tactics' in the First World War, a portion of the force looked after the high flying fighter escort to enable the remainder to have an uninterrupted attack on the bombers. It would appear that Keith Park's No. 11 Group detailed instructions to Controllers and Sector Commanders did not reach the uninformed 'several sources' cited by the DCAS as the basis for his comments. The criticisms were answered in a Minute by Group Captain Crowe, who now had looked into the matter in consultation with Fighter Command, but Douglas was still 'far from happy', feeling that there should be a Group combined tactical plan which allowed specific roles to Wings who would work out their own tactics on the lines of Leigh-Mallory's No. 12 Group Report.[126]

The matter was not allowed to rest there. Sir Cyril Newall, CAS, called a conference to be held in his room at the Air Ministry, on 17 October to discuss Major Day Tactics in the Fighter Force. Director of Home Operations at the Air Ministry, Donald Stevenson, assembled the agenda, together with introductory notes and an Air Staff note on the operation of fighter Wings; this was distributed to those invited to attend, who were: Air Marshals Sir Charles Portal and Sir Phillip Joubert de la Ferté; Air Chief Marshal Sir Hugh Dowding; Air Vice-Marshals W. Sholto Douglas, K.R. Park, Sir Quintin Brand, T.L. Leigh-Mallory; Air Commodores J.C. Slessor, D.F. Stevenson, O.G.W.G. Lywood; Group Captain H.G. Crowe; Squadron Leader D.R.S. Bader and Mister J.S. Orme (Secretary). Referring to the air battles between 8 August and 10 September, the appended introductory notes criticised Keith Park's report of that period saying it did not state how his units were sent into battle, singly, in pairs or larger formations. (This was clearly an error; the report states that pairs of squadrons were used and on some occasions a Wing of two Spitfire squadrons engaged the enemy fighter escort while a similar Wing of Hurricanes engaged the bombers.)[127] The notes went on to refer to the report on five recent No. 12 Group Wing operations provided by Leigh-Mallory, and inferred that the lessons learned should be 'applied generally to enable the fighter defence to operate at maximum efficiency'. (The claims made for the destruction of German aircraft by the Wing, 105 plus 40 probables against the loss of 14 fighters, have since been found to be excessive. Earlier, Air Vice-Marshal Evill in a letter to the Under Secretary of State had told him the figures should be 'regarded only as approximate'. He also commented on how the figures had not improved when the Wing was expanded from three to five squadrons although British losses had. He was 'of the opinion that the AOC No. 12 Group is working on the right lines in organising his operations in strength'.[128] 'His operations' qualified it as being a particular No. 12 Group tactic. The figures Park later quoted when supporting the tactics of his Group were also inaccurate; on 27 September, 102 destroyed, 28 probables for a loss of 15 pilots, for 30 September, 31 destroyed, 20 probables for a loss of 2 pilots.) It was accepted, however, that in the current situation, where raids were made up of fighters and fighter-bombers, the tactics being used were adequate. The agenda was centred almost entirely on the employment of Wings. The appended notes, provided by the Air Staff, which were supposedly a basis for discussion, from which major tactical requirements to meet future mass attacks could be evolved, were in essence markedly critical of the earlier handling of No. 11 Group's Squadrons and an endorsement of No. 12 Group Wing methods.[129] Park reacted angrily, and wrote questioning the validity of their argument, saying the Air Staff had based their recommendations on only the five instances recorded by Leigh-Mallory when his Wing was called upon to reinforce his Group. On the other hand in No. 11 Group three-squadron Wings had been in use for five months when time, space and weather conditions made them practical. By showing comparative figures for the last big attack by the German bomber forces, Park made a favourable comparison between his No. 11 and No. 12 Group records of that day. He laid emphasis on how the geographical situation of his Group did not often allow time to assemble, dispatch and engage the enemy with large Wing formations

> 'before the bomber raids have reached vital objectives' and went on, 'I may be wrong in imagining that our primary task is to protect London, aircraft factories and Sector Aerodromes against enemy bombers, and not merely to secure a maximum bag of enemy aircraft after they have done their fiendish damage.'[130]

Enclosed with his letter to Stevenson, Park sent copies of the tactical orders for No. 11 Group Wing operations which he had given earlier to his Sector Commanders and he asked that they be circulated to conference members beforehand. These effectively answered the Air Staff's criticism and explained why aircraft had been sent to intercept large formations in small numbers and why there had not always been successful co-ordination between the units.

Sholto Douglas presided over the conference in the absence of the CAS, Sir Cyril Newall, who was indisposed. The Minutes record how he outlined three propositions, all of which were couched in terms unlikely to arouse disagreement. They were: to outnumber the enemy; when attacking to have a co-ordinated plan of action (one part of the fighter force to engage enemy fighter escort while the remainder dealt with the bombers) and, if possible, the top layer of the British fighter formation should have a height advantage over the enemy's. This being the ideal, Douglas pointed out it was obviously not always possible to attain this, due to the time factor or the necessity of engaging the enemy before he reached some vital objective, 'and in such cases there might not be time either to collect a superior force or to obtain superior height'. Park offered the view that Wing operations were not always best in countering large formations and it should not be laid down as a general principle; factors of time, distance and cloud were often involved with No. 11 Group operations. He felt the satisfactory results obtained by No. 12 Group had been achieved under ideal conditions when the enemy had already been weakened by the defences in No. 11 Group. Using formations of one or two squadrons, his Group recently obtained results against bombers coming in which compared favourably with those of No. 12 Group Wings. Dowding remarked on the difficulties of deciding which of the incoming raids was the main one; the great problem being how to obtain early knowledge of this. Park related how, during the present 'tip and run' raids, he was employing the reconnaissance Spitfire section for information, supported by a standing patrol by a strong Spitfire squadron which was sent up to 35,000 feet, to cover other climbing units, when first indication came from radar. Leigh-Mallory said he would welcome more opportunities of using the Duxford Wing to help No. 11 Group; he could get a Wing of five squadrons into the air in six minutes and over Hornchurch at 20,000 feet in twenty-five minutes. He added, 'If this type of counter-attack intercepted only once in ten operations, it would be worth it.' After discussion, it was generally agreed that additional fighter support would be an advantage. Squadron Leader Bader from No. 12 Group, a surprise inclusion to the conference (no one of equivalent rank who was experienced in No. 11 Group fighter combat was present), said from his practical experience that time was the essence of the problem; given sufficient warning a large number of fighters could be brought into position and would get effective results. Air Marshal Sir Charles Portal expressed concern about whether concentration of a Wing might adversely affect the efficiency of a Group's responsibility to defend its own area; Leigh-Mallory was satisfied that it would not be incompatible with his general responsibility as Group Commander.

Sholto Douglas summarised the views of the meeting as,

> 'The employment of a large mass of fighters had great advantages, though it was not necessarily the complete solution to the problem of interception. In No. 11 Group, where the enemy was very close at hand, both the methods described by AOC No. 11 Group and those of AOC No. 12 Group could, on occasion, be used, with forces from the two Groups co-operating.'[131]

Dowding said he would arrange for No. 12 Group Wings to participate freely in suitable operations over No. 11 Group area and he would be able to resolve complications of control. It was agreed, where possible, to use larger formations. Dowding, replying to a question from Stevenson, told him co-operation of this kind could in the present circumstances hardly be employed generally throughout the Command as similar conditions seldom arose elsewhere. With reference to the formal agenda, the Minutes of the meeting record, when suitable, Wings of three squadrons should be employed against large formations and, if available, 'without detriment to other commitments' larger formations than Wings should be used; on occasions two Wings together.* Squadrons of a Wing should be based in the same Sector and controlled by the Sector Commander. When the enemy operated in mass formations, the fighter leader could dispense with Sector control and, if given information about enemy movements, he should be responsible for leading his formation to the battle. This proposal came from the Air Staff who realised that squadrons using HF radio would pass quickly out of R/T range of their Sectors. The reasoning was that if the weather was clear enough for the *Luftwaffe* to mount a mass attack, such visibility would be sufficient for the formation to be seen from a distance, thus making ground control unnecessary. Not surprisingly, the Minutes of the meeting were of special interest to Park whose Group had been the target for what he termed 'misinformed criticism' in the Air Staff's note sent out with the Agenda. When J.S. Orme, the Secretary, sent a draft copy to him, he wrote objecting to certain omissions and urgently requested a number of amendments he had written on a piece of paper, which he enclosed, should be included. These were taken from the prepared notes he had used at the conference and from which he had refuted the criticism by the Air Staff. In addition, his amendments recorded how Douglas, Portal and Dowding had agreed that he had followed the correct policy and must continue this against future mass attacks by bombers. He again criticised the manner in which the No. 12 Group Wing operated when over his Group area and made comparisons between the two reinforcing Groups. It would appear from Park's amendments the conference had not been as straightforward as the Minutes suggest, and much antagonism had been engendered beforehand. Other amendments were asked for by Dowding, Brand and Leigh-Mallory. Park's amendment to the Minutes was rejected after consultations with Stevenson and Douglas 'in view of its length'.

---

* This they referred to as a 'Balbo', named after the Italian Italo Balbo who earlier established a reputation for leading large formations of aircraft on long distance flights.

At the end of the conference, Dowding had been asked to report on the position of night interception. He spoke on the problems with serviceability of the AI radar sets and the Beaufighter, but he was satisfied the system was sound in principle. Both Douglas and Stevenson made a point about maintaining civilian morale in London in the face of continued attack during the period in which the system outlined by the C-in-C was being improved. They suggested a temporary Wing of two Defiant and two Hurrricane Squadrons should be formed to specialise in nightfighting; in the style of the 1914–18 War. Dowding argued that continual experiments had been made on this basis and so far the old methods had not proved effective. He was not averse to Defiants being used but 'with great reluctance' he would agree to the diversion of a Hurricane Squadron from day to night work. A preliminary draft of a scheme, prepared by Douglas and Stevenson, was handed to the C-in-C who undertook to examine it.

The following afternoon, Dowding attended another conference at the Air Ministry; Douglas was again Chairman. He was shown a Minute of the Chief of the Air Staff consequent upon a discussion he had had with the Prime Minister. This Minute recorded a decision to specialise three Hurricane Squadrons in nightfighting.* Dowding was strongly opposed to this, regarding it as a waste of dayfighting squadrons. Douglas thought greater success than in the past would be achieved by Hurricane Squadrons which specialised entirely in nightfighting, particularly when the searchlights were fitted with a new radar apparatus. (Dowding had already indicated that this might be the case when this equipment was introduced.)[132]

Behind the scenes further pressure was building up on the leadership of Fighter Command, originating from the Air Ministry and political sources. Already, during the Battle of Britain on 28 August, Sholto Douglas had written to CAS, expressing the view that 'we ought to tackle this night flying problem rather more vigorously than at present'. He complained that the C-in-C Fighter Command was 'pinning his faith almost entirely on the Beaufighter and AI' radar', and suggested that while teething troubles with the new aircraft and its equipment were being sorted out, in the interim period, which he correctly forecast as being a time when things were likely to be extremely critical, certain measures should be taken to

---

* When Leigh-Mallory later took over Fighter Command, he abandoned this practice. His view was that when pilots in single-seater aircraft had been sent up on dark nights, they had to 'spend all their time flying their aeroplanes, and their chances of ever seeing an enemy aircraft were reduced to practically nil'.[133]

bolster the nightfighter force. Dowding had agreed to redirect the Defiant Squadrons but Douglas wanted at least one of Hurricanes to specialise. There was criticism in his letter of the number of non-radar-equipped Blenheim fighters which were being put up at night by Dowding.

'During the last three nights he has put up between 40 and 50 fighters over the whole of England . . . He should, I suggest, be prepared to put up three or four times the number of fighter sorties at night than he has been in the habit of doing.'

Douglas wanted 'fighter' nights and 'gun' nights over London. On occasions when a thin layer of cloud was present at 5,000 feet, aircraft were not illuminated, making Anti-Aircraft gunnery ineffective; on the other hand, if clusters of lights followed the aircraft using sound location, a fighter should be able to see from above its silhouetted shape against the background of illuminated cloud.[134]

Another of Douglas's suggestions was to have the turrets in Blenheims removed to decrease drag and improve its speed by, he estimated, 15 miles per hour. Given Newall's approval, Douglas wished to draft an Air Council letter to Dowding embodying his proposals and formulating an instruction.

Although Hitler decided to postpone the invasion on 17 September, preparations continued. On 12 October he directed that from then on preparations should be continued solely for the purpose of maintaining political and military pressure on England.[135] Measures for a later invasion in the Spring or early summer of 1941 were to be adopted in the likelihood of a reconsideration at that time. Hitler decided to dissipate invasion forces quietly while creating the illusion that they were preparing for an attack on a broad front. Some Enigma decrypts coming from Bletchley Park gave indications of preparation continuing. One rather curious aspect; it would seem that Dowding had not been privy to this important source of intelligence information and had perhaps been receiving some benefit from it only in a filtered form via the Air Ministry. It was at this time Churchill happened upon what he thought was the unnecessarily large circulation of the decrypts and took steps to have it reduced; the Air Ministry, he noted, was the worst offender. Some people were to be struck off the list; others, namely Dowding, C-in-C Fighter Command, Peirse, C-in-C Bomber Command, the First Lord of the Admiralty and the Secretary of State for War, were to be included.[136]

In June 1940, Dr R.V. Jones, a young scientist working for British Scientific Intelligence, had successfully shown that the German Air Force was using accurately laid radio beams over Britain along which their aircraft could navigate and bomb selected targets with great precision; discovery of this, to say the least, came as a great shock, and Joubert de la Ferté was appointed by the Secretary of State, Sir Archibald Sinclair to co-ordinate and direct countermeasures.

In the middle of July, Churchill had written to Dowding asking him to produce a paper on the comparative advantages of summer and winter air fighting. Having seen how ruthless Hitler had been with other countries, Dowding was surprised that attacks by the German Air Force had been restricted to fair military and industrial targets; he was in no doubt that this was the policy. On occasions, it had been difficult to assess what the objective was, but bombs going astray was most likely due to effectiveness of the black-out and difficulty of bomb-aiming at night. He commented,

'The navigation of German bombers at night and in bad weather has been extraordinarily accurate, and there is no doubt that he (Hitler) could lay large areas of our big towns in ruins at any time if he chose to do so.'

He supposed that it was only that the morale effect of British attacks on the people of Western Germany had been such that he dare not risk the effect on his own nation of a retaliatory bombing of Berlin.[137] At this time, their night attacks were small-scale and undertaken by single or small formations of aircraft. There was already a realisation that British bombers could not operate over Germany during the hours of daylight without incurring heavy losses; no long-range escort fighter existed. Dowding's assessment of the effect of seasonal changes was that long winter nights would be a distinct advantage to the British by allowing them to fly the long journey into Germany and back under cover of darkness. On the other hand, it would be equally so for the other side; recognising the inadequacy of British night defences, long nights allowed the Germans to fly over the country for longer periods with comparative impunity. (This proved to be of great benefit to the *Luftwaffe*. The shorter flying distance from airfields in France made it possible for greater bomb loads to be carried and two sorties flown each night.) He remarked on how, on many winter nights, the presence of mist and low cloud made it impossible for any single-seater fighters to operate, whereas on many such nights continental airfields remained clear, allowing bombers, using their navigational methods, to proceed unmolested. If they resorted to indiscriminate bombing of populous areas, the defences would be compelled to interfere with the accuracy of their navigation (the radio beacons and beams) by wholesale 'jamming'. This would initiate a 'jamming' competition and the C-in-C was surprised that this had not already been happening. He had imagined that this would have started long ago with each country 'jamming' its opponent's broadcast until eventually the ether would be filled by a continuous roar preventing radio communications on any wavelength. He said,

'That this has not happened is, I think, due to the conviction of each country that its own radio methods are better than those of the enemy and, therefore, no-one will start a "jamming" competition.'* When related to radar, this situation was not to last. In September, having given up attempts to destroy radar stations by bombing, the Germans resorted to 'jamming'. This increased in October and a number of interference reports were sent to Bentley Priory from stations throughout the chain. Having foreseen this possibility, anti-jamming devices were already installed on the equipment which minimised its effects and reduced the interference to little more than nuisance value.[1] Such attempts to neutralise the Coastal Radar were not expected to cause total failure of the system; it was estimated that 320 jammer transmitters would be required to do this.[2] The Royal Navy began 'jamming' German radar from Dover in late 1940.

Later, clouds of foil strips dropped from aircraft effectively smothered German Radar transmissions. This simple form of countermeasure had been recognised by both sides before the outbreak of hostilities but each recoiled from using it for fear that their opponent, assuming they had not thought of the idea, would quickly copy it and retaliate.

The final part of Dowding's paper to Churchill clearly showed a picture of the inadequacy of night air defences. The new Beaufighter was having many problems and its development programme was so far behind that Dowding had doubts whether it would ever become an effective nightfighter; AI radar, with the big radio manufacturing companies now becoming involved, was making remarkable progress, making it reasonably certain that a practical night interception technique could be developed in the near future.[141] As yet, nowhere in the world had such a technique been developed. The support given by the manufacturers

---

* The Air Ministry view was quite the reverse. Wing Commander E.B. Addison had written in April how they had no desire to start a jamming war, saying 'We have reason to believe that should such a war commence, we might find ourselves inferior in the means of waging it.'[140]

was invaluable; for example, because the RAF was short of technicians, Cossors sent their own engineers to help with installing sets in aircraft. (Work continued on the manufacture of sets at their Highbury, North London, workshop throughout the bombing of London.)

At the end of October, the Prime Minister sent Professor Lindemann Dowding's paper asking, 'Pray comment on this deeply interesting paper written more than three months ago. Mark what has proved fact and what has failed'. Interpreting the word 'wholesale' as meaning indiscriminate, Lindemann criticised Dowding's suggestion that the German radio beams could be nullified by 'wholesale' jamming, pointing out that the frequencies being used by the Germans should be identified and dealt with individually, he explained how this was now being effected. He was sceptical about whether AI in its current form would ever be very effective.

He did not accept that the German bombers could lay large areas of big towns in ruins any time they chose to do so, nor that they were only deterred by fear of reprisals. (By this time the Germans had clearly shown a lack of concern about reprisals; possibly they had studied results of inaccurate British bombing. On the night of 15 November, a few nights after Lindemann's note, the Germans devastated Coventry using the beam technique, when radio countermeasures failed.) The Professor concluded his appraisal of the Dowding paper by returning to his usual theme of using aerial mines and minefields, and suggesting it as being 'the best hope for today'. This, he suggested, could be used until a short wave AI set could be developed some time in the future.

Capitalising on the clever investigative work started in June by Dr R.V. Jones during which time he revealed the presence of the German navigation beams, a tiny section had been set up at Bentley Priory under Wing Commander R.S. Blucke, the most experienced RAF pilot in the use of radio beam flying. From a small office next to the Filter Room, he co-ordinated investigations into searching for the beams, identifying their frequencies and directional bearings. Each night aircraft took off to seek out and report on German radio transmissions. Some of the high masts of CH Radar Stations were also equipped with receivers. A programme for the rapid development of radio countermeasures was already in being. Headquarters No. 80 (Signals) Wing was formed at Radlett on 7 October under Wing Commander E.B. Addison; earlier, in July, he had formed a small section at the Air Ministry to advise on the form of such countermeasures. The technical development of countermeasure devices was put in the care of Doctor Robert Cockburn of the Telecommunications Research Establishment at Swanage.

With concern continuing over the safety of his aircraft factories, Lord Beaverbrook, at the Ministry of Aircraft Production, was pressing for more protection, plaguing Archibald Sinclair by telephone and letter suggesting the Air Staff should do something about it. In answer, Sinclair wrote, with a tinge of sarcasm, 'It is not as you suggest a job for the Air Staff but for your devoted friend the C.-in-C. Fighter Command.' Beaverbrook's letters were passed to Dowding requesting him to do all he could to meet Beaverbrook's requirements. He answered in a comprehensive letter to Sinclair with explanations about what could and could not be achieved with the already over-stretched resources. Copies were sent to Beaverbrook and Sholto Douglas. The latter pointed out the

'C-in-C. is a free agent in the deployment of all components of the defence. He has been given a Directif from the Chief of the Air Staff, endorsed by the Chiefs of Staff to consider the protection of the aircraft industry as his task of first importance'.[142]

Complaints from the Ministry of Aircraft Production about the provision of factory protection continued; the industry was having a hard time. Donald Stevenson, Director of Home Operations at the Air Ministry, repeated Sholto Douglas' remarks in a Minute to Sinclair on 10 December and added,

'The fighter force is already deployed to protect the aircraft industry most effectively. Alterations in the dispositions of Fighter Squadrons could only reduce the efficiency of the defence'.[143]

Nine days after the 17 October conference on Major Day Tactics, the Secretary of State for Air, Archibald Sinclair, visited Duxford in No. 12 Group and listened to complaints about the continuing lack of commitment by No. 11 Group in using the resident Wing. The following week, Harold Balfour, the Parliamentary Under-Secretary of State for Air, a pilot of the First World War, was asked by Sinclair to visit the airfield ostensibly to confirm his own conclusions. Balfour sent his report on 2 November which said how the conflict of operational views was felt acutely by the Duxford units and it was now a personal issue with the pilots who felt resentment against No. 11 Group and its AOC, also with the Air Ministry for allowing matters to develop and continue. They were at the disposal of No. 11 Group and were never called upon to function according to their practised tactics of Wing formation until too late; they were being denied the opportunity of shooting down Germans. They told him the system could be altered but for the resistance of No. 11 Group who objected to their poaching on their territory and were jealous of the Wing formation being likely to shoot down No. 11 Group Germans. They 'knew about the 17 October conference' (this was not altogether surprising as Douglas Bader, their Wing Commander, was there) but the decision of the conference did not seem to have resulted in positive action. (This was incorrect; detailed arrangements between the Groups for the use and control of the Wing were in being. No. 11 Group Controllers were given Park's instructions on 26 October.)[144] Bader apparently had told Balfour of how his Flight Commanders had personal friends in the other Group and they reported how morale was being affected with pilots having to meet enemy forces when greatly outnumbered.

The Adjutant of Bader's Squadron was Flying Officer Peter Macdonald, Conservative MP for the Isle of Wight, who was openly critical of Dowding. He asked Balfour to arrange a meeting for him with Churchill, but Balfour refused; Macdonald did, however, get to see the Prime Minister to air his views.[145]*

A copy of Balfour's report was sent to Sholto Douglas at the Air Ministry and the following day, 3 November, he passed it to Dowding with a critical letter, the substance of which was that the differences between the two Groups had not yet been resolved and it was leading to bitterness between not only the Group Commanders but the Squadrons with the Groups. He wrote, 'This obviously cannot be allowed to go on, and I think that it is for you to put the matter right by an authoritative statement of your views.' He said he was inclined to support Leigh-Mallory's point of view and outlined what everyone had already agreed as being an ideal situation, i.e. outnumber the enemy, the superior numbers of aircraft should have a co-ordinated plan of action and the top layer of fighters to have height advantage over the enemy, etc. This looked perfect on paper especially if the resources to do it were available; the reality was somewhat different. Douglas admitted the time factor frequently negated this when applied to No. 11 Group 'since they have to intercept and attack the enemy before he reaches certain fixed objectives'. He wrote of how he saw every reason to encourage No. 12 Group in their efforts to intercept the enemy on their way home even if they could not arrive in time to attack

---

* Dowding was aware of his political interference. Earlier, in a letter of 9 March 1940 to Stevenson, he wrote about confidentiality, 'You may remember that the settled policy of the Air Ministry had recently to be reversed owing to communications which passed between the Secretary of State and the Adjutant of No. 242 Squadron, who was a Member of Parliament'.[146]

before their objective was reached. This was the complete antithesis of the defence strategy; the squadrons were expected to be in position to prevent the destruction of aircraft factories and airfields. Proposals put forward by Balfour suggesting ways in which No. 12 Group could obtain earlier knowledge of enemy activity via Observer Corps Centres he thought were reasonable. Park, he thought, still had a 'subconscious aversion to another Group coming down and fighting in his area'. He asked that Dowding should go into the whole matter again and settle the question by giving the Groups an authoritative statement of his views.[147]

Dowding passed the Balfour and Douglas correspondence to Evill, his Senior Staff Officer at Bentley Priory, asking for comment. His investigation showed that No. 11 Group were not being obstructive in the transfer of raid information to No. 12 Group, and on the available information, the 'Duxford Wing was called upon with great promptitude'. To get it into action there was now a tendency by No. 11 Group to call for this reinforcement on occasions when it was not absolutely certain that they could be actively employed. Evill then gave his opinion of the current situation on which Balfour's report was founded:

'No one will deny the advantages of a 3, 4 or 5 Squadron Wing against a determined enemy attack whether it be large or comparatively small providing it can bring the enemy to action. A month ago the Duxford Wing, used against strong enemy attacks which took time in their building up over the Gris Nez area, and which came in with determination to reach their objective, would have been very effective. Now, however, against loosely formed high altitude Fighter sweeps there is less time for the Wing to come into action and less for it to bite on when it gets there. The Wing absorbs the energies of 4 or 5 Squadrons which have to be kept concentrated and at Readiness if there is to be any hope of their operating successfully. Even so, it does seem that the time taken to form up is too slow for the present phase of tactics.'

'There are, incidentally, other disadvantages to this Wing operation at the moment. It absorbs 4 or 5 Squadrons out of a very weak Group and thus diverts them from the normal tasks of No. 12 Group, which are the defence of its own area including some highly important industrial districts.'

He wrote of how on 29 October the Wing was operating between 1600 and 1700 hours;

'it was certainly not at Readiness again when the enemy attack on East Anglian aerodromes commenced at 1750 hours. I am inclined to the conclusion that for the moment in the present phase, the use of the Duxford Wing is a mis-employment of a valuable element of our very limited strength. I think that Park was slow to take advantage of the possibilities of this Wing when they were first put forward by No. 12 Group at a time when its operations might have been very valuable,* but for the moment it is probably no longer an economical or effective use of 5 squadrons. There is always a possibility, even now, that the Wing might, with luck, achieve a resounding success, but in this phase I think the odds are slightly against that. It would therefore seem to me reasonable to set a normal limit to the size of the Wing of no more than 3 Squadrons, generally less, according to weather and other indications. But we should do everything possible to arrange our communications so that the full Wing can at any time be brought back into use to the fullest possible advantage.'[148]

This assessment by Evill formed the basis of Dowding's detailed reply to Douglas. In fact, a very high percentage of the reply was written verbatim from Evill's work, including the passage referring to Park being slow to take advantage of the possibilities the Wing idea offered at the time. He added a rebuke to Balfour for listening to the accusations of a junior officer against the AOC of another Group and putting it on paper, hoping the officer would not get into trouble. Balfour, he wrote,

' "ought to have known better". A good deal of ill feeling which has been engendered in the controversy has been directly due to young Bader, who, whatever his other merits, suffers from overdevelopment of the critical faculty.'

Two things were clear to the C-in-C; the Command should take control of such operations when they became necessary and that 'the continuous employment of this Wing of 5 Squadrons cannot be justified in existing circumstances'. Leigh-Mallory, he thought, had many commitments of his own and should 'keep his eye in the boat more'. He informed Douglas of a growing tendency by the enemy to increase its frequency and weight of attacks in the north and west, although it was perfectly obvious he

---

* This criticism appears to be a little harsh. The No. 12 Group Wing was not conceived until 7 September; also at that time there was no means by which No. 11 Group could extend ground control to it.

was attempting to weaken the London defences. He noted the intensity of day attacks on London had fallen off recently and he might soon be compelled to make some redistribution of his force. 'This might give an opportunity of moving young Bader to another Station where he would be kept in better control.' His amazing gallantry, he said, would protect him from disciplinary action if it could be possibly avoided. (There was much concern in high places that the Squadron Leader should not be disciplined.) This reply was sent to Douglas on 6 November. The views of the C-in-C and his SASO, Evill, were as one. The 'authoritative view' asked for by Douglas amounted to a rejection of his personal view; indeed it had provoked a counter-productive response; there was now a strong possibility of the 'Big Wing' concept becoming dormant, it would at best become much restricted, and one of its principal advocates (Bader) transferred to another Station.

Dowding's Operational Instructions issued on 13 November were designed to meet the requirement of the current situation with a view to using the Wing formation only when it was warranted. They stressed the importance of economy in its use being observed, stating No. 12 Group had its own ample responsibilities and so No. 11 Group should take care of itself and call for reinforcements only in special circumstances. These were listed:

'(i)   Enemy attacks that are so strong or so repeated as to approach the limit of No. 11 Group's resources.
'(ii) Dangerously heavy bombing attacks on specially vulnerable points.
'(iii) Enemy attacks directed North of the Thames, particularly when accompanied by other attacks elsewhere in the Group.
'(iv) Special opportunities for the surprise and destruction of enemy formations.'

The reinforcements should, as far as possible, be employed in an area adjacent to No. 12 Group boundary and should have a limited objective, and these tasks should be stated. They should be provided in the strength and at the time and place requested and, for them to do this, adequate notice should be given by No. 11 Group. Tactical methods adopted were to be decided by No. 12 Group, subject to the allotted task being adequately performed. Dowding emphasised the importance of a balance being kept between seizing every opportunity for defeating attacks in the southeast while maintaining strength, and preparation for the defence of No. 12 Group area. He went on, 'No unnecessary strength of Squadrons should be kept at Readiness in No. 12 Group for reinforcement. This strength must be judged in relation to the enemy's tactics'. There was no objection to occasionally employing a large reinforcing formation for the purpose of surprising the enemy if an opportunity arose, or for practice. 'Groups must always be prepared to organise this reinforcement in strength if any change in enemy tactics makes this appropriate.'

Procedure for reinforcing was: Unless further instructions from Command were issued, No. 12 Group reinforcements would not be employed south of the Thames or South Bank of the Thames Estuary. No. 11 Group, working through the Command Controller at Bentley Priory, should give details of what they required and maximum notice given with a preliminary warning if possible. In fine weather, when the enemy was active, No. 12 Group should have two squadrons at 15 minutes notice and their Controller should advise the Controller at Bentley Priory daily at 1000 hours what state they were maintaining. Any greater strength would require a prior arrangement. If a lower degree of readiness were forced on them, No. 12 Group should inform No. 11 Group through the Command Controller; any problems of provision would be passed to the Duty Air Commodore at Bentley Priory for decision. Control of the reinforcing units would be conducted from Duxford and all available Radar information to the latitude of Dungeness–Gris Nez given to them simultaneously with No. 11 Group. (They were already receiving this.) For overland information Duxford would soon be put on the Bromley and Maidstone Observer Corps Centre's teleprinter circuits;* in the meantime, Bromley would pass information of all plots in their area North of the Thames, to Duxford, via Colchester. No. 11 Group were required to tell No. 12 Group all information about raids in their area likely to need their attention.[149] In all a comprehensive plan of action. Radio control of the Squadrons of the Wing would be settled on Duxford Sector Station; this was the nearest No. 12 Group Operations Room to the No. 11 Group boundary. By the middle of November some units, including those participating in Wing operations, had re-equipped with VHF radio which greatly improved ground/air communication. This made it possible for the Direction Finding 'Fixer' stations within the Group to receive 'Pipsqueak' signals when the aircraft were over No. 11 Group area and ascertain their positions.

Group Captain 'Paddy' O'Neil, with responsibility for Air Training at Fighter Command was asked to comment on the draft of a new Air

---

* Observer Corps plots were now being passed by teleprinter to plotters in Group and Sector Operations Rooms.

Fighting Committee Paper produced by Group Captain A.G. Crowe, three days after he had attended the 17 October conference on day tactics and on which his draft appears to have been based. He remarked that it did

'not show sufficiently clearly that the enemy's tactics are continually changing and evolving as we manage successfully to deal with each phase . . . One of the difficulties with these papers at the present time, when tactics are changing so rapidly, is that they are out of date almost before issue'.[150]

Even as 'Paddy' O'Neil was studying Crowe's Paper, tactics were changing. Park had noticed that there was almost continuous activity around the French coast during the latter part of the day and he issued instructions for a Wing of three squadrons to be sent on an offensive sweep through the Dover Straits at this time of the day. At Bentley Priory this indication of quiet confidence was well received.

During the past four months, air fighting had been concentrated in the southeast, the area facing the German-occupied Channel coast. To intercept a raid needed a quick response and a degree of guesswork to decide whether the incoming formation was a feint to draw off the fighters or the main threat; on occasions this too divided into smaller groups which made their way to the targets. Park's brief, complying with the Air Ministry September 1939 Directif to Fighter Command, was to give priority to protection of the aircraft industry, his instructions to No. 11 Group Controllers clearly show that this was seldom far from his mind; the need to preserve his airfields, aircraft and men, out of necessity, soon became of equal standing. To fulfil his commitments required a spread of No. 11 Group resources in depth, and that the squadrons should be disciplined and maintained at a high state of preparation when action was imminent, or that they should be sent up on patrol ready to be directed on to a raid as part of the overall tactical plan.

Of the other Groups, No. 10 to the west was comparatively under strength; it did not become operational until 8 July 1940, after the occupation of France, and as such was fully stretched. No. 12 Group, covering the industrial Midlands, was given adequate means to do it; this area had earlier been thought to be at most risk from long-range bombers coming in directly from Germany prior to the fall of France. However, it would appear that there was only one occasion when the Group was called upon to intercept a large formation (15 August 1940), and the main occupation during daylight was seeking out reconnaissance aircraft, intercepting single or small numbers of aircraft and flying shipping protection patrols, all of which required less than full squadron strength. In the far north, No. 13 Group were similarly occupied and kept at a high state of preparedness, as evidence by them being able to send five squadrons at full strength to intercept the 15 August raid in the Newcastle area.

For No. 12 Group, sharing a boundary with No. 11 Group, it was a frustrating period. While their neighbour was fighting a pitched battle, they, in the main, stood guard and supplied reserves. In this fertile soil of comparative inactivity the seeds of discontent grew and were nurtured by highly placed ambitious men furthering their own ideas.

Douglas Bader, since criticised by some for his part in what became known as the Big Wing controversy, was a leader of quality and, like most leaders, was eager to get into contact with the enemy and was not short of ideas. The indications are, however, that he did not have a thorough understanding of the raid reporting and fighter control system. (His biographer later wrote of how he thought all the technical systems were to hand at Bentley Priory and there was no valid reason why the C-in-C could not have marshalled and conducted the defence from there).[151] There is also a possibility that he was not entirely aware of the confusion he was creating when wandering from the Wing's given patrol area over No. 11 Group; his Sector Controller most certainly did. There was a broad consensus of opinion among Fighter Command leaders that, given the right circumstances; namely, against strong formations; the Wing tactic was worthwhile. Park's main grievance was that it took too long to assemble in the air and so arrived late on patrol; Bader was aware of the time factor and asking for his squadrons to be called on earlier. When conditions allowed, Park was also using Wing formations. Both Evill and Dowding accepted the Wing idea and were critical of Park for being slow to consider the Duxford Wing's possible value on occasions during the period of strong raids; but neither was suggesting a departure from the existing policy in No. 11 Group. According to Laddie Lucas, his biographer, Bader fully understood that while the Wing could be used from Duxford, 40–50 miles behind the front line, the pressure in No. 11 Group ruled out the Wing concept being of general use. Bader realised that such formations were not the answer to every situation. This being so, there appears to be a difference of opinion between what he was advocating and what his Group Commander, Leigh-Mallory, had in mind, as will be seen later.

The largest obstacle to using Wings as reinforcements in other Group areas at the time had been the technical shortcomings of radio communications; VHF in small numbers, was in the process of being re-introduced.* A further impediment was the personal animosity existing between Nos. 11 and 12 Group Commanders.

It would seem that by April the Wing reinforcement policy had lost its earlier appeal. Sir Douglas Evill was instructing his Operations staff to 'Tell Groups that their effort, or lack of effort, is disappointing and that the reinforcement scheme will certainly not work in emergencies if not practised in advance'. He recognised commitments made things difficult and suggested that skeleton exercises should be carried out to get the procedure right. He concluded, 'Ask them to do better in future and to report any practices carried out in their monthly report.'[152]

Soon after the European war was over, senior German Officers were interrogated: *Generalfeldmarschall* Milch, who for a large part of the war was Inspector General of the *Luftwaffe* and Secretary of State for Air, and *Generalleutnant* Galland, Commander of *Jagdgeschwader* 26 during the Battle of Britain and later Inspector of Fighters. Both were quite definite that the whole object of the attacks during the Battle of Britain was to wear down the British fighter force as a preliminary to invasion. Whether the objectives were convoys in the Channel, aerodromes inland, or London, the objective was always the same – to bring the defending squadrons to battle and weaken them. The scope of the battle was, therefore, largely decided by the range of German fighters, especially the Bf. 109. The progressive extension of the offensive inland had been designed to bring Fighter Command up into combat in greater numbers. This, they said, did not mean that there was no special interest in the ground targets they attacked, i.e. fighter aerodromes and destruction of its ground organisation; these they regarded as important.[154] With hindsight, it would appear that the use of No. 11 Group aircraft in small numbers as opposed to use of mass formations, frustrated the German strategy of creating large-scale air battles which would, they hoped, after a number of such confrontations, have seriously weakened Fighter Command.

At Bentley Priory, the ugly reality of war manifested itself. On the night of 16 October a Wellington bomber returning from a raid on Bremen crashed and burst into flames near the tennis courts. Before hitting the

---

* On 18 August, Dowding had decided to re-start the VHF changeover commencing with four squadrons in No. 11 Group Sectors, three in No. 12 Group Sectors and one in No. 13 Group. He instructed that when these came into use, the old HF system was to remain working, making bogus transmissions to create the delusion of nothing having changed.[153] By the end of September only sixteen squadrons had changed over. Six Blenheim nightfighter squadrons had commenced re-equipping on 8 August.

ground, it touched the top of the Sergeants' Mess; had it been a little lower, those inside would have been engulfed. The aircraft belonged to No. 311 (Czech) Squadron. Its radio had been damaged by German AA fire, making it impossible for the crew to get any assistance from the ground in the bad visibility. Wandering low over Stanmore, it is thought to have collided with a balloon cable which sent it out of control. Of the crew of six, only Frank Truhlář, the front gunner, survived the inferno; his turret having become detached from the fuselage, enabled rescuers to drag him out. He suffered severe injuries to both legs, his chest and neck and he was also badly burned.

When Frank was well enough, Dowding hinted to his daughter, Brenda, that it would be nice if she could visit the hospital to see the injured airman, a request she willingly undertook. The visits were not easy as Frank's poor English made communication difficult. He progressed steadily and, typical of Czech aircrew of that time, his great desire was to return to flying. When Air Vice-Marshal Janoušek asked him what he wanted to do when recovered, he said he wished to become a Spitfire pilot.

Truhlář, having had his burns treated by Sir Archibald McIndoe at East Grinstead and passed a medical examination, Janoušek arranged a pilot training course in Canada, and by the Winter of 1943–44 the indomitable Czech was flying a Spitfire as a Flight Lieutenant with No. 312 Squadron. While returning from a sortie providing air cover over the Normandy beach-head on 11 June 1944, the Squadron encountered extremely bad weather with visibility down to 500 yards. One of his colleagues, Sergeant Nosek, was killed when his aircraft hit the ground at Appledram, 15 miles from their home base. Frank managed to find Thorney Island Aerodrome, but the undercarriage of the Spitfire collapsed on landing and the aircraft's belly fuel tank exploded; he was again badly burned. Sir Archibald McIndoe's team at the Queen Victoria Hospital, East Grinstead went to work on him once more.

When the war was over, he was asked to stay in Britain to continue treatment, but instead chose to return home to Czechoslovakia. Somehow he managed to get back to flying, albeit on a very restricted scale. On the ground, life was not at all what returning airmen, some of whom had won high gallantry awards, had expected. The seeds of a totalitarian political regime, which was to suppress the country for many years, were already germinating and airmen were becoming subjected to a campaign to discredit them. Also, Frank became sensitive about the effect his disfigurement was having on some members of the public and, on occasions, took to wearing a light facial mask. Several times he flew over his home town, Lomnice nad Popelkon and to Nova Paka, and it was not unusual, although regarded as irregular by the authorities, for him to perform a few aerobatics over the town. It was there on 3 December 1946 that a Spitfire was seen to circle, do a few aerobatics and finish with a low level run. Sadly, this time a wing of the aircraft struck a building and the machine smashed to pieces close to the house where Frank grew up. Frank Truhlář, a man of great courage, had returned to the place of his birth.[155]

Chapter 9

Dowding and Park Rejected

O n 14 September, with the daylight battle at its height, a critical fraternity was promoting its opinions. A letter had arrived at Bentley Priory from the Air Council saying that the Minister of Aircraft Production, Lord Beaverbrook, had invited Marshal of the Royal Air Force Sir John Salmond, who had retired in 1933 and was now working for him, to undertake a thorough enquiry into the equipment and preparation of nightfighters. (Salmond had written to Beaverbrook on the failure to cope with night bombing.) The Air Council thereupon decided to broaden the scope of this enquiry to cover all matters in connection with air fighting at night. Surprisingly, for such an intricate subject, Salmond's Committee, comprising Air Chief Marshal Freeman, Air Marshal Joubert de la Ferté, Air Vice-Marshal Tedder, Air Vice-Marshal Sholto Douglas, Air Commodores Stevenson and Payne, Group Captain Sowry and F. W. Smith of MAP as Secretary, met on only three occasions – 16–18 September. (Anti-Aircraft Command, in view of its importance, was strangely not represented.) Other people were called before them to give evidence. Their report was, in the main, associated with the supply and development of equipment and training of personnel. It was suggested that plans should be made for the transfer of some single-seater day Squadrons to do night work. Perhaps the most constructive recommendation was to press ahead with the installation of blind landing equipment and navigational aids at nightfighter airfields. The Committee's report was sent to Fighter Command by the Air Council on 25 September with a covering letter stating what recommendations they had already acted upon, and giving instructions to Dowding. In addition, the Air Council strongly advocated the use of the long aerial mine method of interception. They were, incidentally, opposed to the diversion of existing day squadrons on to night work until more squadrons were formed or the scale of the day battle decreased. Dowding was asked for his view on the implementation of certain other proposals; he replied two days later.

Salmond's report with the Air Council's decisions appended, together with Dowding's comments, formed the basis for a high level meeting on 1 October; on this occasion those present were members of the Air Staff, plus the Secretary of State, Sinclair, Salmond and Dowding. Most items were agreed after some alteration of detail. There was only one proposition to which Dowding was strongly opposed and which he regarded as being outside the scope of a committee whose brief had been to look into night fighting and he was very surprised to see it had been introduced. It was a recommendation which implied that delay in getting fighters into the air could be reduced by filtering the CH radar plots in rooms which would be constructed at the headquarters of each Group. This fell more within the province of day operations; at night the time factor was less critical, the procedure in being at the time was for individual aircraft to be sent up to patrol a specific line and be directed only if a 'hostile' was located within that area. The decentralisation idea would entail the dismantling of the existing nationwide Filter Room at Bentley Priory. (Filtering at Groups was already being done at the newly-formed Groups Nos. 9, 10 and 13 only because it was not practical to ask for further telephone lines into Bentley Priory if it were to be done there.) Dowding's principal objection to it was the difficulty of recognition and identification of aircraft. (At this time it required close liaison with all other flying Commands through an Aircraft Movements Officer in the Filter Room to establish this.) He accepted that when IFF was generally fitted and working, his objections would, to a large extent, disappear, but he suggested there would be a delay in passing information to the Air Raid Warning Organisation which governed the country's warning network. He wanted it put on record that in his view the proposal to decentralise filtering would not improve the efficiency of night interception. He pointed out that interception over the sea at night was already being effected in the Groups by them having their Sector Controllers in direct contact with their local Radar Stations, something the committee was already aware of. The meeting generally agreed that building of Group Filter Rooms should commence in order for filtering to be carried out when IFF came into general use.* Throughout the discussions Dowding had conducted himself in his usual forthright manner; on occasion his views had caused details to be altered, on others not. Blind landing systems and navigational aids appear to have

---

* In practice, the IFF system was later found to be not totally reliable, and accurate aircraft identification remained founded on the judgement made at Filter Rooms, where information about aircraft movements of home forces was available.

been his recommendations. If the records of the meeting are to be believed, other than the filtering disagreement, there was a general acceptance of views. Maybe Dowding's overbearing attitude irritated some, but this did not warrant the vicious attack on him which was about to unfold. Indeed, perhaps there was some justification for Dowding to become annoyed; both Joubert and Douglas were members of the very influential Night Interception Committee set up in March specifically to oversee research and development into night interception. In fact both had been Chairmen, Joubert only a few days earlier. Both were well placed to make their contribution but were now being critical.

On the following day, 2 October, F.A. Lindemann, Churchill's scientific adviser and confidant, wrote to the Prime Minister asking, 'Are you satisfied that everything possible is being done to cope with night bombers?'

The day after Lindemann's letter, another criticising the handling of night air defence was sent to him by Eric Seal, his Principal Private Secretary. He said he had been talking to Lindemann and both felt 'that more could be done to counteract the menace of night bombing'. He went on to say the 'Prof' (Lindemann) had 'a lot of suggestions, some of which ought to be tried out'. Churchill 'should send for the responsible Officers, and probe deeply into the details of what they are doing, and ask for day-to-day reports of progress'.* He remarked, 'Dowding has the reputation of being very conservative, and of not being receptive to new ideas.' (Lindemann's 'suggestions' focused on spreading aerial mines in the path of enemy aircraft. His Long Aerial Mine (LAM) scheme, code-named 'MUTTON' by a discerning wit, proved a considerable waste of resources. His schemes in a small way delayed the success of nightfighters by having them grounded when the schemes were in operation. None of the other 'new ideas' were to have any measure of success when tried later.)

Churchill now felt compelled to call a conference to discuss night air defence and asked Lindemann to name those he thought should be present. (Sinclair, Beaverbrook and Newall were not included on his list; it was later amended to accept them!) The Prime Minister asked for Sir John Salmond to be there. (Salmond had had a private meeting with Churchill a few hours earlier; the reason for this will be seen later.)

---

* Churchill kept in very close touch with events. Squadron Leader Joe Kayll recalls how at 6 am he would telephone the Night Duty Officer at Bentley Priory wanting to know what had happened during the night; details of nightfighter victories, *Luftwaffe* targets, etc.

Prior to the meeting, Lindemann sent the Prime Minister a letter, part of which reads, 'Detailed plans for controlled AI interception have been worked out by Sir John Salmond's Committee. Are these accepted and are they rapidly being put into effect?'[153] The Professor appears to have been misinformed; no such plans were made by the Committee. No concrete proposal for specific equipment or a sound technique for directing a nightfighter into a position where it could shoot down an enemy aircraft, which was the basic problem, emerged from their deliberations. The machinery required was still in the research and development stage. This was the very forefront of technology of the day and the greatest hope rested with the Boffins; the solution was not far away.

The conference was held on the following day, 7 October, with Churchill as Chairman. Those present were:- Sir Archibald Sinclair, Sir Cyril Newall, Sir John Salmond, Sir Hugh Dowding, Sir Philip Joubert de la Ferte, Sir Frederick Pile, Lord Beaverbrook, Sholto Douglas, Robert Watson Watt and representatives of the War Office, Admiralty and Ministry of Supply.

The First Minute records that it was broadly accepted that night interception by fighters should be controlled from the ground. The major items discussed were the illumination of enemy aircraft to make it possible for non-radar-equipped fighters to intercept, and the technical problems experienced with the Beaufighters and the installation of their AI radar. They dealt with radar control of guns and searchlights and the requirement that a high standard of personnel and training was necessary. (At the time, tuition was being carried out by Professor P.M.S. Blackett and a team of scientists.) The final part of the agenda centred on Lindemann's aerial mine ideas. Throughout the meeting there was general acceptance of the practical steps taken, most of which were already underway; some were ideas Dowding had already implemented. Churchill then asked Dowding if he agreed with the recommendations of the Sir John Salmond Report, and once more the argument arose whether decentralisation of filtering had been relevant to the enquiry into night air defence, and whether it was worthwhile. It was agreed that this and any other points Dowding thought not relevant to night interception should be put by him to the Prime Minister afterwards.

Dowding corresponded with Churchill, outlining his objections to the filtering proposal. The Air Staff, supported by Archibald Sinclair, pursued the matter – Churchill asked them to reconsider; he was not sure of the soundness of the scheme 'in view of the strong reasoned opinion of the C-in-C'. Sinclair wrote to Churchill saying the Air Staff thought it 'an undoubted fact that time was saved in getting the squadrons into the air by filtering at Group Headquarters'. In the view of the Air Staff, when more intense operations began in the following Spring, perhaps 2,000 or 2,500 aircraft would be in the air over the coast at one time, and impossible congestion would arise at Command Filter Room.

It would seem the proposal put forward that decentralisation was a nightfighting issue had somehow become, according to these figures, a dayfighting one. Another point raised was the possibility of the entire filtering system being destroyed if Bentley Priory were bombed. As has been seen, provision for this was already in being by having a standby room at Leighton Buzzard. Sinclair estimated the cost of building three Group filter rooms would be £25,000 each, possibly more, and the estimated date for completion would be the following Spring. Churchill sent Sinclair's letter to Dowding with a covering note asking that the arguments it contained and the authority behind it should be carefully weighed. He asked for the C-in-C's observations; the cost of building the Filter Rooms, he said, was not relevant; there would be no harm in 'having them under our lea for next Spring'. He added, 'Pray keep this communication as strictly personal and make no reference to it in any official correspondence'.

The desire of the Prime Minister that the correspondence should be kept on a confidential basis gave Dowding the opportunity to express his feelings. There were a few minor inaccuracies in Sinclair's Minute, he wrote, but the only one of importance was his statement about it being an undoubted fact that time would be saved in getting squadrons into the air by filtering at Group Headquarters – it was substantially untrue – radar plots were 'told' to Group Headquarters without delay, the average transmission time being less than 15 seconds (roughly the time taken to actually say the words). Sinclair had described the Salmond Committee as being 'authoritative', but Dowding questioned the depth of examination of the problems, remarking on how the Committee had completed its task with phenomenal rapidity (three days). He had given evidence before it and could not remember the matter of filtering ever being mentioned (it had been), and was extremely surprised to find it was included in their recommendation. He commented on the likelihood of congestion arising in the Filter Room and the contingency plans to avoid it. Using a diagram, he explained how the benefits of 'range cutting' in the Filter Room would be lost. When creating the system Dowding had started with the idea of decentralised filtration but had abandoned it. He now thought the change, on balance, would not have sufficient advantage to justify the cost and effort.

It would appear that Dowding now felt the Fighter Command system was being threatened by the degree of interference from outside his Command. (He knew nothing of the effort being made to discredit him personally.) He wrote, 'The fact is that the metaphorical edifice which you have seen in my Operations and Filter Rooms has been built up, brick by brick, under my own eye during the past four years.' He recalled the poor state of defences when he took over. The letter continued,

> 'The system I have devised may not be perfect, but it cannot be improved by disruptive incursions on the part of people who do not understand it as a whole ... My main grievance, however, is in the matter of the expenditure of my time in arguing with the Air Staff every intimate detail of my organisation. Surely a Commander-in-Chief should be left to manage his own affairs if the general result is satisfactory. I have expended not less than fifty hours of my time on this controversy.'[158]

Churchill wrote to Sinclair asking if it was really true that time was saved by filtering at Group. Churchill asked for a study to be carried out and it concluded that with decentralisation none of the original process was omitted and none added. It could, therefore, be assumed that there would be neither saving nor loss of time in respect of the number of links through which the information passed. It suggested the main factor in favour of decentralisation was the avoidance of future congestion at Command with the continued expansion of the radar chain.[159] The argument used by the Air Staff that Group filtering would save time was based on a false premise; it was hoped that Operations and Filtering work could be done on the same table, thus removing the need for 'telling' plots between the two functions. Calculations showed the size of the table would be so large (50 × 60 feet) that plotting by hand during intensive operations would be impossible. Separate tables using the existing procedure continued.[160] (By May 1941, some were having second thoughts about decentralisation. Sholto Douglas, now AOC-in-C Fighter Command, wrote to Chief of the Air Staff Portal: 'My predecessor was strongly opposed to decentralisation ... I think the present centralised system works quite well from the point of view of efficiency, and I do not think there is much to be gained by the proposed change.'[161]

The Prime Minister was now under political pressure to get rid of Dowding. It came in the form of a letter dated 6 November from Sir Reginald Clarry, MP, Chairman of the 1922 Conservative Private Members Committee. He wrote of how 'the Executive Committee were requested to meet and hear certain criticisms of the Fighter Command (RAF) brought forward by several members. This meeting was held and I was requested to represent to you the lack of confidence in which Sir Hugh Dowding is held in certain quarters of the personnel of the Force, and the grave concern felt by my Executive'.*

This brought forth a rebuke from the Prime Minister. He replied that questions of high appointments were continually in his mind and he had many sources of information and opportunities for forming a right judgement. He made sure that the best men were chosen but also to make officers discharging tasks of extreme difficulty feel confident that they would be supported and protected while they did their duty. He wrote, 'I do not think it would be at all a good thing for the 1922 Committee to become a kind of collecting house for complaints against serving Commanders-in-Chief or other important officials.' The Committee were none too pleased the following month when the Chairman reported that the Chief Whip had informed him that the Prime Minister contemplated asking Cabinet Ministers not to address party committees such as the '1922 Committee'.[162]

* Unfortunately this meeting was held in secret session and no records are available. On 16 October, Committee members had also asked for a secret session debate on 'Air raid defence generally, and especially of London'.

Chapter 10

Dowding Retired

In November Dowding suffered a stunning blow which was to haunt him for the rest of his life. He was sacked from his job as C-in-C Fighter Command and replaced by Sholto Douglas whose conception of air defence strategy, as has been seen, was far removed from that used in the Battle of Britain by Keith Park. It thus became convenient that Park should be removed, and this occurred on 18 December; perhaps not surprisingly, Trafford Leigh-Mallory took over No. 11 Group.

As early as 7 December 1940, a somewhat pushy Leigh-Mallory had already spelled out his plans to Sholto Douglas on the subject of 'Organisation of Wings' and, 'assured that the principle of operating our fighters in large formations has been agreed to', gave full rein to his imagination. Little thought appears to have been given to the proven tactical expertise of a very clever enemy. He reasoned that the largest formation operated so far had been five squadrons – sixty aircraft, and thought it should be possible to operate three Wings of three Squadrons each, amounting to 108 aircraft in one general formation. Leigh-Mallory suggested seven Wings in Fighter Command; No. 10 Group would have one only, made up of Spitfire and Hurricane Squadrons (mixed); No. 11 Group would form four Wings, two purely of Spitfires, with two others mixed. The No. 12 Group area should have two Wings made up from Spitfire and Hurricane Squadrons (mixed). His memorandum went on to state where the allocated aircraft should be based and made recommendations about the selection of Wing Leaders. At the heart of Leigh-Mallory's plan was the unpredictable factor: 'If the Germans are operating in very large formations, bombers and fighters . . .'.[163] No reference was made as to how other raids would be repelled, many of which had earlier caused considerable damage, or whether the Wings would remain on the ground, as they had done in No. 12 Group, while waiting for a mass attack to occur.

On receipt of the letter at Bentley Priory, Group Captain G.M. Lawson of the Operations Section, who, like everyone, favoured fighter operations

179

in strength, wrote a minute to Douglas Evill outlining certain operational objections which he thought, to some extent, negated the value of such large formations.

He itemised the impracticalities of using the suggested large formations, many of which had already been well aired, i.e. time spent in the air while forming up, inflexibility and the high degree of organisation required, etc. Leigh-Mallory's scheme, he thought, would to some extent involve breaking away from the existing Sector organisation. Lawson indicated his personal preference for the No. 11 Group system of using pairs of squadrons working together with similar sized formations when combating heavy raids. He thought Leigh-Mallory's ideas were worth trying but not on the ambitious scale proposed.[164] Evill was also critical. In a Minute to the C-in-C he recorded his unease about Leigh-Mallory speaking of the 'principle of operating our fighters in large formations' and giving 'no recognition to the other factors of time and space which have to be taken into account in meeting the German attacks, particularly in No. 11 Group'. Leigh-Mallory had placed some importance upon squadrons taking off as a Wing and Evill commented, 'I do not regard this as practicable in the advanced Sectors of No. 11 Group if the Germans recommence any serious bombing of aerodromes by day, and to my mind this will certainly be a feature of any renewed offensive.'[165]

On 17 December, Douglas put his personal view in the form of a Minute:

'I am very much in sympathy with the AOC No. 12 Group's proposals. I am convinced that we must try and get larger formations of fighters operating against the enemy mass formations when he starts employing them again, which he undoubtedly will do. We must try and outnumber the enemy in the air instead of always being ourselves outnumbered, which has been the rule heretofore. There is a good deal of feeling on this question, both inside and outside the Command. We must therefore give the AOC No. 12 Group's proposals every possible support.'

He was 'not very much impressed' with the list of disadvantages related by Lawson, and continued:

'There is however one big and obvious disadvantage about large formations of fighters, viz. that they will obviously take longer to intercept and may therefore fail to intercept before the enemy reaches and bombs his objective. On the other hand, I have never been very much in favour of the idea of trying to interpose fighter squadrons between enemy bombers and their objective. The best, if not the only, way of achieving air superiority is to shoot down a large proportion of enemy bombers every time they come over. It would be better to do this before they reach their objective if possible, but I would rather shoot down 50 of the enemy bombers after they have reached their objective than shoot down only 10 before they have done so.

'It seems to me that No. 11 Group have been rather hypnotised by this idea that they must meet the enemy before he reaches his objective. The result has been that single squadrons, or at the best Wings of two squadrons, have been pitted against vastly superior numbers. The results have not been too bad, but I am sure they would have been better if we could have taken on the enemy mass formations with much larger numbers working as a coherent whole.

'It is also possible to some extent to mitigate this one big disadvantage by putting up one or two squadrons as goalkeepers to worry the enemy formations while they are over their objective, giving time for the fighter "balbo" to get round behind the enemy and intercept them on the way home.'

Douglas went on to quote the difference in results between large and small groups at the time of Dunkirk, and concluded:

'I therefore approve generally the proposals of the AOC No. 12 Group. Please instruct the AOCs No. 10, 11 and 12 Groups to organise Wings on the lines suggested.'[166]

This was the view of the new C-in-C Fighter Command: he had long held this opinion. As early as August 1938 when the debate on future fighter strength for home defence was on, he had written,

'It is immaterial in the long view whether the enemy bomber is shot down before or after he has dropped his bombs on his objective. Our object is *not* to prevent bombers reaching their objectives, though it would be nice if we could, but to cause a high casualty rate among enemy bombers, with the result that the scale of attack will dwindle rapidly to bearable proportions.'[167]

This was more than a minor shift of emphasis and questionable whether this policy followed his summary of the views of the 17 October Meeting on Major Day Tactics. (See pages 153, 154 & 155.) It was now Evill's and Lawson's job to try to make it work. Lawson commented, 'The scheme is rather ambitious and is dependent upon the introduction of VHF in sectors not already equipped before it can be fully implemented.' On

22 December similarly Evill minuted, 'It is a matter of regret that the reinforcing arrangements are still comparatively restricted by the technicalities of communication.'[168]

The manner in which Dowding's period of office at Bentley Priory was terminated was incredible. At the time Archibald Sinclair became Secretary of State for Air in the new Churchill administration in the middle of May, Dowding was approaching the latest advised date for his retirement. This was to be 14 July; several other retirement dates and deferments had already passed. With only ten days to go before the expiry date and at the commencement of the Battle of Britain, a further request was made by CAS (Newall) asking that he should accept a further deferment until October. Where earlier, retirement would have been acceptable, Dowding now felt the current situation made it prudent that he should remain in office until the Spring of 1942, a time suggested earlier for his retirement. This view he expressed when replying to Newall. He sent a copy of the letter to Sinclair who replied on 10 July that he agreed with the deferment to October decision, adding the comment, 'I could give you no higher proof of my confidence in you and, although perhaps it seem superfluous, let me add the assurance of my full support'. On that day a 'Private and Confidential' letter was sent to Sinclair by Churchill. It said,

'I was very much taken aback the other night when you told me you had been considering removing Sir Hugh Dowding at the expiration of his present appointment, but had come to the conclusion that he might be allowed to stay on for another four months. Personally, I think he is one of the very best men you have got, and I say this after having been in contact with him for about two years. I have greatly admired the whole of his work in the Fighter Command and especially in resisting the clamour for numerous air raid warnings, and the immense pressure to dissipate the fighter strength during the great French battle. In fact he has my full confidence. I think it is a pity for an officer so gifted and so trusted to be working on such a short tenure as four months and I hope you will consider whether it is not in the public interest that his appointment should be indefinitely prolonged while the war lasts. This would not, of course, exclude his being moved to a higher position, if that were thought necessary. I am, however, much averse from making changes and putting in new men who will have to learn the work all over again, except when there is some proved failure or inadequacy.'[169]

On 12 July, Sinclair met Churchill and discussed the retirement and the following day the Prime Minister invited Dowding to dine at 'Chequers'. He told him he had secured his confidence, wished him to remain on the Active List for the time being, without any date for his retirement being fixed. He said he had written to Sir Archibald Sinclair on the subject; as has been seen, he had also spoken to him. Dowding referred to the conversation he had had with Churchill the previous night in a private letter to Sinclair on 14 July. A misunderstanding arose between Churchill and Sinclair over whether there had been a decision in their discussion on 12 July to the effect that a review of the October retirement arrangement would be made in a month's time. The Secretary of State had jotted down a note in red pencil on Churchill's letter to this effect. It would seem Dowding's letter to him two days later telling him what Churchill had said had not been queried because a month later correspondence was re-opened with the Prime Minister. Churchill's understanding was that Dowding had been given an indefinite wartime extension. On 10 August 1940, he wrote,

'It is entirely wrong to keep an officer in the position of Commander-in-Chief, conducting hazardous operations from day to day, when he is dangling at the end of an expiring appointment. Such a situation is not fair to anyone, least of all to the nation. I can never be party to it.'

Replying, Sinclair said how he had now consulted Newall who would write to Dowding withdrawing the October time limit to the period of his Command. This letter, sent by him on 12 August, said he was 'now glad to be able to say that it had been decided to cancel the time limit to the period of your appointment as C.-in-C. Fighter Command'. Perhaps the most remarkable aspect was how retirement of a Commander because of his age could be considered while he was conducting a battle for the survival of his country. (As a matter of interest, the Prime Minister was in his 66th year.)

In the following weeks the battle for control of British skies continued with increasing ferocity and resulted in the successful preservation of the British Isles from German invasion, but there were shocks on the way.

Unknown to Dowding and Churchill, the fruits of high intrigue were reaching maturity.[170] Elderly and much revered Marshals of the Royal Air Force Sir John Salmond and Sir Hugh Trenchard, both of whom had for many years been far from the centre of RAF affairs, were conspiring and exercising their influence. On 25 September Salmond, in a letter to

Trenchard, wrote of how he had written to Beaverbrook on the failure to cope with the night bombing and from it had come his enquiry into the night defences. He said he completed the report two days later (on 17 September) and on it put a private note to Beaverbrook to say he considered Dowding should be dismissed. He related that Beaverbrook rejected the idea and refused to become involved. Salmond went on to say how Beaverbrook held Dowding in high esteem and this conviction was also held by the Prime Minister. He said he had then gone to see Sinclair and told him that Dowding should go; he could see Sinclair was scared about bringing the matter up even though he knew that the CAS (Newall) and the Air Staff, as far as he could tell, were unanimous in supporting his view. Salmond realised Sinclair was going to do nothing. Salmond said how he had attended an Air Council meeting to discuss his report and beforehand let it be known to CAS (Newall) that he intended to bring up the question of Dowding after non-Service members had left. During the meeting, however, a somewhat perturbed Newall passed him a note requesting him not to do so; Salmond thought a first class opportunity for Air Council members to make their views known had been lost. This attitude he found difficult to understand because only a few days earlier, Newall had endorsed the idea of sacking Dowding because of his intransigence about accepting the Air Staff's latest ideas on nightfighting. (It would seem that they wished to sack the C-in-C Fighter Command not because he was guilty of poor judgement but because of his lack of enthusiasm for experimentation with their 'new ideas'. It is perhaps not unreasonable to ask why such 'ideas' were not forthcoming before the nightfighting crisis arose.) Salmond's letter maliciously attacked Dowding, whom he considered to be enjoying a reputation gained by the efforts of the dayfighter pilots. He did, however, concede much of their success was due to him. Salmond's letter went on to say how during his argument about the dismissal of Dowding with Beaverbrook, he had been reminded of Newall's responsibility for air defence. Salmond was happy to see both men dismissed. He supported this view by listing a number of, what he thought to be, serious errors of judgement made by Newall. (These assertions appear hardly credible when seen in the light of the prevailing circumstances of the time and they, rightly or wrongly, give the impression of Salmond being out of touch with the true situation.) Salmond concluded his letter by asking Trenchard to use his influence with Beaverbrook because he firmly believed that by having Dowding and Newall in Command, the highest standard was not being achieved. On the day of Salmond's 25 September letter, his

Report together with the Air Council's conclusions arrived at Bentley Priory; this was the first occasion Dowding had seen them. No debate had taken place and, without hearing Dowding's explanation, Salmond was already calling for his dismissal. The meetings on night air defence came later.

It will be recalled that Salmond had requested a private meeting with the Prime Minister in a letter sent on 5 October. It was worded as follows: 'I am most anxious to put to you the case for a change in the holder of the important position of C.-in-C. Fighter Command.' He mentioned his enquiry into night air defence, 'the result of which, together with what has since occurred, make a change, in my opinion, imperative'. He added, 'this opinion is also very strongly held by most, if not all, Service members of the Air Council.'[171] Churchill met him the following day and ferociously defended Dowding. He also dismissed the opinion of his scientific adviser, Lord Cherwell, who was a supporter of Salmond's views.

Trenchard was also busy manoeuvring behind the scenes. In a letter to Salmond dated 4 October 1940, the day prior to Salmond's request to see Churchill, he wrote of his efforts to obtain the dismissal of Dowding. He felt it would be too difficult for Portal (who was in the process of taking over from Newall as Chief of the Air Staff) to sack Dowding unless enough influence could be imposed to enforce it. That is not to say that Portal would have agreed to become involved in the conspiracy anyway. Trenchard recognised his influence as being more in the world outside the Service and promised to continue his activity in that direction. He furtively advised Salmond how he never mentioned their collaboration, thinking it would be more effective if they were both seen to be acting on their own, but each reaching the same conclusion.[171] Coincidentally, several days later, the Big Wing dayfighter controversy and criticism of dayfighter tactics came to the fore. At the top of Salmond's earlier letter to Trenchard his handwritten note continued, 'After three weeks I met him (Churchill) again at the "Other Club", he said I was right, D. had gone "but it nearly broke his heart". Had the P.M. not agreed, I had decided to appeal to HM' (The King). The *tête-à-têtes* of the two RAF ancients at 'Brooks Club' seem to have proved fruitful. Sir Cyril Newall was replaced as Chief of the Air Staff by Sir Charles Portal in October, becoming a Marshal of the Royal Air Force and taking over the Governor-Generalship of New Zealand.

There is a possibility that, with the benefit of hindsight, Sir John Salmond may have later changed his opinion. In an article on the Battle of Britain written for *The Daily Dispatch* newspaper on 25 September 1943, he wrote,

'Fortunate, too, were we in having as Supreme Commander of the Fighting Squadrons a man who knew the job in all its technical and operational detail and had been in the saddle during the three years before the war, Air Chief Marshal Sir Hugh, now Lord Dowding.'[173]

On 13 November, Dowding met the Secretary of State for Air, Sir Archibald Sinclair, at the Air Ministry; Sinclair told him of the need to strengthen the British organisation for selecting, modifying and purchasing aircraft and armament in the United States of America. He told Dowding that the project was primarily the concern of Lord Beaverbrook who had asked for his services and he, Sinclair, 'had formed the opinion that to make Sir Hugh Dowding available for this undertaking would be the best disposition of our resources'. He had agreed to Beaverbrook's request. Beaverbrook was, of course, well aware of the intriguing going on within the Air Force. Dowding replied that he did not suppose that an answer would be expected straight away. The Secretary of State stressed the importance of the mission and hoped it would not be refused. Dowding asked if it was to be only a temporary mission and if he would be returning, at its conclusion, to his Command. Sinclair then told him of his intention to appoint Sholto Douglas to take over Fighter Command. Dowding asked for a night to think things over and also expressed a wish to see the Prime Minister; Sinclair agreed, adding that perhaps after having thought about it he would feel that this was unnecessary. Dowding answered that 'he certainly would wish to see the Prime Minister'.[174]

Churchill told him how he felt about him being replaced and, according to Dowding, expressed surprise that it should have been done 'in the moment of victory'.[175] This part of the conversation and the Prime Minister's apparent lack of opposition to the change were to mystify Dowding and impair his judgement of Churchill thereafter. He was unaware that, without the Prime Minister's support, he would have been replaced much earlier. When the concerted clamour for his removal had reached such a high level, Churchill felt compelled to accept the change. While Dowding concentrated all his energy on preserving the country from defeat the machinations of a few well placed individuals had sought to discredit him.

After Dowding had gone, Churchill wrote to the lately installed Chief of the Air Staff, Portal, telling him how he was sending Dowding to the

United States 'in the public interest'; the purpose of the mission was to get their war aviation developed along the right lines. Dowding had expressed doubts about his ability to fulfil this mission but, Churchill continued, 'Personally I think he will perform the task very well, and I will give him a letter for the President'. Giving Portal a monitory hint, he added, 'I have a very great regard for this officer, and admiration for his qualities and achievement.'[176]

On 17 November, Dowding wrote his final report on the progress of night interception. It covered a wide field, reporting on his visit to see the experimental GCI station at Durrington on the occasion of its first operational trial. (Production of these new stations had already been given the go-ahead.) Dowding's lengthy memorandum embraced most technical aspects of nightfighting, giving a clear and perceptive, up-to-date picture of the current state of affairs. In it the ingredients for the future success of nightfighting were visible.[177]

Before he left Fighter Command, he sent a message to all Operational Stations and Units:

'My dear Fighter Boys,
'In sending you this my last message, I wish I could say all that is in my heart. I cannot hope to surpass the simple eloquence of the Prime Minister's words, "Never before has so much been owed by so many to so few." The debt remains and will increase.
'In saying good bye to you I want you to know how continually you have been in my thoughts, and that, though our direct connection may be severed, I may yet be able to help you in your gallant fight.
'Good bye to you and God bless you all.'

He was now well over fifty-eight years old and for the past four years had been occupying a position where the burden of Command had increased to almost unbearable proportions. For many weeks, both day and night, his people had been defending the country against an opponent of great strength and guile. This had literally been done in full view of the public and political gaze. Not surprisingly, he was now very tired. His work was done. He finally left Bentley Priory on 24 November 1940.

Charles (Chic) Willett, a member of his staff remembers:

'The strain of the great problems and lack of sleep began to show. There were times when I saw him almost blind with fatigue; he obviously needed a long rest, he was becoming burned out. When Dowding was eventually replaced, he came along to each office and said, "I think

187

you know that I am going, thank you very much." On the morning of his departure, Sholto Douglas came to take over and walked into the office while Dowding was writing at his desk; he finished what he was doing, looked up at Sholto Douglas and simply said, "Good morning", and was away.'

He sailed for the United States on 18 December. Beaverbrook, looking for further employment for him, wrote to Sinclair informing him that the time had come to make a selection of a successor to Sir Wilfrid Freeman, Senior Air Force Officer at the Ministry of Aircraft Production. Beaverbrook had recently mentioned Dowding as a likely candidate. Both Sinclair and Portal were insisting that the position should be filled by an Air Force Officer. Beaverbrook baited them, asking, 'Would the appointment of Sir Hugh Dowding be well received in the RAF?' Sinclair replied,

'Certainly it would be acceptable to the Royal Air Force in a sense in which the appointment of no civilian, with the exception of Sir Henry Tizard, would be acceptable. On the other hand, since you asked my opinion, I am bound to tell you frankly that I think the appointment of Sir John Salmond or of Sir Edgar Ludlow-Hewitt would be more acceptable.'[178] (Sir Henry Tizard was later appointed.)

The mission to the United States was clouded by controversy, with Dowding expressing views on equipment which were not exactly those of the official line; there was also dissension about him taking an interest in affairs outside of armaments. Complaints were sent to Beaverbrook; at one stage Lord Halifax, the Ambassador, asked whether it was possible to contrive an excuse for his early return to England. Knowing of the recent intrigues at home, Beaverbrook replied, 'It is necessary, of course, to bear in mind that he is not at all popular with some RAF personnel.'[179] Dowding toured United States aircraft companies and commented favourably on a number of their latest construction and design innovations. On the other hand, he was critical of the lackadaisical attitude of many of the British Air Commission members, remarking, 'It is no exaggeration to say that many now fail to realise that there is a war on.'[180] 'There was scathing comment in his personal notes on the organisation of the Commission, its size and what he considered to be unnecessary perquisites given to staff. The scheme for ferrying aircraft to Britain, he thought, was a "muddle" and lacking in organisation. On the whole there was little likely to have endeared him to members of the Commission.' He was given the opportunity to renew his acquaintanceship

188

with the radar scientist 'Taffy' Bowen who was now working there on a collaboration mission. Bowen gave him a flight demonstration of the new AI 10 set and he was clearly delighted with it. When writing to U.S. General Cheney he congratulated everyone concerned and told him to get it into production even though the British had not as yet got a suitable aircraft available likely to exploit its full potential.

When Dowding returned from his mission in May 1941, Beaverbrook had left the Ministry of Aircraft Production and J.T.C. Moor Brabazon, the distinguished pioneer aviator, had succeeded him. The problem of what to do with the ex-C-in-C Fighter Command began to cause him embarrassment, and he reminded Sinclair that the Ministry of Aircraft Production arrangement was only for the duration of the American Mission. Several ideas were then put forward by Sinclair in correspondence with Churchill. One was that he should become Governor-General of Southern Rhodesia, another, that he could have a dual role as Inspector-General with Sir Edgar Ludlow-Hewitt. Churchill suggested the possibility of putting him in charge of the programme for air ferrying aircraft and equipment from the United States; the Americans were pressing for a speeding up of the process. (After a discreet enquiry, he found the Americans were not in favour of Dowding.) He then proposed that Air Marshal Barratt should be transferred to this job and his position in Army Co-operation filled by Dowding. Sinclair and Portal objected strongly, pointing out how using him in an Operational Command would run contrary to a recently declared Higher Appointments Policy. They proposed Sir Frederick Bowhill should be appointed instead. Churchill showed his displeasure, emphasising 'as Minister of Defence I am bound to take a direct part in all high appointments in the Fighting Services'. Part of the Sinclair reply spoke of the difficulties of finding employment for Dowding and explaining the impossibility of providing him with an operational Command now the retirement policy was in place. He recognised the Prime Minister's anxiety that he should remain in the employment of the State. At the end of June 1941, Sir Arthur Street, Permanent Under-Secretary of State for Air, wrote to Dowding on behalf of the Air Council asking him to write a Dispatch on the Battle of Britain. The letter finished by saying that with the conclusion of the work they would have no further employment to offer. 'You will accordingly be placed on the retired list from 1st October next.'

The dispatch was finished and submitted to Sinclair in late August 1941.

When Dowding's retirement was Gazetted, it created interest and a

189

degree of unfavourable comment in the Press. The reaction by Churchill on seeing the official announcement in his newspaper was electric. He wrote to his Chief of Staff, General Ismay, on 22 October,

'Pray enquire from the Secretary of State for Air and the Chief of the Air Staff in what circumstances and on what grounds Sir Hugh Dowding has been retired from the Air Force? Was he retired at his own request? Was he retired in virtue of some automatic age limit?'

Ismay made enquiries and the following day received a further Minute from Downing Street; on this occasion it was very strongly worded. It said,

'Wait upon the Secretary of State with this Minute and inform him that the Prime Minister and Minister of Defence cannot agree to the retirement of Sir Hugh Dowding. In a matter of this importance affecting an Officer who commanded in the decisive Battle of Britain, the Prime Minister should have been consulted beforehand.

(2) The enforced retirement from the Active list of Sir Hugh Dowding cannot be accepted. The Gazette must be cancelled in this respect, and the form of announcement must be settled forthwith.

(3) No important decisions about the appointment of Commander-in-Chief or the retirement of an officer of the highest consequence are to be taken by any of the Service Departments without consultation with the Prime Minister. This principle is fully recognised by the other Service Departments.'*[181]

Sinclair wrote to Ismay,

'I am extremely sorry to see from the Minutes which you showed me from the Prime Minister that he thinks that I have treated Sir Hugh Dowding with less than the consideration which is due to the victorious Commander in the Battle of Britain; and that I should have consulted him before releasing the brake, which I have applied for five months, to the routine process of retirement.'

He said he had discussed the Prime Minister's strongly expressed wish

* It is of interest to note that on the first draft of the Minute (later crossed out by him), Churchill refers to a suggestion that he was contemplating six weeks earlier replacing Air Marshal Tedder with Dowding in the Middle East. He had been persuaded against this by Sinclair and Portal. Churchill made this point when reminding them that they were aware of his intention to keep Dowding in active employment.

190

that Sir Hugh Dowding should be found employment with CAS (Portal), and was prepared to offer the job of examining the Establishments of the Royal Air Force in the United Kingdom and report on what manpower reduction could be made without prejudicing its operational efficiency. (A shortage of men was forecast for 1942.) If he agreed, he could be employed as a retired officer with a 25 per cent increase in pay. The alternative was to cancel his retirement and employ him on the Active List; this course would entail losing the 25 per cent increase and arouse public comment and questions in the House of Commons on the cancellation of the Gazette; this publicity would be distasteful to Sir Hugh Dowding himself. On the 24th, Churchill indicated his approval to Sinclair of the arrangement and selected the option of cancelling the retirement.

Portal wrote to Air Marshal Sir Christopher Courtney, Head of the Establishments Committee, and explained how the Minister of Defence (Churchill) had not been notified of Dowding's retirement and 'when he saw the announcement in the newspapers, he decided that, in view of the high service rendered by Dowding in the past, some further employment must be found for him'.[182]

Sinclair invited Dowding to see him on 28 October 1941 and told him about the work. The following day, writing from his home in Wimbledon, Dowding turned it down. His wish to remain retired was accepted by Sinclair but not by Churchill who asked to see him. The discussion was very frank. Afterwards, Dowding made a note: 'I said that I should work with the utmost reluctance under Sir Archibald Sinclair, whom I dislike and distrust. He said (Churchill), "He is one of my oldest friends and I don't think he has ever spoken badly of you, though others may have", or words to that effect.'[183] He was astonished to hear Churchill remark that he had known nothing about the retirement and only learned of it when reading the newspapers. There was some discussion about the possible publication of a small book Dowding had finished writing a few days earlier. On the main issue Churchill was to have his way. However unpalatable the prospect of working with the Air Ministry, he returned to active service. By the time most of the task was done; he had had enough. On 18 June 1942, he wrote to Sinclair asking that he should be put on the Retired List 'at his own request'. In a further letter he complained of Staff Officers being guilty of inertia, obstruction and supplying false information. A certain officer, namely Sir Wilfrid Freeman, was impertinent and being supported by Sinclair. Clearly a recent discussion with the Secretary of State had been acrimonious; in the last paragraph he wrote,

'Finally

I must disassociate myself from your views that it is an act of disloyalty to the Air Force to take action which will result in defects at the Air Ministry being brought to the notice of the Prime Minister.'

On his retirement it was necessary for the King to sign the submission. On 17 July 1942 the King's Private Secretary, Sir Alexander Hardinge, wrote to Sinclair,

'. . . at the same time His Majesty wished me to raise with you the question of his being promoted to Marshal of the Royal Air Force on retirement. There may be all sorts of difficulties of which the King is not unaware; but it has always seemed to him that Dowding performed a really wonderful service to this Country, in creating and putting into practice, the defence system which proved so effective in the Battle of Britain. His Majesty would be most grateful if you would give this suggestion your consideration.'

After discussing it with the Chief of the Air Staff (Portal), Sinclair answered, welcoming the appreciation His Majesty had of Dowding and continued,

'But I have reached the conclusion, after careful consideration, that there are certain objections to his promotion to Marshal of the Royal Air Force at the present time. In the first place, the Battle of Britain was fought nearly two years ago and it might well be asked why, if he was not promoted at the close of the Battle of Britain, he should now receive this award. But a more serious objection, surely, is that Sir Hugh Dowding has, with his Majesty's approval, already retired once. While I could not have recommended promotion when he retired last October, it would certainly have been understandable then; but I cannot help feeling that promotion now in lieu of reversion to the retired list would be a matter for comment . . . When rewards come to be made at the end of the war, Sir Hugh Dowding's name might be considered along with those of other senior officers of the Royal Air Force who have rendered outstanding war Service.' [If still in office he] 'should certainly then wish to consider the claims of Sir Hugh Dowding to some reward'.

Hardinge replied,

'His Majesty entirely recognises the force of your argument against promoting him to the rank of Marshal of the Royal Air Force at the present juncture; the King is quite satisfied to know that his services will come up for consideration of one kind or another at the end of the war. His Majesty did not as a matter of fact realise that he had already retired once before.'

R. H. Melville, Sinclair's Private Secretary, wrote to Portal,

'You have already been informed that Sir Alexander Hardinge withdrew the proposal that Sir Hugh Dowding should be promoted Marshal of the Royal Air Force. You may wish to see the correspondence which has passed between the Secretary of State and Sir Alexander Hardinge on the subject.' [The letter ended,] 'I should add that the final paragraph of the Secretary of State's letter is specifically worded to avoid any commitment to consider promotion to Marshal of the Royal Air Force for Sir Hugh Dowding. I informed Sir Alexander Hardinge that it was unlikely that this particular reward would in any event be recommended. He accepted this position.'[184]

Churchill, however, was not satisfied; on 11 May 1943, after Dowding had relinquished his post as Air Aide-de-Camp to the King, he wrote to him,

'I should be glad to know whether you would allow me to put your name forward to The King for the honour of a Barony. I am proposing this in view of your memorable services to this country during the Battle of Britain.'

Dowding chose the title 'The Lord Dowding of Bentley Priory'. By now he had settled into civilian life.

On 9 May 1945, the day after the end of the war in Europe, Sir Archibald Sinclair wrote to Dowding,

'On this historic day I send to you on behalf of the Air Council a message of cordial greeting. It was under your inspired leadership that the Battle of Britain was won and our island citadel was saved. The whole nation, indeed freedom-loving men and women the world over, will always gratefully remember you and the gallant "few" who fought and flew under your command.'[185]

About three weeks later, at the time of his retirement as Secretary of State for Air, he also wrote a letter to Sholto Douglas, Dowding's successor at Fighter Command, part of which said, 'I felt as though I had won a battle when I got Fighter Command into your hands, and, looking back, how right I was.'[186] The letter to Dowding was one of a number of congratulatory messages sent out by the Air Council to prominent Air Force figures, and it fell to Sir Archibald Sinclair to compose the one to the ex-Commander-in-Chief Fighter Command.

Chapter 11

Fighter Command on the Offensive

W hen Douglas took over Fighter Command in November 1940, of the fifty-two day squadrons only half were Category 'A', suitable for the front line. He asked the Air Ministry to expand the fighter force to eighty day squadrons and twenty of night fighters; they settled on a figure of sixty-four for the day work. Three new Fighter Groups, Nos. 9 and 14 in the North and No. 82 in Northern Ireland, would be in being by the end of 1941.

When touring aerodromes, the new C-in-C was often being asked by pilots to provide aircraft capable of better performance at altitude; Hurricane pilots complained of being unable to compete with the Bf.109s above 20,000 feet and those flying Spitfires were similarly affected about 25,000. Keith Park had already reported how, when engagements were taking place above this height, the performance of enemy fighters was vastly superior. Air Vice-Marshal Sandy Johnstone CB, DFC, AE, then commanding No. 602 Squadron, later commented,

'Although we could coax the Mk. 1 Spitfires up to 33,000 feet, they were literally hanging on their props at that height and would probably have stalled on the spot from the recoil of the guns if they were fired. Once they (Bf.109s) began to appear at these great heights, we just left them to their own devices and waited for them to come down to a level of our own choosing; generally around 27,000 feet, then we could deal with them more easily. Needless to say, they seldom accepted the challenge and seemingly preferred to keep out of harm's way.'[187]

When Leigh-Mallory took over from Keith Park, who was about to be moved to No. 23 Training Group, Douglas wrote to him saying that the biggest problem to overcome was the night bomber and if it was not solved 'we may even lose the war'.[188] Douglas acknowledged the Directif giving priority to protection of the aircraft industry and considered, 'No formal variation of this directif was needed to make it clear that the defeat of the night bomber must be one of my main tasks.'[189] This was an obvious and accurate assessment. He was already in dispute with the Air Ministry, having learned of their decision to postpone further supply of the nightfighter version of the Beaufighter; all future production was to be directed to Coastal Command. He wrote to CAS (Portal), reminding him of poor serviceability of his aircraft and suggesting more interceptions could be achieved if more Beaufighters were operating. Portal replied saying how certain powerful forces were working to hand over Coastal Command to the Admiralty and to keep it, it was necessary to give priority to all of the Command's requirements. (The 'powerful forces' were the First Sea Lord and Beaverbrook.) He told Douglas more numbers would do no good

'until the problem of shooting down the bombers is solved . . . so far as I know, you have not a single crew which can yet intercept and destroy night bombers with any regularity, and so long as this persists I regard the problem as completely unsolved and the provision of a larger number of aircraft as a requirement of secondary importance'.[190]

By the following April, Douglas was able, statistically, to prove his case. Portal wrote to Beaverbrook,

'We want immediately a much greater number of Beaufighters for Fighter Command to enable them to take toll of the enemy night bombers. In no other way can we lessen the night attacks on your aircraft factories.'[191]

By the end of February 1941 shipping losses to German U-boats and long-range aircraft were very serious. Fighter Command was called upon to assume more responsibility for the protection of East Coast traffic. On 9 March, a formal Directif extending this was issued; defence of the Clyde, Mersey and Bristol Channel became the Command's primary task, superseding that of the aircraft industry.

By now the Command was also flying over the continent in strength, seeking to destroy enemy aircraft; its radius of activity was being strictly limited by the short range of the fighters. In cloudy conditions small numbers were sent out; in clear weather large formations with a few bombers as bait were flying CIRCUS operations. These resembled some of the early tactics employed by the *Luftwaffe* during the Battle of Britain, but there was one fundamental difference; unlike the British, the Germans were not defending their own land, a few bombs on occupied territory did not goad them into retaliating. In fact, during the early part of 1941, many of their battle-worn fighter units returned home to rest and train. Results then were disappointing; after six months just twenty-three of the enemy were claimed against a loss of thirty-one pilots. No major engagements had been fought. The *Luftwaffe* was surreptitiously moving its aircraft into positions ready for an attack on Russia, in the East. On 17 June, Portal issued instructions for an intensified campaign to try to hold these aircraft in the West but by the latter part of July the losses were so high that it brought into question whether 'Circuses' should continue. Since 19 June, no less than one hundred and twenty-three pilots were lost. Douglas was far from happy. On 29 August he wrote to Sir Wilfrid Freeman at the Air Ministry, 'From the parochial Fighter Command point of view this particular war has ceased to pay dividends. How long ought we to continue with these offensive sweeps on the present intensive scale?'[192]

German pilots were puzzled by the aims of British strategy and contented themselves by using small numbers of aircraft to nibble at the fringes of the large British formations and by exploiting every favourable opportunity for a quick kill. Eventually only two single-seat fighter *Geschwader* remained in the West between the Franco–Belgian frontier and Brittany. During the period of intensified operations, they cut back to between 160 and 200 serviceable aircraft.[193] By the end of August 1941, this figure had fallen to just 97 serviceable machines. (After the war, German records revealed that only 81 of their aircraft had been lost during the entire daylight offensive. Fighter Command claimed 355 aircraft destroyed.) By the autumn such offensive operations by Fighter Command were temporarily phased out. The prospect of bad weather and the need to conserve aircraft made the campaign unsustainable. Meanwhile a policy of denying use of the English Channel to German shipping was vigorously pursued; night offensive 'intruder' operations over the Continent were continued.

As in all air warfare, each side sought dominance over the other by improved performance of their aircraft and equipment. Fighter Command was having a few problems. The Hawker Typhoon single-seat fighter, introduced into service at the latter part of 1941, was having engine problems and structural failures; its performance at altitude was poor. The supply of Beaufighters remained inadequate; in July interest focused on the use of a new twin-engined, all-wooden aircraft, the De Havilland Mosquito, for nightfighting, which eventually established itself as the best nightfighter of all.

With the Spring of 1942, offensive operations were resumed and continued to be costly. The latest Bf.109(F) and a fine new radial-engined fighter, the Focke-Wulf 190, were outclassing the best the British could put into the air. Their general performance particularly at high altitude, was proving to be of great tactical benefit to German pilots. Rolls-Royce were at the time developing a new engine, the Merlin 61, and Sholto Douglas wrote to the Air Ministry in April asking for early steps to be taken to fit one hundred of them to Mark V Spitfires. This combination, designated the Mark IX, proved so successful that it largely redressed the dominance of the German machines and was later produced in very large numbers. The C-in-C was clearly impressed with the new Merlin engine. A few days after urging the Air Ministry to fit it to the Spitfires, he was writing to them again,

'It seems quite clear that our best hope of outmatching the Hun fighter force next Spring is the proposal to put the Merlin 61 into the Mustang, and to persuade the Americans to produce this aircraft in considerable numbers'.[194]

This idea had first been spoken of a few days earlier. The Mustang until then was in use as a photo reconnaissance, ground support fighter, another of the American aircraft with poor altitude performance. However, when fitted with the Rolls-Royce engine, it became arguably the finest piston-engined fighter of the war.

On 28 November 1942, Sholto Douglas left Fighter Command to take up an appointment in the Middle East and his position at Bentley Priory was filled by Trafford Leigh-Mallory. With the United States now in the war, the plans for the eventual defeat of Germany were already being prepared. Sections of the three British armed Services were working at Norfolk House in St James Square, London to lay some of the groundwork for an invasion of Northern France. Group Captain Tom Gleave arrived in early September and became Group Captain Air Plans under Air Commodore Victor Groom (now Sir Victor). Planning was conducted under the code name 'ROUND UP', subsequently renamed 'OVERLORD'. In mid Summer 1943, Lieutenant-General Sir Frederick Morgan, Chief of Staff to Supreme Allied Commander (COSSAC) took up residence; the Supreme Commander, General D. Eisenhower, was appointed later. Morgan's arrival heralded a further stage of the planning process; each member of the British staff was paired with an American counterpart. Tom Gleave, now Head of Air Plans, began working with Colonel 'Pete' Phillips (United States Army Air Force). When they had written the first draft, 'Pete' appraised it and translated it into American. Leigh-Mallory was given added responsibility for the planning and preparation for the Air Operation in August 1943 as Air Commander-in-Chief (Designate) and on the formation of the Allied Expeditionary Air Force (AEAF) in

November, took over command. The new Force grew out of Fighter Command and the remaining structure became the Air Defence of Great Britain under Air Marshal Sir Roderic Hill who undertook the defensive responsibilities hitherto undertaken by Fighter Command, and included the early protection of the invasion forces during the initial stage of the assault. He was responsible to Leigh-Mallory now Air Chief Marshal Sir Trafford, as was Air Marshal Sir Arthur Coningham, Commander of Royal Air Force Second Tactical Air Force, and Major-General Lewis H. Brereton, Commander of US Ninth Air Force. However, Leigh-Mallory delegated operational control of the planning and operations of both RAF and US Tactical Air Forces to Air Marshal Sir Arthur Coningham who became known as the Commander, Advanced Allied Expeditionary Air Force, with Headquarters at Hillingdon House, Uxbridge. Leigh-Mallory's Headquarters were at Stanmore. This was a natural choice for the headquarters of air operations; it was already the hub of a vast communications network and the only place in the country where a comprehensive visual display of air activity over the British Isles and the proposed invasion area could be seen. With space at Bentley Priory already at a premium, expansion to take in OVERLORD planning staff brought about an overflow into the Stanmore and Elstree districts.

Air Marshal Sir Douglas 'Zulu' Morris, then a Group Captain and second-in-command at North Weald, was called to Bentley Priory by Leigh-Mallory:

'He said, "I want you here tomorrow morning to start a new headquarters for me." I replied, "Yes Sir!" and that was how the invasion headquarters for the Air Component, soon to become Headquarters of the Allied Expeditionary Air Force, came into being. At nine o'clock the following morning I went off to find a suitable building and chose "Kestrel Grove", a large house close by in Hive Road, but very soon the organisation outgrew the building and more offices were sought elsewhere.

'The various branches had planning meetings; it was then up to me; they decided what they wanted and I, with my small staff of five or six people, processed it. Our part was to provide the manpower and equipment for the projects. At meetings at the Air Ministry I would say, "I want fifty men, or perhaps a hundred, even a thousand" and they would ask why and I would say, "Sorry I can't tell you." It was all very secret. I then told them where the men and equipment were to be sent. Once there, training etc. commenced.

199

'Building up the invasion air force was an enormous undertaking and as time went on, finding locations for the units we were creating became increasingly difficult. It took an age arguing with the Air Marshals about where the units should be settled; I recall being so frustrated on one occasion, I said to one, "You are a bloody bastard, you will not agreed to anything." Having blurted it out, my immediate thought, being a Group Captain, was, "My God, this is the end, you've done it now." To my surprise he simply said, "Of course I won't." Strangely he became more amenable afterwards. Everything was designed to be able to move forward at the right time as the ground forces moved deeper into Europe.'

To make way for senior officers about to conduct the air war from down 'the hole', the No. 11 Group Filter Room was relocated in August 1943 at 'Hill House', a large house on the right of the hill going down into Stanmore; this was just prior to AEAF Headquarters being set up in the area. At this time the combined services establishment had already reached 3,022 people; (nearly a year later the RAF and WAAF, figure alone had risen to 2,934). The need for more accommodation for personnel led to more private houses being requisitioned.

As D-Day, 5 June, approached (it was later put back to the 6th because of bad weather), conferences of US and RAF Commanders were held in the War Room down 'the hole' each morning. They were given a weather forecast, reports on Naval activity and Military Intelligence, and an appraisal of German Air Force performance. Commanders usually gave an account of raids carried out by their respective air forces during the previous twenty-four hours. Further operations were discussed and assigned to the heavy bombers of US 8th Air Force and Bomber Command; medium and fighter-bomber operations were co-ordinated with the strategic heavy bomber programmes. Each week a list of targets, with selected priorities, was issued by the Chief of Operations at AEAF Headquarters 'Kestrel Grove'. From the underground block at Bentley Priory the Air Commanders directed the most potent weapon of destruction yet known to man.

The task of Leigh-Mallory as Air Commander was not made easier by disagreements about the best way to support the invasion force by disrupting the enemy's supplies and reinforcements. Professor Solly Zuckermann, a scientist employed in air planning, realised that destruction of important centres in the railway network would achieve the desired effect. But what became known as the Transportation Plan was opposed by commanders of the heavy bomber air forces who were actively engaged in Operation POINTBLANK, a directif issued nearly a year earlier for the destruction of the German fighter force and its supporting industry. Lieutenant-General James Doolittle of the US 8th Air Force, was directing daylight operations against the German aircraft industry and airfields, lately concentrating on the oil industry; meanwhile, Air Chief Marshal Sir Arthur Harris was directing Bomber Command efforts at night on industrial cities. Both thought their particular strategy would win the war and neither wished to be diverted from it. A compromise was reached which allowed for both air forces to be used in the Transportation Plan for the period prior to OVERLORD. In spite of differing opinions on policy and clashes of personality, the air plan was accepted. From early May, effort was directed on to the pre-invasion target programme.

Into the already contentious situation a further and not altogether unexpected factor had been thrust upon the planners of OVERLORD. It had long been known, from some impressive research by Dr R.V. Jones and his colleagues of British Scientific Intelligence, that the Germans were working on the development of 'V' weapons (*Vergeltungswaffen*), Retaliation Weapons. One, the V1, was to appear in the form of a small robot aircraft transporting nearly one ton of explosive, another, a long-range rocket with a similar payload – the V2.

In the Autumn of 1943, the French Resistance was reporting the building of peculiar concrete structures with attendant buildings on small sites in the hinterland of Northern France. Photographic Reconnaissance brought forth further evidence; many more were discovered within a radius of 130–140 miles of London. Scientific Intelligence identified them as launching sites for robot V1 flying bombs, the ski-shaped constructions being launching ramps. The seriousness of the threat led to a diversion of some of the bomber effort on to their destruction.

While this bombing (codenamed CROSSBOW) progressed, German engineers were surreptitiously producing and putting in place a more simplified version of the launching apparatus and many of these sites remained undetected. The Allies, seriously overestimating the damage they had done to the V1 programme, returned to their bombing campaign and the air support of the D-Day invasion forces. Neither Air Marshal Hill, C-in-C of the defence forces, nor General Pile, commanding AA gun defences, had sufficient intelligence information to speculate on what the weight of the flying bomb attack would most likely be and where it would be directed. A plan was devised which would allow for a rapid redeployment of defence forces should the attack develop on Southern

201

embarkation ports now overflowing with men and weapons for the D-Day operations or, alternatively, if it were to be directed against London. Soon after 4 a.m. on 13 June, a week after the successful OVERLORD landing in France, the first of many V1 'Doodlebugs' was launched against England; the target was London and its citizens. Thereafter the number of flying bombs increased to alarming proportions as more of the hidden modified sites were brought into use.

The Intelligence Section, accommodated in huts in the grounds at Bentley Priory, was particularly hard pressed. Eileen McCormack (née Montgomery) was a WAAF member serving then:

'Our section was assigned to sifting ordinary private citizens' mail captured in raids by the Resistance in France, Belgium and Holland. Each letter was scrutinised and important items heavily scored. The letters were usually of a personal nature; relatives, friends or perhaps to military personnel from home. There would be remarks such as "Some soldiers have arrived in the village and we have been asked to billet them." Another might say, "We can no longer go to the park as it has been closed to the public; the Army are doing something there", and such like. From this private correspondence, information was gleaned on troop movements and other military developments. There was concern about Hitler's "V" weapons and I recall specific information being sought on the location of launching ramps being erected in France; the closing of a park mentioned in a letter was the clue to one site. We sent reports to Uxbridge, Photo Reconnaissance took photographs of suspect areas and, if our suspicions were confirmed, they were passed to the bomber force for action. On many evenings as the Lancaster bombers droned overhead on their way to the Continent, we knew what their target was.'

A very serious blunder had been made by those responsible for direction of the flying bomb countermeasures. Earlier, in May, the 2nd Tactical Air Force and the US 9th Air Force were given an instruction that emphasis given to CROSSBOW should be 10% and 'This effort should not exceed 10%'.[195] At this time the US 8th Air Force had carried out a few raids on the sites; Bomber Command operations had ceased weeks earlier. Such was the miscalculation that two days after the D-Day landings, a Chiefs of Staff Sub Committee met to discuss dismantling AA Command.[196]

Now, no effort was spared in seeking out and bombing the 'ski' sites and supply organisation. With the characteristics of the bomb now fully revealed and experience in combating the weapon growing, Roderic Hill and Frederick Pile set about reorganising the defences. In the early stage of the bombardment the fighters proved to be the most effective; they were patrolling over the sea and inland to the edge of a gun zone behind which was a balloon zone protecting London. Hill's Deputy SASO at Bentley Priory, Air Commodore G. H. Ambler, suggested how the efficiency of the defences could be improved by radical changes in the zones of action afforded to the aircraft and gun components. Heated arguments were also occurring; pilots were complaining of gunners shooting at them. Hill, convinced of the efficacy of Ambler's ideas, called a meeting of Air Defence Commanders and advisers on 13 July. All agreed to the proposed changes. At a conference earlier in the day, Hill had mentioned likely changes. Leigh-Mallory directed that 'the disposition of defences should not be made without a trial on a small Sector'.[197] The new plan was for all guns to be moved to the coast to fire out to sea and a short distance inland; fighters would operate out to sea in front of and behind the gun zone – balloons remain in existing positions. The plan entailed an enormous movement of many hundreds of guns and many thousands of personnel. A vast signals network was required. Amazingly all the heavy guns were in situ in three days and the light guns two days later. Ignoring Leigh-Mallory's advice, Hill gave the order for the moves. Two days later, advising the Air Ministry of what he was doing, he stressed that it was merely a tactical redeployment of resources although it did involve changes in the plan previously approved by them. People at the top were not pleased. Air Marshal Bottomley, DCAS, wrote on their behalf censuring Hill for not having consulted them. Hill, in return, replied, trying to disguise the truth, that he was making a tactical re-orientation of the defences. This new plan used the guns more effectively; firing out to sea they could now use shells fitted with proximity fuses which exploded when in the vicinity of an object, a hazard overland. For Roderic Hill, who took full responsibility for the move, the success of the redeployments was fortunate. The CAS (Portal) had already distanced himself from it. At a meeting of the War Cabinet, he 'expressed some doubts whether the rearrangement would in practice prove to be an improvement on the previous system'.[198] With 'ski' sites being overrun by advances on the continent and the highly successful air defences, the flying bomb campaign was finally neutralised. At the time when defence chiefs were congratulating themselves on the successful outcome, the first V2 long-range rocket hit London. Although AA Command began working on an idea, as yet there was no defence and fortunately the Germans were unable to sustain attacks of the same severity as those of the V1s. The rockets ceased when ground forces pushed their launching area beyond range of Britain, by which time the fate of Germany was almost sealed.

When hostilities ceased in Europe at midnight on 8 May 1945, celebrations at Bentley Priory (once more Headquarters Fighter Command, having reverted to the old title in October 1944), were well organised. There were Thanksgiving Services, free beer at lunchtime and a dance in the evening. An enormous cake, weighing nearly two hundredweight and decorated to represent an airfield, was provided by the Mess Staff; a large bonfire continued to blaze into the early hours. The next day, perhaps not surprisingly, was designated as one of rest. The following Saturday, after a Thanksgiving Parade and march past, Sir Roderic Hill left to take up an appointment on the Air Council. The killing and destruction had ceased, but for Roderic Hill and many thousands of others, the anguish continued. The war had recently cost him the life of his son.

Appendix 1

Evidence from Squadron and Group Operations Record Books

Information recorded in Squadron and Group Operations Record Books is not always reliable, e.g. the No. 12 Group book shows that on 24 August 1940, the day North Weald was bombed, and two days later when Debden was attacked, No. 66 Squadron was sent to reinforce No. 11 Group, also on the day of the raid on Debden, No. 229 Squadron is recorded as having been sent. On both these days neither Squadron's Operations Record Book makes mention of this. Of the other two Squadrons stated as having reinforced No. 11 Group, it would seem No. 19 got airborne soon after the North Weald raid, but No. 310 took off nearly 1 hour 20 minutes later. When Debden was hit, No. 19 Squadron's Spitfires took off 31 minutes after the bombing and six Hurricanes of No. 310 Squadron left Duxford (8 miles away) ten minutes after the attack, but were able to intercept some raiders when they were going home; whether these were from the Debden raid is not known. From the evidence, although Park did not specify dates when complaining about the late arrival of 12 Group reinforcements 'late August', these were the attacks to which he referred. If the books are to be believed, other than an abortive patrol over North Weald by No. 310 Squadron in the late afternoon of 18 August, no other assistance appears to have been sent to No. 11 Group prior to then.

Curiously, his appreciation of the co-operation received from No. 10 Group may well have been based on an agreed code of practice for reinforcing; a study of Operations Record Books of that Group and its Squadrons gives no indication of reinforcements ever being sent to No. 11 Group before the date of Park's initial criticism made in instructions to his Controllers. (27 August.)

As a generalisation, what does become clear from the records of this period is how little the Squadrons in No. 12 Group were being operated at full squadron strength. Other than the interception of the 15 August

North Sea raid on Humberside by No. 616 Squadron, there is no recorded evidence to suggest the squadrons were ever employed in protecting their Group area in anything other than single aircraft, a Section of three aircraft or a Flight of six aircraft. A similar picture is created by No. 13 Group's records; here again 15 August was unusual in that full-strength Squadrons Nos. 41, 607, 605, 79 and 72, plus the Blenheims of 219 were put up to defend the Newcastle area.

Normally there was little call for the use of more aircraft in the north; daylight raids were very small. Heavy raids on the industrial Midlands were confined to the hours of darkness; there can be little doubt that some squadrons sent down from the north to replace exhausted units of No. 11 Group before this policy was dropped in early September 1940, lacked experience for the tooth and nail conflict there. Within days, their losses were so high that some had themselves to be replaced: those remaining had good leadership and learned very quickly.

Appendix 2

Historical Notes on Bentley Priory

T he mansion originated from a small house bought from James Duberley, an Army Contractor, by the Honourable John James Hamilton, later Ninth Earl and First Marquess of Abercorn, in 1788.

John Soane, the eminent architect, was commissioned by Hamilton to design the total transfiguration of the house and estate and worked on the project for sixteen years. First drawings were completed at his office at Welbeck Street in 1789 and were for a breakfast room, library and 'Tribune' now usually referred to as the 'Rotunda'; later in the year designs were for a dining room, music room and an additional withdrawing room.

When the Marquess died in 1818, he was succeeded by his grandson who had not yet reached the age of consent and resided at Bentley Priory, when not at school at Harrow, with his guardian Lord Aberdeen. He later became the First Duke of Abercorn.

In 1848 the entire freehold estates at Stanmore were put up for sale by auction. (The Priory estate now said to be upwards of 500 acres. The other property, Stanmore Park, which was acquired in 1840, said to have been upwards of 1,400 acres.) The sale appears not to have proceeded. That same year, the ailing Dowager Queen Adelaide, widow of William IV, negotiated a three year lease during which time she was visited by Queen Victoria and the Prince Consort. The old Queen's residency was very short; she died on 2 December 1849.

On 14 April 1853, the now 455 acre estate passed into the hands of John Kelk, a building contractor, who was known for his work on railway construction. A price of £41,000 plus £500 for fixtures was agreed commencing with a £5,000 deposit. Four years later, Kelk's advisers discovered that certain parts of the estate were of copyhold and wastehold tenure and the price was reduced by £1,000; he did, however, agree to purchase an additional strip of land for £225 which had not been included in the original transaction. The new owner carried out alterations including construction of a clock tower and Tuscan portico at the rear.

In December 1881, Frederick Gordon bought Bentley Priory for £75,000, £55,000 of which was conditionally lent to Gordon by Kelk. By adding an extra wing accommodating bed chambers, Gordon, a hotelier, extended his business; he was also responsible for extending the railway into the Stanmore district. Much of the land, said to be 466 acres when purchased from Kelk, was sold off for building plots varying from three to twenty acres.

By June 1895, the hotel had failed and the property was for sale but it was not until 1907 at the time of Gordon's death that it finally changed hands. The building, now furnished with thirty bedrooms, became a private boarding school for about seventy young ladies of wealthy parentage and this survived until December 1924. It remained empty until 25 March 1926 when a decision on its future was finalised. The estate was divided; the largest portion, about 240 acres, was purchased by a syndicate which subsequently sold it off as building plots; the largest plot, 90 acres, was obtained by Middlesex County Council. The house and 41 acres of land was bought by the Air Ministry for £25,000.

An RAF Signals Unit arrived and on 25 May 1926 Headquarters Inland Area was officially installed.

Appendix 3

Treasury Inter-Services Committee Estimate of Expenditure on Radio Direction Finding Chain (CH Radar)

On 19 December 1935, the Treasury sanctioned expenditure for the establishment of four Stations; this also took in the cost of the Research Station at Orfordness. These were to be constructed for Service trials at a cost of *£68,000*. By August 1937, the experiments had been so successful that with only those at Orfordness, Bawdsey and Canewdon in operation (the other two at Great Bromley and Dunkirk were yet to be completed), it was decided to go ahead with the whole chain, making twenty in all. To bring the original five stations up to the design standard of the proposed fifteen new ones, a further outlay of *£137,000* was estimated. The probable average cost of each of the new stations was said to be:

Land	£3,000
Towers	£28,000
Power supply, electrical distribution, stand-by plant, etc.	£8,000
Operational buildings	£3,000
Roads, path and fencing	£5,000
Quarters for two warders	£1,200
Contingencies	£3,800
Total	£52,000

The fifteen stations would cost £780,000.

The twenty stations would each require a further £16,000 for more powerful apparatus, costing £320,000 in all.

The total cost for the Chain would be £1,305,000.

The annual operating cost was estimated at £174,000, made up as follows:

Pay of Personnel	£57,000
Works maintenance	£20,000
Transport	£10,000
Electricity, fuel and water	£2,000
Telephone rentals	£60,000
Maintenance of equipment	£25,000

The Treasury gave sanction for the proposal on 13 August 1937

Appendix 4

The Protection of the Aircraft Manufacturing Industry

The Chiefs of Staff 17 September 1939 Directif given to the Air Officer Commanding-in-Chief Fighter Command for the 'protection of vital points in the aircraft industry against air attack', listed the following areas:

Derby and Crewe (Rolls-Royce)
Bristol (Aircraft and Engine Factory)
Sheffield
Brooklands (Vickers and Hawkers)
Kingston (Hawkers)
Southampton (Supermarine)
Birmingham and Coventry
Castle Bromwich (Nuffield)
Wolverhampton (Boulton and Paul)
Hucclecote (Gloster)

A further appreciation was being prepared.

A paper appended to the Directif drew attention to the Coventry and Sheffield areas, the former producing by far the largest proportion of light alloy components; similarly the latter produced steel materials. It advised that Derby and Bristol were the most vital areas in connection with Aero Engine Production. If serious damage were inflicted on the locations mentioned, the whole of the industry 'would be virtually paralysed'.

Appendix 5

Members of the Air Council and Department of Chief of the Air Staff – October 1940

Members of the Air Council in October 1940

Sir Archibàld Sinclair, Bt – President
Captain H.H. Balfour – Vice-President
Marshal of the RAF Sir Cyril Newall – Chief of the Air Staff (succeeded by Sir Charles Portal from 25 October 1940)
Air Vice-Marshal (acting Air Marshal) E.L. Gossage – Air Member for Personnel
Air Marshal Sir Christopher Courtney – Air Member for Supply and Organisation
Air Vice-Marshal A.G.R. Garrod – Air Member for Training
Sir Wilfrid Freeman – Representing Ministry of Aircraft Production (later Vice-Chief of the Air Staff)
Sir Charles Craven
Sir Harold Howitt
Sir Arthur Street – The Permanent Under-Secretary of State for Air

Members of the Department of Chief of the Air Staff in October 1940

Air Chief Marshal Sir Charles F.A. Portal – Chief of the Air Staff
R.S. Crawford – Private Secretary
J.S. Orme – Assistant Private Secretary
Air Chief Marshal Sir Wilfrid R. Freeman – Vice-Chief of the Air Staff
Air Vice-Marshal W. Sholto Douglas – Deputy Chief of the Air Staff
Air Vice-Marshal R.H. Peck – Assistant Chief of the Air Staff (General)
Air Commodore (Acting Air Vice-Marshal) R.H.M.S Saundby – Assistant Chief of the Air Staff (Operational Requirements and Tactics)
Air Marshal Sir Philip B. Joubert de la Ferté – Assistant Chief of the Air Staff (Radio)
Wing Commander J.E.W. Bowles – Assistant Director of Air Tactics (ADAT)

References

References prefixed P.R.O. refer to Public Record Office Crown Copyright material.

1 PRO AIR 2 1812
2 PRO AIR 2 1812
3 PRO AIR 2 1389
4 PRO AIR 2 1389
5 PRO AIR 2 1389
6 PRO AIR 2 1389
7 PRO AIR 16 260
8 PRO AIR 2 3034
9 PRO AIR 2 1812
10 A.F. Wilkins in *Bawdsey, Birth of the Beam* by Gordon Kinsey: Terence Dalton
11 PRO AIR 2 2145
12 PRO AIR 2 2145
13 PRO AIR 20 2095
14 PRO AIR 2 3579
15 Lady Betty Pretty in a discussion with the author.
16 From the text of BBC programme *The Forgotten Leader* – 1971
17 E.G. Bowen *Radar Days*: Adam Hilger
18 PRO AIR 10 5485
19 PRO AIR 10 5485
20 PRO AIR 16 129 *Preliminary Report on Home Defence Exercise 25 August 1939*
21 PRO AIR 16 261
22 PRO AIR 2 4195
23 PRO AIR 24 507
24 PRO AIR 16 129
25 PRO AIR 16 677
26 PRO AIR 16 37
27 PRO AIR 16 37
28 PRO CAB 79 1 War Cabinet Meeting 22 September 1939
29 PRO AIR 20 2055
30 PRO AIR 8 287
31 PRO AIR 8 287
32 Air Chief Marshal Sir Hugh Dowding *The Battle of Britain Dispatch – 20 August 1941*
33 PRO AIR 8 287
34 PRO AIR 8 287
35 PRO AIR 8 287
36 PRO AIR 8 287
37 PRO AIR 16 190 *Fighter Policy September 1939 – May 1940*; Dowding correspondence with the Air Council
38 Correspondence between the author and Professor Hanbury Brown
39 PRO AIR 26 186
40 PRO AVIA 7 124
41 PRO AVIA 7 344
42 PRO AVIA 7 344
43 PRO AIR 2 7180
44 David Pritchard *The Radar War*: Patrick Stephens
45 Conversation between Air Vice-Marshal Peter Chamberlain and the author
46 Correspondence with the author
47 Correspondence with the author
48 Sadie Younger's correspondence with the author
49 PRO AIR 2 2599
50 PRO AIR 20 2095
51 PRO AIR 20 2061 Notes on Fighter Command activities over the Continent
52 PRO CAB 65 13
53 Paul Reynaud *In the Thick of the Fight*: Cassell & Co. Ltd, London.
54 PRO CAB 79 4 133rd COS Meeting
55 PRO CAB 65 13

56 PRO AIR 16 359
57 PRO AIR 20 4341
58 PRO AIR 8 287
59 John Colville *The Fringes of Power*:
   Hodder and Stoughton
60 PRO AIR 41 14
61 PRO AIR 41 14
62 PRO AIR 20 4341
63 PRO AIR 20 4341
64 PRO CAB 79 4
65 PRO AIR 16 900
66 PRO AIR 8 287
67 PRO AIR 8 287
68 PRO AIR 8 287
69 M.A. Liskutin, DFC, AFC *Challenge
   in the Air*: William Kimber
70 PRO AIR 20 4341
71 PRO AIR 24 507
72 PRO AIR 2 3080
73 PRO AVIA 7 438
74 PRO AVIA 7 438
75 PRO AIR 24 526
76 PRO AIR 20 7701 Conference held
   at Karinhall 15 August 1940
77 F. H. Hinsley, *British Intelligence
   in the Second World War* – Vol. 1:
   HMSO, London
78 Alfred Price, Figures from *Pictorial
   History of the Luftwaffe*: Ian Allen,
   London
79 Air Chief Marshal Sir Hugh Dowding
   The Battle of Britain Dispatch – 20
   August 1941
80 PRO AIR 24 526
81 PRO AIR 2 2964
82 PRO AIR 20 251
83 PRO AIR 16 99
84 PRO AIR 20 4341
85 PRO AIR 2 3559
86 PRO AIR 20 251
87 PRO AIR 20 7701
88 PRO AIR 16 1067 Keith Park
   Report – *Air Attacks on England
   between 8 August and 10 September*.
89 PRO AIR 20 4684
90 Correspondence between Audrey
   Brown and the author
91 PRO AIR 41 12
92 PRO AIR 20 7701 Translation of
   captured German documents
93 PRO AIR 41 16
94 PRO AIR 16 1067 Keith
   Park Report – *Air Attacks on*

*England between 8 August and 10
   September*
95 PRO AIR 16 735
96 PRO AIR 41 16
97 PRO AIR 25 197
98 PRO AIR 20 251
99 PRO AIR 20 2062
100 PRO AIR 25 197
101 PRO AIR 16 365
102 PRO AIR 25 197
103 PRO AIR 16 1067
104 PRO AIR 20 2062
105 PRO AIR 16 668
106 PRO AIR 20 4338
107 PRO AIR 16 901
108 PRO AIR 16 901
109 PRO AIR 16 217
110 PRO AIR 41 16
111 PRO AIR 16 901
112 PRO AIR 41 16
113 PRO AIR 16 638
114 PRO AIR 16 375
115 PRO AIR 16 735
116 PRO AIR 16 282
117 Keith Park, *German attacks
   on England 11 September–31
   October 1940.*
118 Peter Flint *RAF Kenley* (information
   supplied by Group Captain Myles
   Duke-Woolley): Terence Dalton
119 PRO AIR 16 98
120 PRO AIR 25 197
121 Air Chief Marshal Sir Hugh
   Dowding, *The Battle of Britain
   Dispatch* – 20 August 1941
122 PRO PREM 4 68/9
123 PRO AIR 41 16
124 PRO AIR 16 330
125 PRO AIR 16 330
126 PRO AIR 2 7281
127 PRO AIR 16 1067
128 PRO AIR 16 735
129 PRO AIR 2 7281
130 PRO AIR 16 735
131 PRO AIR 20 2062
132 PRO AIR 20 2062
133 PRO AIR 24 511
134 PRO AIR 20 2062
135 PRO AIR 20 7000
136 Martin Gilbert, *Finest Hour:* William
   Heinemann Ltd
137 PRO PREM 3 22/2
138 PRO AVIA 15 366

139 PRO AIR 41 12
140 PRO AIR 2 8344
141 PRO PREM 3 22/2
142 PRO AIR 19 157
143 PRO AIR 19 157
144 PRO AIR 41 16
145 Harold Balfour, *Wings over Westminster*: Hutchinson
146 PRO AIR 20 251
147 PRO AIR 16 375
148 PRO AIR 16 375
149 PRO AIR 16 375
150 PRO AIR 16 282
151 Laddie Lucas, *Flying Colours*: Hutchinson
152 PRO AIR 16 375
153 PRO AIR 2 2946
154 PRO AIR 41 16
155 Squadron Leader M.A. Liskutin, DFC, AFC and A. Vrana (No. 312 Squadron), letters
156 PRO AIR 16 387
157 PRO PREM 3 22/5
158 PRO AIR 16 677
159 PRO PREM 3 16
160 PRO AIR 41 18 and AIR 20 5192
161 PRO AIR 2 5230
162 Minutes of Committee Meeting 18 December 1940
163 PRO AIR 16 367
164 PRO AIR 16 367
165 PRO AIR 16 367
166 PRO AIR 16 367
167 PRO AIR 2 3034
168 PRO AIR 16 375
169 PRO AIR 19 572
170 RAF Museum B.2638 – Salmond Papers
171 PRO PREM 3 22/7
172 RAF Museum B.2638
173 RAF Museum B.2638 (Article written for Kemsley newspapers.)
174 PRO AIR 19 572 (On the cover of this file of the Secretary of State for Air's correspondence is written, 'Keep closed for 100 years'.
175 Robert Wright, *Dowding and the Battle of Britain*: McDonald.
176 PRO PREM 3 466
177 PRO PREM 3 22/2
178 PRO AIR 19 572
179 PRO PREM 3 466
180 RAF Museum AC 71/17/2 – Dowding File, Dowding's personal notes – Tour of Aircraft Plants in America
181 P.R.O PREM 4 68/9
182 RAF Museum – Dowding File AC 71/17/2
183 PRO AIR 19 572
184 PRO AIR 19 572
185 RAF Museum
186 Sholto Douglas, *Years of Command* Collins
187 Air Vice-Marshal Johnstone, letter to author
188 PRO AIR 24 508
189 PRO AIR 16 846 Report by Marshal of the Royal Air Force Sir Sholto Douglas
190 PRO AIR 16 622
191 PRO AIR 20 2899
192 PRO AIR 20 2778
193 PRO AIR 41 18
194 PRO AIR 27 509
195 PRO AIR 37 1443
196 General Sir Frederick Pile, *Ack-Ack*: Harrap
197 PRO AIR 37 563
198 PRO AIR 20 6016

Bibliography

Narrative of the history of Operational Research Section Fighter Command Edited by H.M. Barkla
Air Historical Branch Narrative – Fighter Control and Interception
Air Historical Branch Narrative – Air Defence of Great Britain, Radar in Raid Reporting
Air Ministry Pamphlet 1942 – Radio Location Systems of Raid Reporting
Air Ministry Pamphlet – Filter Room Standing Orders
Air Ministry Pamphlet – Standard Notes on RDF Training
Dispatch 'The Battle of Britain' The London Gazette – Air Chief Marshal Sir Hugh Dowding, G.C.B., G.C.V.O., C.M.G., A.D.C.
Air Operations Fighter Command, 25 November 1940 – 31 December 1941 (Report) – Marshal of the RAF Sir William Sholto Douglas
Air Historical Branch Narrative – Vol. IV The Beginning of the Fighter Offensive 1940–41
British Air Policy between the Wars, H. Montgomery Hyde – Heinemann
British Air Strategy between the Wars, Malcolm Smith – Oxford University Press
The Narrow Margin, Derek Wood and Derek Dempster – Hutchinson
The Rise and Fall of the German Air Force 1933–1945, – H.M.S.O., reprinted by Arms and Armour Press
Years of Command, Sholto Douglas with Robert Wright – Collins
Flying Colours, Laddie Lucas – Hutchinson
Bawdsey, Birth of the Beam, Gordon Kinsey – Terence Dalton
The Radar War, David Pritchard – Patrick Stephens
In the Thick of the Fight, Paul Reynaud – Cassell
The Fringes of Power, John Colville – Hodder and Stoughton
Challenge in the Air, M. A. Liskutin – William Kimber
British Intelligence in the Second World War Vol. 1, F. H. Hinsley – H.M.S.O.
Pictorial History of the Luftwaffe, Dr Alfred Price – Ian Allen
RAF Kenley, Peter Flint – Terence Dalton
Wings over Westminster, Harold Balfour – Hutchinson
Dowding and the Battle of Britain, Robert Wright – McDonald
Ack-Ack, General Sir Frederick Pile – Harrap

Index